Confessions

of a Happily

ORGANIZED

Family

Deniece Schofield

BETTERWAY BOOKS
Cincinnati, Ohio

ISBN 1-56865-958-X

Edited by Donna K. Collingwood
Production edited by Jennifer Lepore
Cover designed by Chad Planner
Cover photo of *The Multi-Purpose Stand That Brings Order* courtesy of Lilian Vernon Catalogs.

TABLE OF CONTENTS

INTRODUCTION

Before this goes one sentence further, let me stop right here. I know you don't have time to read this book. This book is my version of chicken soup. If it's used correctly, it'll cure just about any family management problem you might encounter. So, how are you going to find time to read it? I've got a few ideas.

• If family interruptions are a problem, it might help to read the book standing up. Not just standing there, but with one hand on the vacuum cleaner or holding a bathroom brush. The object is to look like you're working so no one will bother you. After all, no one will want to get your attention because they won't want to be drafted.

I learned this trick as a child. After being put to bed I'd often sneak out to the living room and stand silently watching the TV. I'd never say anything because if my mom was aware of my presence, she'd send me back to bed. (When people don't want to do something, they keep a low profile.) If anyone suspects housework is in progress, I can guarantee they'll keep a low profile. You'll be able to read for hours uninterrupted.

• Use waiting time. Put the book in the bathroom, under the front seat of the car or tucked in your purse or pocket. I can read volumes in a grocery store. It seems like I always get in line behind a person who doesn't even start looking for her checkbook until the checker gives her the total. Then the search for the pen starts. She has to rummage through her purse. Giving up, she asks to borrow a pen. Then it usually takes more than twenty-seven seconds to find the ID for cashing her check. She always has coupons (even expired ones that have to be refused). If you spend a lot of time in the grocery store, you should be able to knock off this book in no time.

• Actually, you don't really have to read the book. You can browse through the index or table of contents and pick out problem areas you're dealing with: laundry, homework, getting the kids to clean up their rooms, mealtimes, traveling with kids, moving, babies, whatever.

Now that you've got lots of time to read, let me tell you about this book. It begins where *Confessions of an Organized Homemaker (Confessions I)* left off. In that book I talked about toys, puzzles and games; sewing, craft and workroom supplies; a paper-handling system; kitchen organization; a storage system for seldom-used articles. These topics (and many others) are covered completely in *Confessions I*. So, for maximum benefit, use both books as your complete guide to home management.

Throughout *Confessions II* I've chosen to use masculine pronouns; this is for brevity only and indicates no sexual bias. Besides, I'm the mother of four boys so I usually think in terms of the masculine pronoun. I frequently use the words "house" and "home." Please interpret that to mean whatever you live in—whether it's a condo, a camper, a loft or a villa.

Through experience, experimentation and correspondence with people across the country, I've uncovered solutions to many common problems. After reading this book you'll know how to get your kids to clean up their rooms (and other impossible tasks), and you'll know how to store everything from buffalo heads to bowling balls. You'll know how to make every family trip fun and memorable long after the suitcases are unpacked. You'll discover the secrets of self-motivation and tips to motivate others so you won't have to do everything yourself. Even things like homework and hints for a no-mourning morning are covered. In short, you'll know how to jump-start your whole family!

I'm not a child psychologist and you won't hear a lot of "how to raise your kids" advice from me. That kind of counsel is fairly easy to come by nowadays and from more reliable sources. Many doctors broadcast on the radio and are only a phone call away. One thing I will say, though (and this is important)—Organization will never take the place of discipline. You can have everything in your home exactly where it belongs. You can have the most sanitary house on the block. But, if you don't discipline children and control unwanted behavior, things will never be organized.

I once listened to a famous family psychiatrist speak about disciplining children. He explained that basically the process was simple: Set an example. Then, he added three other steps:

1. Ignore whatever undesirable behavior you can ignore.
2. When behavior cannot be ignored, follow through with the logical consequences of that behavior.
3. Catch the child in the act of good behavior and reward it openly.

The philosophy of this book is based on example. As an adult, you need to learn, live and teach correct principles of order and organization to your children. I'll give you lots of ideas on how to do what brings you the most joy and satisfaction while you enjoy the peace and comfort of orderly surroundings.

No, I don't have all the answers. Our family get-togethers are sprinkled with now-famous stories of who did what to whom. Like Jeff crushing a bag of potato chips and hiding the crumbs all over the house:

underwear drawers, houseplants, high atop closet shelves. Then there's the one about Jim Jr. shutting his little brother in the car trunk. And we can't forget about Brian hopping out of the clothes hamper in the bathroom when a guest was using the facilities. Have you ever had a child hide in the laundry chute because he didn't want to walk to school? Ever had a child climb into the freezer because he was hot and wanted to cool down? Did any of your children write letters to another child telling her they didn't like her? Ours have.

I was so grateful when our kids stopped stabbing the toothpaste tube with safety pins and stopped taping firecrackers to the legs of their G.I. Joes. One of our boys used to sneak tampons to use as parachutes for his action figures. No, I'm no child psychologist. I struggle with the same things you struggle with. But, yes, it is possible to raise kids from tots to teens and beyond in an organized, orderly home— without doing it all yourself and without using a whip and chair a la Barnum and Bailey.

Maybe you plan to do a lot of organizing when the baby goes to college. (One lady told me she's not getting new carpeting until the baby's toilet trained.) Meanwhile, don't you long for someone to take out the trash without being asked? Have you ever heard the words, "What can I do to help?"

There's no need to wait. You can have things the way you want them—right now. As you absorb the following material, you'll discover many ideas to help you reach your goal of organized living with kids.

Think of these ideas as pieces of ripe fruit hanging on a tree. Carefully select the fruit you can use. After you choose, use and modify each idea to fit your circumstances, select a few more pieces of "fruit."

As you begin to make changes, work quietly. If you start to scream, nag and threaten, you won't generate much enthusiasm among the ranks. Next, work slowly so you can maintain each new system and develop it into a good habit, while you teach the family to do the same. Above all, be determined. Whenever you undertake any type of improvement program, everyone else in the family thinks you're going through a stage that will soon pass, so they don't take you seriously. Only quiet determination will bring them around, so let them know *this* time you mean business—and stick with it.

When you're in the middle of getting things in order you might want to give up and wonder if it's worth all the trouble. It is worth it! When I hit bottom years ago my goal was to be able to nurture my family, manage my home and still have time and energy left for personal development. The methods outlined in this book teach you how to reach that blissful state. Remember just about any program in the world will work if *you* work. (It's sort of like dieting.) Another thing I learned is to keep starting over when you mess up. You'll get to your goal if you don't stop starting over.

As you assimilate this information and make it a part of your life— as your family becomes happy and organized—you'll notice a boost to your self-image, your energy level will increase, responsible attitudes will develop in your children, and you'll get the help and free time you so desperately need. The answers are right here between the covers of this book. So what are you waiting for?

CHAPTER ONE

Does Your Family Need This Book?

Let's begin by taking a test to see how organized your family is right now. There are ten questions. Choose one of the four responses listed for each question. Which answer most closely depicts your family lifestyle?

1. Where do your family members put their clothes at the end of the day?

   A. Sorted into laundry hampers.
   B. Hung up on chair backs, doorknobs and stair railings.
   C. On the floor by the clothes hamper or piled in a chair.
   D. Wherever they take off their clothes.

2. How do your family members record telephone messages?

   A. All messages are recorded on a central telephone log.
   B. On Post-it Notes, scratch pads and "While You Were Out" forms.
   C. Messages are frequently written on the kitchen counter, on studs in the basement, on matchbooks, napkins, coloring books or on exposed areas of flesh.
   D. All telephone messages are memorized. That's easier than trying to find a pen.

3. What does your bathroom look like?

   A. Spotless, sterile and antiseptic, yet charming.
   B. We play a game at our house. We try to decide what each toothpaste glob in the sink looks like (Abraham Lincoln, McGruff the Crime Dog, a racoon, a maple leaf . . .).
   C. Our bathroom looks like Henry's Hair Emporium on a busy day. Wet towels, hair spray, shampoo, conditioner, blow dryers, curling irons, curlers, brushes, combs, bobby pins, clips, hair ribbons . . .

D. I couldn't tell you. I'm afraid to go in there.

4. If you were looking for hats, mittens and boots, where would you find them?

A. Hats and mittens are in a pocketed bag hanging inside the closet door. Boots are on a boot tray on the closet floor.
B. Tossed in a box on the closet floor.
C. Wet mittens can always be found in any coat pocket. Hats are on the kitchen table. Boots are usually forgotten at school.
D. In a pile on the floor inside the front door.

5. How was your last road trip?

A. Great. Everyone had a good time—even Mom and Dad.
B. I don't think the kids believed us when we said we were going back home if they didn't stop fighting. We had to tell them over and over.
C. We had to enforce the rule, "No teasing, touching or looking at your sister."
D. Wonderful. We each had our own video games and Walkman. We hardly even spoke to each other the entire trip.

6. What do you do with school papers?

A. More memorable items are saved and mounted in scrapbooks.
B. All school papers are placed in boxes. The boxes are given to the children when they turn eighteen.
C. Displayed on the refrigerator door, bedroom doors, walls, bulletin boards, closet doors, windows, corkboards or any visible, vertical surface.
D. Piled up chronologically on top of the refrigerator, microwave, dining room table, bookshelves, desks, kitchen counter, end tables, nightstands, dressers, TV or any visible, horizontal surface.

7. How often do you go grocery shopping?

A. We check the current month's meal plan and shop accordingly once a month. We buy fresh produce and milk once a week.
B. Three times a week on the way home from soccer practice.
C. Every day when I find out what each person wants to eat. (We don't have a single meal that everyone likes. So, around here it's like feeding time at the San Diego Zoo.)

    D. Every day at 5:30 P.M. I'm usually on my way to the store anyway to pick up some aspirin or Prozac. (Wondering all day what I'm going to fix for dinner gives me a stress headache.)

8. When you take the clothes out of the dryer, do you:

    A. Fold (or hang) them and put them away.

    B. Pile them on top of the bed, sofa or dryer with the promise to fold them later.

    C. Fold them and promise to put them away later.

    D. There's nothing to fold. We only wash something when we need to wear it.

9. You just learned you and your family are moving to another state. Do you:

    A. Go to the store to stock up on corrugated cartons and color-coded labels. Subscribe to the newspaper in your new town. Get a change of address kit from the post office.

    B. Cry. Tell the kids to cry.

    C. Get a box of chocolates and read a romance novel.

    D. Try to be understanding when the realtor suggests you wait to show the house to prospective buyers until *after* you've moved.

10. How do you store bats, balls, hockey sticks, rackets and other sporting gear?

    A. We have a sports storage unit installed in the garage. It hangs right above the parking stalls for the kids' bikes.

    B. Most of this stuff is thrown in a large heavy box affectionately called the ball box.

    C. Usually in the backyard, the neighbors' backyards and on the kitchen table.

    D. In the driveway.

Now, count up the number of As, Bs, Cs and Ds you scored. If you marked mostly As you should be writing books, not reading them!

Mostly Bs? You're not in too bad of shape but there are still a few chuckholes to be paved along the way.

Mostly Cs? Do you need this book? Yes!

Mostly Ds? Let me just say this: Your becoming a happily organized family is comparable to the Pope changing religions. But it *could* happen.

The purpose of getting things organized is to provide yourself and your family with a tidy, comfortable home—a place where you and others want to spend time. But you can overdo it. If every (or nearly every) answer was an A, ask yourself honestly what kind of feeling there is in your home. Do you allow people to sit, stand or walk if there's not a slipcover or plastic mat? Do you ask people to move frequently so all the couch cushions will receive equal wear? Have you ever discarded a newspaper or magazine before anyone had a chance to read it? Too sterile an environment can paralyze family growth and happiness. People leave when they want to relax and enjoy themselves.

I received a letter that helps make this point. A woman told me she and her husband had invited some people over for a get-together. One of the guests mentioned he hated to touch anything and really felt uncomfortable sitting down. The house seemed so perfect, he didn't want to mess it up in any way.

Organization and cleanliness are means to an end. In and of themselves they're worthless. The object of efficient home management is to do the right job right. If you spend hours ironing sheets, underwear and shoelaces, you're probably doing the job right—but are you doing the right job? Probably not. Remember moderation is the key to successful home management. Here's an example:

We have a friend who lives in a historic mansion. It's a beautiful home, professionally decorated, full of antiques. Around every corner of every room is an interesting bit of architecture or a pane of original leaded glass. In this setting it would be natural to feel ill at ease just as the man did in the letter I mentioned.

But despite all these accoutrements our friend has managed to make this home warm, welcoming and inviting. Something is always bubbling on the stove or baking in the oven. Fresh flowers are frequent visitors. There are always a few school projects prominently displayed. A plastic-covered map of the world is on the dining room table to encourage educational family dinner times. Soft music is usually playing in the background. No matter when you drop in, you are made to feel like they've been eagerly anticipating your arrival. I love to be in that home and I always want to stay once I get there.

This home feels so good *in spite* of all the trappings—not *because* of them. This same warm atmosphere can be created in just about any circumstance—whether it's a mansion or a mud hut.

In contrast, we have another friend who lies on the floor to read the paper and watch TV—because as a youngster he was never allowed to sit on the furniture. Though he has no reason to continue the practice, that childhood habit has become natural to him.

And I remember when, years ago, a little neighborhood girl was hit by a car. Though she luckily was unhurt, she feared what her mother would say when she saw her torn clothing.

Pay attention to the messages you're sending your family. Don't ever give them the impression the house is more important than they are. Somewhere along the line we've come to the conclusion that the house has to be cleaner and tidier for people who *don't* live there.

So, if you scored all As, I'm recommending you relax and lighten up a little. However, this is not a license for sloppiness. Some people live in virtual squalor and justify it by saying they'd rather spend time with their kids than clean house. This, too, has an adverse effect.

What we're looking for is a middle-of-the-road approach, and I can't paint the lane lines for you. Only you can do that. Be honest with yourself and discover if you're guilty of tipping the scale one way or the other. If you're too close to the situation, talk it over with your family or with a friend who has the courage to tell you the truth. You cannot become a happily organized family unless you find that comfortable fine line between perfection and pigsty.

If you scored a lot of Cs and Ds on the test, don't despair. Millions of people are in the same situation. After completing this book and applying its principles, your score will change drastically. I promise.

How can I make such a claim? For starters, you'll experience a raised consciousness toward order. You will become painfully aware of times when you put things here "for now." As you bring order to a drawer, shelf or room, and make sure the new system is maintained, your children will begin to have a clear vision in their minds of where things belong. (Have you ever noticed what a mess people can make when they're looking for something? Orderliness will prevent that.) If things don't have a specific spot all their own, they'll never be put there! I know from experience that when you mix chaos with kids you have an insufferable situation. With five kids, if we didn't have a least a semblance of order, I would have been in "the home," cowering in a corner of a padded cell.

The kids will begin to enjoy the good feeling they get when things are orderly. Besides, when a room is in apple-pie order, any irregularities are immediately obvious (unmade beds, clothes dropped on the floor, etc.) and kids learn what each lifestyle (clean or chaotic) feels like. Chances are, they'll choose the former. Then, and only then, will chaos begin to give way to neatness and you will gradually be set free.

NEGATIVE REWARDS

Obviously, organization is my favorite subject. How could such a boring subject be so satisfying? Let me explain. At our house we work on a system of negative rewards. By that I mean I don't hear too much about it when I do things right, but I hear plenty when I mess up! Sound familiar?

After spending hours on all fours cleaning the refrigerator, I can't remember ever hearing *anyone* say, "Gee, the refrigerator looks great!" And no one ever says, "I'm so glad all the buttons are on my shirt this morning," or, "It was swell of you to get all those stuck Cheerios off the kitchen floor," or, "Aw shucks, dear, you made the bed!" But boy, do I hear about it if there's a button missing, a sticky floor or an unmade bed. Sometimes it seems there's a universal misconception that I have exclusive rights to the sewing box, mop and linen closet. (I've been doing my best to reconceive that idea, though.)

You too may have noticed doing housework is like filling a sieve with water. Phyllis Diller summed it up nicely on a *Tonight Show* appearance, "Cleaning the house while the children are growing is like shoveling snow before it stops snowing."

Negative rewards. We face them daily. Do it right and no one remembers, but do it wrong and no one forgets. Maybe you've noticed there's not a lot of glory at home. We don't often receive accolades or pats on the back (with the obvious exception of Mother's Day or Father's Day). And where are my loyal supporters the rest of the year? Why, they're spilling milk in my clean refrigerator, throwing gum wrappers in their sock drawers and volunteering four hundred cupcakes for the next PTA meeting (usually this evening). No wonder we conclude organized living is best left to the childless, the single or to incredibly stout-hearted parents!

THE GOOD LIFE

All this leads me to why getting things in order is exciting! When you have a closet, cupboard or drawer in perfect order, that one little area seems to say, "You're doing a wonderful job! Keep up the good work!" What motivation. It's terrific to feel those words, because chances are ten to one you'll never *hear* them.

Every day I get letters from people all over the country. Invariably I get one that says, "Today I cleaned out my closet. Every five minutes I go in there—*just to look at it!*"

Organization feels good, and that good feeling spills over into your disposition. It can improve your entire outlook on life. Organized living sets you free from feelings of despair, and stress is greatly reduced. You experience a feeling akin to relief.

Madison Avenue has made a fortune selling the "good life." Look at any billboard. Check any magazine ad, TV commercial or listen to the radio. Everything for sale in this country is guaranteed to give you that "good life," whether it's a glass of milk, a knife full of peanut butter, a car, a pair of jeans or a socket wrench. Nothing is exempt from this marketing strategy.

Yes. Everyone is cashing in on the "good life." I, too, offer it to you—free of charge. All it takes is some forethought, a little time and some good old-fashioned work.

Christopher Robin (from A.A. Milne's *Winnie-the-Pooh*) said it best, "Organizing is what you do before you do something, so that when you do it, it's not all mixed up."

If you want organized living with kids, you can have it. Stick with me and we'll work together—gradually, smoothly and systematically—down the road to emancipation.

CHAPTER TWO

Goal Setting

I t's only fitting I should write a chapter on goal setting: I'm the all-time champion. I set goals like crazy: run four miles a day; learn to make drapes (and make drapes for every room in the house); quit eating candy; write at least two pages daily in my journal; and get up at 5 A.M. every day for the rest of my life.

Well, here I sit—the bruised veteran of every physical fitness program devised by man. I gave my stationary bike away. The kids use my jogging trampoline for their "who can get their fingerprints highest on the wall" contests, and my leg warmers (years old now) are in the garage keeping the water pipes from freezing. My "drapes" are now Levolors. I will always love candy, and every time I gobble down another piece I address a silent prayer to Richard Simmons. My journal is no threat to the *Diary of Anne Frank*, and every morning at 5 A.M. my mattress reaches out its big strong arms and pulls me relentlessly back into bed.

These futile attempts at goal setting haven't discouraged me, though; my failures have taught me so many things, I can honestly say I'm grateful for most of those hard knocks. If the words "unmotivated, weak, unselfdisciplined, sniveling, pathetic creature," ring a bell, you must be giving yourself the same lecture I used to give myself every time I messed up. Now, I know better.

Here's where I went wrong: the key to successful goal realization begins with setting goals correctly—something I had never done. But before we go through the specific steps involved in setting reachable goals, let's get down to the grass roots. Why are goals necessary in the first place?

Without goals, things that don't matter in the long run take over your life. You start thinking, "If I can just make it through today and stay out of the headlines I'll be okay." We get so wrapped up with socks, pancakes and paychecks we never get on to the more important things.

Without goals, you're always a spectator in the great game of life.

You sit on the sidelines watching others achieve and score. You only wish for a piece of the action. Remember, you can't score unless you have a goal. And any running back worth his salt will tell you that you can't score unless you have the *ball!*

Become a goal seeker. With the goalpost in sight, you're not only in the game and in on the game plan—you've got the ball. Now *that's* exciting. You're in charge. You're dictating the course of your life. (Yes, I know what happens to the guy who gets the ball—he's pushed around, tackled and piled on. But before he hits the turf he squeezes out just a few more inches.)

Natural energy is released when you enjoy what you're doing. If you know about "runner's high" you know it's partly a physiological phenomenon—but it can also be attributed to simply achieving a goal. The pursuit of a lofty goal helps you direct and channel energy. It gives you a reason to get out of bed in the morning.

Goal setting saves time. Most of us fritter away a good portion of our lives by scheduling daily tasks without regard to the total picture. We shoot arrows without aiming at the target. We work more, accomplish less. With an outlined course to follow, daily activities take on new meaning as they guide you in the right direction.

It is the nature of a human being to pursue a goal. When that basic need isn't being fulfilled, feelings of discouragement, general dissatisfaction and sometimes depression set in.

Every tick of the clock is a piece of your life. Make the most of it. Get up and goal!

GOALTENDING

OK! You're all fired up, but where do you start?

All it takes to start is to sit down and think. There are a lot of questions you can ask yourself to help the goal selection process begin: What would you do if you had more time? What would you do if you had only six months to live? What do you want to be doing in five years? What do you want to accomplish during your life?

These are a few ideas to stimulate your thinking. I hope, though, you're more in tune to yourself than I am. Whenever I come across such questions I either draw a blank or become profound and get bogged down. Personally, I find success with questions like: What do you want less of? (Stacks of papers on the dining room table, dirty laundry, weeds in the lawn . . .) A question phrased that way automatically tells you what you want more of.

Another successful method (for me, at least) is to use goal setting to solve problems. For example, ask yourself, "What bothers me most about my life now?" "Can I make any changes that will make me more successful? If so, what are they?" "Am I happy with my environment? If not, why?" "I could function more effectively if . . ." "What jobs am I procrastinating on?" "What activities would I like to eliminate completely?"

Another way to discover goals you're truly interested in pursuing is to pay attention to what you do all the time. If you're constantly cleaning house, do you secretly want a house just like the Seven Dwarfs had after Snow White moved in? If you spend your free time reading *Sports Illustrated*, watching Monday night football, and being a professional fan in general, maybe you have the unspoken goal of being physically involved in the sports world.

What really turns you on? If you wouldn't dream of missing the Furniture Fix-Up Guys, maybe you'd like to pursue a latent desire to restore your antique trunk or teach classes in furniture repair and refinishing.

Maybe you've always dreamed of a trip to Australia or of having a cabin in the mountains. Shake the cobwebs from your mind and start jotting down some ideas. (Since you're reading this book, you obviously have the goal of organizing your family.)

This is the point at which I always used to stop. My list of dreams, goals and ambitions was written in black and white. Now, I'd fantasize, everything would be wonderful and I would live happily ever after—wrong! So far, all we've done is to wish for what might be.

THE TEN COMMANDMENTS OF GOAL SETTING
(Now pay attention because a few pages down the road you'll be learning how to help your kids set their goals!)

1. *Conceive it, believe it and achieve it* is your new fight song. Remember—what you see is what you get. If you can't visualize yourself eventually achieving a particular goal, reword it, change it—until you can actually believe in its ultimate fulfillment.

2. *Make the goal specific.* To say "I want to be physically fit" isn't specific enough. This is better: "I want to be physically fit. I will have reached that goal when I weigh 185 pounds with body fat not to exceed 15 percent." The latter goal statement lists the requirements for meeting the goal, so you'll know when you've made it.

Be sure you've written down exactly what goal you're after—not just a way to get there. If you've listed "get up every morning at 5 A.M.," that is probably not a goal. More likely your goal is to have two hours of uninterrupted time and to get a jump on the day. If so, getting up at 5 A.M. is just one way of accomplishing that goal. You can achieve the same results by staying up later at night or by delegating more of your morning responsibilities. Do you need a two-hour block of time, or can you use your lunch hour, coffee breaks or the baby's nap time? Can you arrange for an older child, spouse, friend or relative to hold down the fort occasionally while you go to the library, visit a friend or barricade yourself in your bedroom?

When I set my 5 A.M. goal, I think I was more concerned about how wonderful it would sound when I told people that's when I got up. So I fought my natural tendencies (to stay up late) and failed miserably. I found I could get the same results much easier by staying up late and getting up at the regular time each morning.

Realistic goal setting involves three steps:

First, list your resources. Do you have any special talents and skills (don't forget personal commitment, willingness to work hard, etc)? Would family members or friends be willing to help? Perhaps these folks can give physical help, donate or lend materials, offer their knowledge and advice, or introduce you to an influential person.

Second, brainstorm. Jot down every conceivable way the goal can be accomplished. (Ask your kids. They look at things so simply, they often come up with great ideas!) Talk to the friends you listed as resources. Note every idea, no matter how stange it may seem. Then, as you scrutinize your list of possibilities, you can combine and create, modify and minimize, substitute and rearrange.

Third, explore all the alternatives in order to come up with the quickest, easiest and best way for you to reach your goal.

3. *List your goal activities.* Every goal has three parts. First, you have the big, main goal. Second, you have a list of subgoals, which are activities to help you accomplish the main goal. Third are minigoals, a series of little jobs that make up the subgoal. Minigoals are tasks that can be accomplished in one day (or better yet, one hour).

It works much like an outline. When you plan your goal you write up the outline:

I.   Main Goal
    A. Subgoal
       1. Minigoal
       2. Minigoal
    B. Subgoal
       1. Minigoal
       2. Minigoal

When you start working on the goal, you start at the bottom and work your way up.

A while back I read about a fellow who was eating a car. Believe me, he didn't sit down with a knife, a fork, a checkered bib and dig in. This guy *knew* how to tackle a big job. He had the entire car ground up one fender at a time. Gradually, he worked his way through the doors, the engine, the fenders and the upholstery. Now, there's a great goal-setting lesson in there somewhere.

Minigoals are the stuff main goals are made of. They give you a successful experience every time you accomplish one. Each time a minigoal is satisfied, you gain a renewed sense of motivation and determination to keep pressing forward. Minigoals make your self-confidence grow and flourish. They exercise and strengthen your ability to discipline yourself.

We all know muscles have to be stretched and flexed gradually until you can bend over straight-legged and touch your toes. But have you ever stopped to think that self-discipline works the same way? To a person with a short temper, "No yelling at the kids" is like doing the splits at his first gymnastics class. Start with small successes: I will not yell at the kids during breakfast today.

Gradually, and almost painlessly, you can reach the goal just by taking small, predetermined steps.

4. *Establish the order* in which subgoals will be worked on. Take the case of my brother, George Wheeler. An avid do-it-yourselfer. George's main goal is finishing off his basement.

Here's a rough list of his subgoals:

- Plan the layout
- Studding
- Rough wiring
- Rough plumbing
- Drywall
- Hang doors
- Ceilings
- Finish walls and ceilings
- Finish wiring
- Cabinets and finish woodwork
- Floors
- Finish plumbing

In the interest of space I've already listed the subgoals in priority order. This is just a logical definition of how the main goal must be advanced.

(Bear in mind that within each subgoal are a lot of those minigoals—the bite-sized pieces that further the goal in small snatches of time.)

5. *What resources do you need?* Know what this goal is going to cost you in terms of time and money. This step is both essential and rewarding. Essential in that adequate planning depends on your resources. Will you have to finish the basement as you can afford it, or can you have all the supplies delivered this afternoon? Will you be working on the project alone in your spare time, or will you have frequent and willing recruits?

This step is as rewarding as it's necessary. Most of us think in terms of barriers. "I can't do this because I don't have any power tools." "As soon as I get started, the phone will ring." "I've never installed a shower before." This planning step gets you past the barriers because it forces you to search out resources and ways to overcome your self-proclaimed obstacles.

6. *Give yourself a deadline.* Decide when you'd like each subgoal to be completed and jot down the dates. Then, starting at the bottom of your outline, assign completion dates to each minigoal.

To clarify this, look at the chart on the following page. The subgoal is: Plan the layout. The completion date is June 1. Starting at the bottom of the list of minigoals (City Hall—building permit) you work backward from June 1 and eventually work your way back to May 19, which then becomes your starting date for this subgoal. (This is not as complicated as it sounds!)

7. *Use my handy form.* I use this form for lots of things. If I'm working on a craft project, reading a long, important book or improving a character trait, I break the job down and fill out the form. For an involved project like the basement, you would fill out one form for every subgoal.

This form is vital to scheduling your time and handling your finances. By knowing up front how much time and money you need for your goal, you can avoid overextending yourself in either area.

For example, the week you'll be in Cleveland is not the week to schedule the studding. The week you have to pay for Karen's retainer, Josh's new school shoes and your hunting license fee is not the week to have the supplies delivered C.O.D.

Let's see how a less concrete goal like becoming a happily organized family would work. Right from the start, breed success into your planning session by involving the whole family (or as many as you can round up).

Start by asking, "How can we become a happily organized family?"

GOAL: Finish the basement
Subgoal: Plan the layout

Minigoals	Completion Date	Resources Time	Money
Call bldg. inspector to find out codes	5-19	15min.	
Sketch rough layout	5-25	3 days	
Buy new tape measure	5-25		$5.95
Plan wiring layout	5-30	2 hrs.	
City Hall—bldg. permit	6-1	1 hr.	$50.00
Subgoal Totals	6-1	3 days, 3:15	$55.95

Jot down all the ideas as they're given to you (or appoint a scribe). Here's a sampling of possible responses:

- Get to school on time.
- Get up earlier.
- Read some books about the subject.
- Plan menus.
- Have cleaner bedrooms.
- Coordinate family and individual activities.
- Do the laundry on a routine schedule.

Next, choose one area to focus on even if several things are in dire need of attention. Taking on too much may discourage everyone and defeat your purpose.

Let's say the family votes to zero in on the bedrooms. Decide exactly what you want to accomplish so you'll know when the goal has been met. For example, let's assume you state your goal as follows: Goal: To have all the bedrooms kept orderly five days a week for three months.

Continue the discussion by asking everyone to air their gripes. What are the problems with bedrooms; what are the causes of these problems? (List them.)

Mom's gripes: In the kids' rooms the beds aren't made and when they are, they're done sloppily. Dresser tops are always heaped with junk. The closet doors are left open. Clothing is crammed and jumbled in the drawers. In the master bedroom newspapers and dirty dishes are left lying around. The drapes are ugly.

Dad's gripes: Ditto with the kid's bedrooms. In the master bedroom pantyhose are always hanging from the shower rod. Laundry is folded on the bed.

Kids' gripes: Bunk beds are too hard to make. No place to put school papers. Can't hang picture posters. Need desks.

Now that the goal is clearly stated and problems are well-defined, brainstorm and decide how to overcome the chaotic bedrooms.

Here's an abbreviated list of possible solutions:

- Get fitted quilts for bunk beds.
- Give each child a large container for "treasures."
- Purchase bins for school papers.
- Designate *one* wall for posters, pennants, etc.
- Get up earlier to straighten things up before work or school.
- Discard old clothes; pack seasonal clothing away.
- Build study tables for the kids' rooms.
- Get an over-the-door dryer rack to hang pantyhose on.
- Stack newspapers neatly on nightstand.
- Return dishes to the kitchen.
- Purchase new drapes for the master bedroom.
- Fold laundry on card table in laundry area.

Once you've chosen remedies that will work best for you, break down the main goal (clean bedrooms) into subgoals. Here's a portion of the finished outline.

I.   Main Goal: Bedrooms neat and orderly five days a week for three months.
    A. Subgoal: Beds easier to make.
       1. Check mail-order catalogs for fitted bunk bed quilts.
       2. Check favorite stores for quilts.
       3. Purchase spreads.
    B. Subgoal: No junk or school papers on top of the dresser.
       1. Purchase bins for school papers; bins will go on the closet shelf.
       2. Purchase under-the-bed boxes for "treasures."
       3. Hang posters, pennants, pictures, etc., on the northwest bedroom wall.
    C. Subgoal: Drawers cleaned out.
       1. Remove all clothing from drawers.
       2. Put clothes in three piles—out-of-season, give away, won't fit (store for other sibling to wear); discard unwearables.
       3. Replace only current season's wearables in the drawers.
       4. Use drawer dividers to separate socks from underwear.

With the goal well outlined, you've got a road map that leads you directly to your desired destination—clean bedrooms. If you'd like, you can transfer this information to the goal form and assign deadlines, etc.

You'll notice on our list of solutions a few items that cannot be broken down: Get up earlier to straighten rooms; return dishes to kitchen and stack newspapers; fold clothes in laundry area, etc. These may be grouped on one form, placed on a checklist to chart progress, written on a big poster as a reminder or whatever.

8. *Be flexible.* If you fall down the stairs and break your legs, you'll have to put the basement on hold for a while. Sometimes things beyond your control will temporarily prevent you from continuing your program. All these plans are written on paper, and while you should take them seriously, check and revise them from time to time as situations warrant.

9. *Be enthusiastic.* Enthusiasm releases energy. Our oldest son, Jim, is real testimony to that fact. Jim, by nature, has one speed: S-L-O-W. (We put markers down during the day to see if this kid moves.) One particular night his boys' chorus was performing in concert with the girls' chorus. With blinding speed, Jim bathed, dried his hair, splashed on the aftershave and dressed. He was ready to go in fifteen minutes flat! (I'm still amazed I could use the words "blinding speed" and "Jim" in the same sentence.)

I know it's hard to be enthusiastic sometimes. When the baby is toddling through rush-hour traffic and your son is perched atop the neighbor's twenty-foot pine begging you to take his picture, you may well decide to chuck your whole goal, let alone enthusiasm.

Sometimes you just have to pretend. Feign enthusiasm long enough for the real excitement of accomplishment to take over.

10. *Reward yourself.* Be proud of every little accomplishment. Treat yourself to something you enjoy. I keep a running list of things I enjoy doing and choose rewards from it. Whenever I feel a surge of interest or excitement, I jot down what it was that made me feel that way. Certainly my moods change. What motivates me one day leaves me flat the next. But my list is long enough now that I can usually find an interesting reward.

Is That All There Is?

Years ago we lived in a town that was devastated by a flood. Homes were lost, roads were broken up and many priceless possessions were either saturated or buried by the thick wall of mud that plunged down the mountainside. Some homes were completely filled with mud.

One such house was standing structurally undamaged, yet everything inside was virtually useless. The owners of this house decided to do what they could to save the structure. With the aid of many volunteers, the house was shoveled out pail by pail and the interior was gutted until only the wall studs and frame were left.

A while after the rebuilding process began, however, the breadwinner in this family quit her job! She had only two or three years until her full retirement, but she retired anyway and lost most of her benefits. Her attitude was, "I've worked all my life for *things*, and in five minutes, everything was gone. What's the use?"

While you'll agree this seems a bit drastic, I can't help but sympathize with this woman. Permit me a bit of philosophy: Our lives need to involve more than things. Setting and achieving goals gives us more than material possessions to hang onto. Goals give direction to the humdrum of daily living. They build character, strengthen the family and fill lives with meaning.

Think back over the last ten years of your life. If you feel "there's got to be more to life than this," you probably haven't been setting those goals.

Alexander Woollcott said, "Many of us spend half our time wishing for things we could have if we didn't spend half our time wishing."

GOAL FOR IT

"Why should I plan goals when I can procrastinate?" you ask. "After all, procrastination puts things into perspective automatically."

Good point. It's true that when you procrastinate, your priorities are set for you. When something becomes a crisis you know what has to be handled first. You needn't make any decisions.

And, of course, at the end of the year when the Procrastinator's Club of America publishes their predictions for the *preceding* year they're always 100 percent correct. Not too shabby.

Procrastination adds a dimension of excitement and stimulation (not to mention high blood pressure, stroke and heart disease) to what may otherwise be a dull, uneventful life. You can imagine how boring things would be around here if we didn't run out of gas two or three times a month. What would we laugh about when we're gathered around the dinner table? Besides, now I have a collection of "just try to top this" stories I can use at our next party.

Procrastination is comfortable for a while. It keeps us safe from confronting whatever it is we're putting off. When I first started to work on this book, I was procrastinating like mad. I was afraid I couldn't do it, afraid I couldn't meet my deadline, afraid I couldn't think of anything to write about. So I sat around thinking up chapter titles, scribbled down and filed various ideas, shuffled papers and sifted through a large stack of books. Finally, I realized what I was doing and got on my mettle and just plain started writing. That's all it took.

Anyhow, I understand procrastination. I know how easy it is to fall into the trap and I know its destructive effect.

Procrastination is a deadly time and energy enemy and must be avoided at all costs. It is the biggest single cause of crises. When you're first aware you're procrastinating, stop and ask yourself these questions:

What am I afraid of?
Is there a small portion of the job I can do now? (Think of something—anything—that will advance your goal.)
How long is it really going to take?
What is my reward if I finish just one minigoal?

Staying on Track

Self-motivation is built into this goal-setting program if you'll just give it a chance. The need to achieve can and will be learned if you'll consistently set attainable but challenging goals—goals that require just a little stretching.

Elbert Hubbard has said that the line between success and failure is so fine sometimes all that's needed is a single extra effort to bring victory over our apparent defeat.

When you begin feeling tired and frustrated, it's best to stop. You want as many pleasant associations with your goal as possible. Try to end on a positive note and at a point of accomplishment. Don't stop in the middle of a sentence or a row of knitting. The reason for this is only logical—it makes your next start-up time that much longer. You'll waste time deciding where you were and what you were doing. Whenever you're working on a project and need to stop before the project is completed, make a note about what you were doing or what to do next. This practice alone will shave minutes off each "start-up" time.

Sometimes it may take some evaluation on your part to discover why you stalled. Maybe you'll find a solution to prevent its recurrence.

Interest also feeds self-motivation. Find out more about your chosen project. The more you know and learn the more engrossed you become. Get more information, but don't use this as an excuse to procrastinate. I kept putting off starting this book under the guise of "I need more information." It got to the point that gathering facts kept me from writing. So learn about your goal and as soon as your interest is sparked, get busy. You can always continue your quest for knowledge as you go along.

Interruptions and distractions will rob you of enthusiasm, so avoid them if you can. But never, I repeat never, let an imperfect situation be an excuse to do nothing. That is why minigoals are so helpful. They can be accomplished quickly without having to wait for large blocks of time to magically appear.

Now that you're an expert goal setter, let's move on to the kids. How can we help them reach their full measure? (You may want to become well acquainted with the goal-setting process and feel comfortable with it before teaching the methods to your kids. If so, skim over the following material and come back to it when you're ready.)

SETTING EXAMPLES

Helping your children set goals is admittedly easier when they're young—and it's a lot more fun.

When Johnny says, "When I grow up I want to be a policeman," do you say, "That's nice. Finish your soup"? Or do you gather a bunch of Johnny's friends and schedule a tour through the police station? Do you encourage his dream, or do you let it pass, knowing next week he'll want to be a house painter? Our reactions to our children's goals and ambitions determine, to a large extent, what they ultimately *do* about their lofty aspirations.

Goal setting for kids is not quite as exacting a science as it is for adults. After all, I can't picture one of the kids tripping into the house after school and saying, "Well, it's time to fill out one of Mom's goal forms. Gee, I just can't wait to get started!"

The children can be guided subtly, though, by asking questions, by getting involved (as much as you're wanted), e.g., scheduling those tours through the police department, reading books, cutting out pictures for scrapbooks, etc. All this must be done objectively, without censure. (Provided the child's goal isn't immoral, illegal, fattening or distasteful!)

Involving the Kids

Children need little advice if they see good examples. One of the most effective ways to teach children how and why to set goals is to involve them in many of your own goal-setting sessions, and always involve them when family goals are being discussed and planned.

Some families set aside an hour a week or an hour a month for a joint meeting in which family goals are discussed:

> "Should we get a new dining room table or a snowmobile?"
>
> "Where should we go on vacation this summer?"
>
> "Let's start eating more nutritious foods. What kinds of things should we buy (or not buy)?"
>
> "We need to have more peaceful mornings. What can we do to get ready on time without fighting and screaming?"

If goals are participative, more cooperation is inbred. When the children feel like they "own" a piece of the project, they give a little extra effort (at least) to help it succeed. This whole process conveys a sense of belonging and unity. Everyone learns that his actions contribute to an embracing whole.

Children need to be interviewed, however casually, from time to time. Here is a stimulating list of questions that will evoke many enlightening responses from your children. Try a few out for size.

1. If you could trade places with someone else, who would it be?
2. If you could go anywhere on a vacation, where would you like to go?
3. What famous person do you admire most?
4. Who are your favorite movie stars, singers and sports figures?
5. What is your favorite sport, favorite movie and favorite song?
6. What do you remember about fifth grade (or whatever)?
7. What would you like to change about yourself?
8. What would you like to change about the world?
9. What would you like to do in your spare time?
10. If you had a million dollars, how would you spend it?
11. If you wanted to do a secret good deed, what would you do?
12. What would you like to change about our family?
13. If you could give any gift in the world, what would you give and to whom?
14. Do you have a wish you're trying to make come true? Can you tell me what it is?
15. What talent would you like to develop?
16. What are the most important things in your life?
17. What are you most thankful for?

Here are some other topics for discussion: school, good books they've read, career development, the child's physical and emotional health, personal appearance, feelings of self-worth, dating, relationships with friends, religion and family standards. The whole purpose here is to keep a tab on where your kids are right now (likes, dislikes, dreams, ambitions) and what they're doing to move toward where they want to be.

The pursuit of a goal will encourage wiser use of time. I'm not recommending inflexible, rigid time controls, just a gentle pulling in the right direction. Remember, it's the constant tap, tap, tap of the hammer that sets the nail in place.

Teaching a child to plan can begin when the child is very young. Teachers often encourage kindergarteners to place their cutout pictures on the page before they apply the paste. They learn to gather everything they need before they play a certain game, and they're taught to leave a lot of room on the line when they're printing a long word.

A jigsaw puzzle can provide a good lesson in planning. If you simply put the pieces on the floor and ask a child to assemble it, he has a hard time. But present him with a plan (the picture of the puzzle) and he can put it together in no time.

A small child can be told a plan is simply looking ahead—seeing the finished puzzle picture. But a plan doesn't work all by itself; once the plan is in order, we must *do* something. Following a recipe, sewing from a pattern, building a model, writing a story or planning a birthday party are all concrete examples of how planning works in a child's life.

My son Steven learned how to plan at an early age (it must have been in school or by accident). One day he decided to build a fort, but before he started, he grabbed a pencil and paper and wrote, in his best second-grade printing: 3 afgans, 1 table, 2 sheets.

With older children, the best approach seems to be asking questions, for example: "What have you got planned next week?" "What are you going to do about your incomplete in English?" "Do you still enjoy your artwork as much as you did last year?" Asking questions puts the responsibility on the child to determine solutions. It also forces them to think and plan ahead. "*Do* I like art as much?" "What am I going to do next week?"

Setbacks

It's bound to happen. Goals are not reached; reports are past due; games are lost; wrong notes are played during the recital. What then? How can you keep failure from eating away the self-confidence and self-discipline you've tried so hard to foster?

Try to find out why the failure occurred.

- Did your child do the wrong thing?
  Is Mary playing the violin when she'd rather be playing ball? Did Quinn tackle a complicated model without first trying the snap-together variety?
    Make sure the child isn't taking giant steps when baby steps are called for. Also, be sure you're not treating the child as an extension of yourself (e.g., you got straight As and *he's* going to get straight As; you played the harp and *he's* going to play the harp).
- Did your child do the right thing wrong?
  Sometimes the child is ill-prepared for something he wants to do. For example, Ed wanted to try out for concert choir, but he missed too many rehearsals. Did Henry get a bad grade on his report because he didn't follow the directions?
- Is the child doing too much?
  Maybe your child is overinvolved. Homework, school reporter, chorus, student body officer, band, pep club, etc. There's a limit to how much can be handled and still done well.
- Has the child reached his saturation point?
  From your own experience, you know how exciting it is to do something you truly enjoy. But when you've done it over and over the pleasure wanes—and you back off for a while until you're in balance again.
    Your children can have those same feelings of saturation. Brian gets awfully sick of baseball come July. But when April rolls around again, he's outside swinging the bat.
- Is the child comparing himself to other people?
  That's almost a ridiculous question because even as adults we continue to struggle with this problem. Explain how foolish it is to compare yourself with others.
    Stress your child's unique qualities. Explain that everyone in this world has strengths and weaknesses. No one has them all. Encourage him to measure his own progress against himself. Star charts, plus-minus charts, or journals are good for this.

When Steven was in speech therapy he had a plus-minus chart to fill out every day. Whenever he held his tongue in the correct position for fifteen minutes, he got a plus. When he bit his fingernails (an absolutely forbidden vice for children with tongue thrust problems) he got a minus. Each week he tallied up his plus column and tried to beat his previous record.

Keep stressing the positive. Generally, the child will see he's not so bad after all. But when failure occurs, it often helps to get the child to quickly think about his strengths, his positive qualities. After losing a basketball game is a good time to have Brian explain to you how a three-point shot is scored or a 2-1-2 zone works. If Susan has just lost the student council elections, tell her you'd like to hear her play the Beethoven piece she performs so beautifully. Tell Jim how much you've enjoyed using the plant stand he made for you in woodshop. These have to be sincere nonmanipulative attempts to draw the child out of the dumps. Nothing but time will completely heal the wounds, but the kids still need those gentle reminders that there's a successful self behind that temporary failure.

The Time Is Now

Don't lose today by waiting for a brighter future. Each person in your family can begin molding his future right now by becoming a goal seeker. If you want success for tomorrow, you must work for it today. The time is now to get up and goal.

CHAPTER THREE

It's About Time

Y ou must be kidding! Goals are the *least* of my worries right now. My 'to do' list reads like a training manual for the folks at Ramada Inn and Mister Rogers's neighborhood. I have to take the little kids to preschool, get the other kids on the bus, clean the house, prepare the meals, do the laundry, mend, iron, do the yardwork, maintain the car and wash the dog. I'm also president of the little theatre group, a volunteer at the drug crisis center twice a week, a Sunday school teacher and a member of the state legislature. In my spare time you'll find me carpooling children to soccer games, dancing lessons and swimming pools. And oh yes, I work full-time, so I'm gone from home about ten hours a day!"

All I can say is, "Whew!" Actually, this scenario is not as far-fetched as it sounds. For example, one afternoon I received a phone call from a woman in North Carolina who painted a similar picture and begged me to help her. She was a widow and had the added burden of tackling this moil alone.

As I recall, I didn't offer any words of profound wisdom, but I do remember how good that conversation was for me. It opened my eyes and made me realize there are millions of men and women in the same fix. How do they handle it all? How do they pull it off?

My curiosity led me to investigate. I studied people and asked questions like, "What's your secret?" "What motivates you to get everything done?" "How do you manage your busy schedule?" Through good books, I also consulted with experts.

Here's what I discovered. The sum total of my research is twofold. First, there are certain common denominators basic to each successful system; and second, *no one* gets *everything* done! No matter how universally competent someone appears on the surface, no one is all things to all people, handling everything perfectly.

These people, these superachievers, have been known to bag large numbers of misplaced articles and stash them in the hall closet to escape the eyes of unexpected guests. They put dirty dishes in the oven for the same reason and have been seen stapling merit badges onto Boy Scout uniforms. Yes, those folks who seem to successfully negotiate kids, careers and car pools have learned the fine art of selected neglect. (More about this later in the chapter.)

OK, then, let's begin by revealing those common denominators. After all, what have you got to lose but a few headaches?

Remember, the people I studied are all winners. They are not necessarily wealthy or endowed with superhuman qualities. They are normal, everyday individuals who spend time doing things that bring them joy and satisfaction. They make the most of their lives.

GOAL FIRST

The first step, they all agree, is to set goals. By now, I hope the reasons are crystal clear. You can't manage your time unless you know where you're going. How can you decide what to do today if you don't know what needs to be done this week, this month, this year? Effective time management begins with effective goal setting.

I won't belabor the point. Suffice it to say that *not* setting goals is worse than taking four kids to Kmart the day before Christmas.

Simplify Your Life

Keeping your selected list of goals uppermost in your mind, let's advance to the second step—simplifying your life. In light of your priorities you can now determine which of your tasks are important and which are not. Most of the time we're caught up in a flurry of activities—generally more than we can handle effectively. Relataively few bring us closer to a chosen goal.

Assume, for the sake of example, you're the person who, with raised eyebrow and clenched jaw, attacked my goal-setting program as an exercise in futility. Pretend that bottomless pit of a "to-do" list is yours.

To begin with, let's set the Ramada Inn stuff aside. (In chapters 5–9 we'll discuss housecleaning and getting the kids to help.) For now, let's get right to the outside demands on your time:

- President of little theatre group
- Drug crisis center volunteer
- Sunday school teacher
- State legislator
- Full-time job

Now review the goals you set for yourself in chapter 2. Jot them down next to the list of your outside activities.

In *The One Minute Manager* (Kenneth Blanchard and Spencer Johnson, Berkeley Books), the authors ask a piercing question: "Does your behavior match your goal?"

Let that sink in for a mintue. Are any of these extraneous demands moving you closer to achieving a goal? That should be the criterion for swinging or not swinging the axe.

What you do daily should lead you to what you want. If your main goal is to improve the quality of life in your community and make it a better place to raise your family, you're right on target.

However, if time is a problem you may have to decide which of those time demands have the richest payoff in terms of moving you closer to your goal. A time management law (known as the Pareto Principle) states that 80 percent of the desired results come from 20 percent of the activities. So skim off the cream and dump the milk.

On the other hand, suppose your main goal is to become a proficient calligrapher. Your "to do" list is going one way and your goal is going the opposite way. Remember, what you *do* is what you get.

If you're constantly bored in certain social settings, while attending meetings that don't go anywhere or accomplish anything, or if you feel certain to-dos are a real waste of time, take courage and head these annoyances off at the pass. That's right. Let 'em have it—right between the eyes! (Ruthless, aren't I?)

Simplify the Kids

Let's move on to the delicate topic of children's activities. Sometimes it's necessary to axe a few of the kids' comings and goings. I believe fully in the principle of getting children involved with lessons, sports, academics, etc., in order to build self-esteem and give them skills for their future, but you can overdo it.

Why are the children so involved? Is it so you'll be seen as a better parent than Mr. Jones down the street? Are you concerned your child be as well accepted as so-and-so's? Did you always want to be a ballet dancer, or whatever? Is the child involved because of peer pressure— "Everyone else is doing it"? Be honest with yourself. Children build self-esteem in part by having successful experiences. When they're worn too thin they don't do anything as well as they might otherwise.

If the children's outside demands are creating a severe financial burden and/or causing contention, stress and anxiety at home (not to mention time jams that disrupt all normal and necessary family activity), ask yourself if the positive results outweigh the negative.

I know this is a sensitive issue, but as long as I'm in this deep, I want to add one other thing. My husband Jim and I have interviewed hundreds of teenagers. One of the questions we asked the kids was, "If you could change one thing in your home, what would it be?" A large majority cited things like, "I wish my parents didn't fight so much," or "I wish things were more peaceful at home."

These "I wish" statements frequently expressed a desire for a lack of conflict in the home. Other interview answers indicated that the home was ill-managed generally because of improper time use.

So go ahead and let the kids get involved, but take it easy. This would be a good time for a family meeting. Discuss the need for limits. Tell the children how much time you have available (and when) and then let them choose activities (within set boundaries) most meaningful for them.

What else could you eliminate from your life? Take a look at this checklist and maybe you can choose one or two things to eliminate that will help alleviate some time jams.

Some Elimination Possibilities

- TV
- Newspapers, magazines, etc.
- Your job (Maybe you could find one closer to your home or, if possible, investigate part-time work or job-sharing options. Perhaps you could even work at home a few days a week.)
- Your house (Maybe a smaller place would be easier to keep up. Maybe you could find a house closer to your job.)
- Going to or giving parties, excessive telephone socializing, coffee klatches, drop-in visitors, meetings
- Manicures, pedicures, weekly hair appointments
- Theatre, movies, plays, concerts
- Excess possessions (The more you have the more you have to take care of.)
- Houseplants, unnecessary yardwork
- Pets
- Gourmet cooking, cake decorating
- Sleeping in or going to bed early
- Waiting time (waiting in doctor's office, standing in lines, waiting for other people—kids, spouse, repairperson)
- Looking for things

- Over-cleaning the house (daily dusting, scrubbing the garage floor, sterilizing the window tracks)
- Excess paperwork
- Time-consuming appliances (ovens you have to clean, freezers you have to defrost)
- Car (Think of all the chauffeuring you'll avoid, servicing time and money you'll save. Maybe you just need to upgrade your car so you won't waste a lot of time waiting for it to be repaired.)
- Surfing the Internet (I know of so many people who spend literally hours on the Internet every day, just surfing and chatting. Imagine the time and money you could save by taming this one little habit.)

One of the superachievers I mentioned earlier is the mother of eleven children; yet she seems to manage everything with ease. When I asked her how she does it, she answered, "I select what I'm going to neglect." She not only plans what she's going to do, but what she's *not* going to do. I put her method to the test and I'm a convert for life. I learned that when you make a conscious decision not to do something, it's a real relief!

Following a housekeeping schedule (as you'll see in chapter 5) is a good example of selected neglect. Often when I'm working around the house my conscience begins to nag. "You should move the furniture and vacuum under it." "Dust the Levolors." "Wash the windows." Sometimes, in order to silence the harping, I say right out loud, "That's scheduled for another day. Today I can neglect it." It's instant peace of mind.

There's another benefit, too. Do you ever experience feelings of guilt or inferiority when you walk into your neighbor's house and see twenty-one quarts of freshly canned tomatoes sitting on the counter, clean sheets on the clothesline snapping in the wind, and a recently scrubbed kitchen floor?

I used to feel envious until I found out about selected neglect. Now I say to myself, "I didn't scrub the floor because I didn't *plan* to."

You'll be more successful with this book if you choose to neglect certain ideas or suggestions. What may seem like a marvelous idea to some may seem like just a lot of hard work to you.

So make those conscious decisions—what goals to pursue (step 1) and what to eliminate (step 2). Step 3—calendaring your time—will explain how to get your plans into action.

YOUR POWER TOOLS

Just as a skilled cabinetmaker relies on the finest power tools to create quality furniture, a skilled time manager depends on power tools as well. And what are those tools? First, a planning notebook; second, a family organizer and for some, a family calendar as well. Let's look at each one separately.

If I were to ask by a show of hands how many of you have ever heard: "Make a list of things you want to accomplish today, put the most important one first, and tick each item off as you complete it," everyone would have his hand waving in the air. Sure, we've all heard it a hundred times—but how many of really *do* it?

My research revealed an important fact about planning. Winners and losers both know the principle of using a calendar, appointment book or planning notebook. The difference is, winners *use* them every single day. That's the bottom line.

My husband frequently has his nose in a book entitled *Coaching the Zone and Man-to-Man Pressing Defenses*, by Neal Baisi. He's always got a game plan in his head and a clipboard on his arm, drawing Xs and Os much like John Madden on Sunday afternoon. Jim has a defensive strategy for every offensive play, and he uses these plays and maneuvers as game situations dictate. Jim said something once that so impressed me, I jotted it down. He said simply, "The purpose of a coach is to get you somewhere you can't go by yourself."

My planning notebook is my coach. It reminds me of the game plan so I can truly be the victor with the spoils—my completed goals. My "coach" tells me when and what to modify as the day progresses, thus assuring optimum results.

The Planning Notebook

The planning notebook I use is $5\frac{1}{2}'' \times 8\frac{1}{2}''$ loose-leaf divided into sections, the first one being the calendar section. The notebook holds daily pages (one per day) where I record to-dos, appointments and notes. There are also twelve monthly calendars so I get a quick overview of what each month looks like.

At the end of the calendar section I keep a "running to-do list." This is where I jot down jobs I need to do (or delegate) but I can't decide when we'll do them. Since I can't assign them to a certain date, I put them on the running to-do list so I won't forget them. During my daily planning session, I check the running to-do list and select a few of the items and get them done.

The other sections in my notebook contain things I want to have with me to refer to. I have a goals section, a menu planning section, a list of books to pick up at the bookstore or library and a section for great flashes of inspiration, to name a few. Everything I need is in one place; it's always with or accessible to me.

I take my notebook everywhere. I have a slipcover on it that converts it into a purse—so it's actually a purse and a planner in one. If your planner is too cumbersome to tote to the symphony or out to dinner, leave it in the car and stick a few note cards in your purse or pocket. (For information about my planning notebook and purse planner, please write to Home Management, P.O. Box 214, Cedar Rapids, IA 52406.) *Confessions of an Organized Homemaker* details the specifics of my daring system.

Get yourself a calendar, an appointment book, a small notebook— anything you can use to make permanent notes and reminders. You can't get where you want to go without one. The system you choose should be big enough for you to record everything you need to record, but small enough so it's portable.

Use It!

Once you've got your equipment in place, force yourself to use it. Make yourself sit down and plan what your course of action will be for the next day.

It's important to plan tomorrow at the end of today. Why? Tonight you'll have your goals in mind with sheer determination to advance them. Naturally, you'll plan to accomplish the most important things first. However, if you try to plan in the morning, all you'll see will be stacks of sticky dishes, mountains of dirty laundry and a hungry baby clinging to your knees. What do you think you'd schedule then? Sure, the urgent stuff. Except for the baby, the other things aren't that important, even though they have to be done. Besides, nowadays most of us are scurrying off to work and directing so much traffic in the morning, there's just not time to plan.

It's easier to keep your priorities straight before you face the harsh realities of the day. In the morning, recheck your plans. If someone wakes with a fever, if the car battery is dead or if a blizzard hit during the night, you may need to make some adjustments.

Of course, some things must be done: dishes washed, lawns mowed and spelling words studied. What seems best is to block out a few hours (or whatever you can afford) to wrap up all the must-do's. Sometimes you may have to block out the time in fifteen-minute increments, espe-cially if you're out of your home several hours a day. What isn't accomplished in the set time can wait until tomorrow, be delegated or forgotten. If you're not careful, routine jobs will fill your entire day and you'll find yourself dealing with problems rather than opportunities.

If you have a hard time setting your daily priorities, try this. Ask yourself, "If I could do only one thing today what would it be?" That answer is your number one priority. This task should be the one that has the greatest impact on one of your personal goals. Then go on to, "If I could only do two things today, what would they be?" Now, you've got your number two job, and so on.

Even if you don't have time to plan, plan anyway. You'll find the total time spent on a project decreases in proportion to the amount of time you spend planning. Honestly, when you then cast your bread upon the waters it comes back buttered!

One word of caution—don't become a *rigid* planner. Leave spots for relaxation and inevitable interruptions. If you're a homemaker you may find it helpful to plan without too strict a deadline. For example, when I plan to have the kitchen clean by 8 A.M., washing done by 10:15, dinner ready by 11:45, I tend to snap at the kids when they interrupt and put me behind schedule. I'm upset with the person who calls on the phone, again frustrating my plans. While deadlines are important, you may need to use more general terms at home, e.g., kitchen cleaned, washing done and dinner ready before lunch.

Another technique I like is the "highest-priority tasks this week" method. Take a Post-it note and jot down those highest priority tasks. This should be a short list of things you'd like to have done by the end of the week—clean out the garage, plant the garden, read the Gospels in the New Testament. The sticky note can be moved from page to page all week as a gentle reminder of your goals.

Whenever you have a few extra minutes, perhaps you can do something to move your goal along towards the finish line. You may not have time to wash all the windows in the house, but can you clean one or two of them? You can work on the garden one row at a time, straighten one corner at a time, and read the New Testament one chapter at a time. It's the best way I know of to get things done without wasting time and to be less irritated by interruptions.

An effective planner groups similar tasks together so as to have a large time bonus when the jobs are completed. For example, when you make several phone calls you handle them as a large job so you get down to business faster and get the whole job done quicker, leaving leftover time in one useful chunk. The same goes for running errands, vacuuming, or shoveling snow.

The Family Calendar

In addition to having a planning notebook you might consider using a family wall calendar. (Note: It is, however, advisable to use only one system. When two or more calendars are being used it requires added effort and time to duplicate the date and you usually wind up with bits and pieces of information on each calendar. Thus, neither is complete nor 100 percent accurate. Some families benefit from using both systems, though, so I'm including it as an option. You can make the decision that's best for your circumstances.)

The family wall calendar can be a monthly calendar with large squares, one of those big plastic-laminated wall planners you wipe off and reuse month after month, or you can make an enlarged version of the following weekly planning sheet. Here you record the time of Jeff's football game, the weekend Lisa is going to the mountains with her friend's family, your next business trip or vacation. Record such seasonal activities as bottling fruits and vegetables, changing the furnace filter, rotating the tires, fertilizing the lawn. As added incentive, be sure to jot down the dates you plan to go to the zoo, the amusement park or the children's museum. The wall calendar can also be used to schedule household chores.

Because the kitchen is the pivotal place for most family activities this is a good spot to hang your wall calendar. If you don't like the looks of it, hang it just inside a cupboard or closet door, or around a corner where it's less conspicuous.

This type of system can keep the family aware of everyone's comings and goings so adequate planning can be maximized and problems minimized. Just be sure you frequently check this family calendar against your own planning notebook so both are kept current. If you find using two calendars is more than you can handle or have time for, drop the wall calendar. The planning notebook is too vital to eliminate.

In our home, everything is pegged to my planning notebook. The whole family realizes its importance and knows if they need a ride somewhere, birthday treats for school or an early dinner on game night, it has to be written down or it's forgotten.

Each one of our children has a weekly planning sheet, and information pertinent to each child is transferred from my notebook onto his sheet once a week. (More about this and a copy of the planning sheet appear in the next chapter.) Because planning a week in advance is easier said than done, I also check with everyone daily to find out what's on the docket. You may also find it useful to exchange photocopies of your week's plans with your spouse.

WEEK OF _____

CALL	THINGS TO DO	PEOPLE TO SEE	CORRESPONDENCE

Monday _____ — Goals: _____
8
9
10
11
12
1
2
3
4
5
6
7
8
9

Tuesday _____ — Goals: _____
8
9
10
11
12
1
2
3
4
5
6
7
8
9

Wednesday _____ — Goals: _____
8
9
10
11
12
1
2
3
4
5
6
7
8
9

Thursday _____ — Goals: _____
8
9
10
11
12
1
2
3
4
5
6
7
8
9

Friday _____ — Goals: _____
8
9
10
11
12
1
2
3
4
5
6
7
8
9

Saturday _____

Sunday _____

The Family Organizer

I was first introduced to this power tool by Harold Taylor, president of Time Management Consultants, Inc., and author of *Making Time Work for You* (Dell Books), and I will be forever in his debt. This organizer saves so much time and eliminates so much clutter, it's a *must* for every home.

What is it? It's a three-ring binder (ours is a full-sized 8½″ × 11″) that holds everything from telephone logs to baseball game schedules.

The purpose of the family organizer is to hold and organize all the papers that anyone in the house has to look at or refer to. Instead of keeping those papers magnetized to the front of the refrigerator, stacked on the counter, or tacked up club-sandwich style on a bulletin board, keep all the papers behind tabbed dividers in the family organizer.

The book holds anything you want it to hold. Here are some ideas: emergency phone numbers, sports rosters and schedules, church phone directory, housekeeping schedule, community calendar, high school calendar, lists of videos available at the video store, facts for the babysitter, the kids' planning sheets (explained in the next chapter), menus for take-out from favorite restaurants, school lunch menus, information or telephone call lists for school, church or auxiliary groups or clubs anyone is involved with.

While it's important to determine what sections will best serve the needs of your family, here are two that should be required: the telephone log and the phone directory.

If you have tiny scraps of paper, envelopes, business cards and matchbooks covered with phone numbers, if you waste a lot of time looking up phone numbers, if your kids can't find anything (but the wall) to write messages on—this form is definitely for you. When one is filled, you can file it away for fast future reference. (Be sure the family rule is "no doodling" on the telephone log.) Enlarge the sample telephone log (see the following page) to 8½″ × 11″ and try it out for only a day. You'll be convinced of its effectiveness.

Next, the phone directory has names and numbers of the kids' and your close friends so you and the children can find each other if you need to.

Also, include the numbers of your favorite stores and restaurants (also note the times they open and close), numbers for the library, school, church, theaters, video stores, plumber, mechanic, doctors, veterinarian, pharmacy. Just include all the numbers you call frequently so you won't have to continually look them up in the phone book.

Make up as many sections as you need and place each behind a tabbed divider to make the information easy to find. I can't stress

Telephone Log

Date	Message for	Caller	Phone #	Message

enough how helpful this book is!

If it's possible, store the family organizer next to the busiest phone in the house. (You might want to have a phone log by each phone.) If you don't have room to store the book by the phone, store it as you would store a regular telephone directory. But—make the family organizer very accessible. If it's hard to get to, no one will use it.

Your power tools are a calendar or planning notebook and the family organizer. If you only choose two ideas from this whole book, these are the ones!

DELEGATION

The fourth and final common denominator in the quest for a winning time management formula is delegation.

Most of us have heard about how much time delegation saves. Many of us have fantasies of happy, agreeable children resounding glad tidings of "What can I do to help, Dad?" In our dreams we see them leap to any undone task. Be honest. Have you ever heard the words, "I'd be happy to, Mom?" Me, either. But I do get my minimum daily requirement of "Why do I have to do all the work around here?" And, "But I didn't make the mess." Applying what we learn about delegation will bring our home lives closer to our fantasies.

Delegation is such an important issue (and probably the reason you're reading this book) that I'm devoting an entire chapter to the subject. You'll learn all about it in chapter 8—after we take a look at everything that needs to be done.

There you have it! The common factors that make up a successful family time management program.

1. Set your goals.
2. Simplify your life.
3. Plan and calendar your time.
4. Delegate.

To say this four-step success program is easy would be as misleading as the phrases, "some assembly required," "virtually spotless" or "wrinkle resistant." Yet, taken one step at a time, it's not overly taxing or complicated; in fact, it's quite logical.

Set your goals. Keeping your direction in mind, streamline your life and carefully plan and schedule your time, delegating whatever you can. Don't you think it's about time?

CHAPTER FOUR

Family Management
and Motivation

I don't know which has caused me more grief over the years, the words "gross," "sick" or "but." "But, Mom, *he* started it." "But I haven't had time to practice." "But that teacher doesn't like me." "But I won't have any time to play." "This food looks gross. Oooo . . . sick."

When you get right down to it, kids have a lot of time management problems. Let's see: don't forget to bring something to school on Friday for show-and-tell; reading records are due on Monday; the science project is due next month; posters for school elections must be up by Tuesday morning; bring a sack lunch for the field trip Thursday; the seal costume for the first grade circus needs to be finished this week; the Excel program is held every Wednesday after school for forty-five minutes; baby-sitting this weekend; tuba lessons Saturday afternoon. Add to this maze household chores, doctors' appointments, sporting events, things they just plain want to do, and you'll get the picture. Kids are busy.

My main concern as a parent is that the children use their time wisely. If they're involved in constructive activities, I'm not so concerned if they don't always do a lot of extra housework. What I'm after is an overriding feeling of being a responsible, contributing person.

For example, one of our boys wanted to be an orthopedic surgeon. He worked hard at school and got good grades. He was also a sports fanatic and fairly gifted athlete. From the time he was very young, he wanted to go to a Big Ten school on an athletic scholarship. Even as a youngster in elementary school he anxiously pursued those goals. In the fall and winter he played basketball, either at a regular practice or league game, about six days a week. In the spring and summer he'd follow a similar regimen with baseball. He wasn't just goofing off. When he'd work out in the gym, he'd run for miles dribbling through his legs, shooting layups and working on his left hand. Naturally, working out this much and maintaining his grades, he wasn't available to do a lot of housework. But we were behind him all the way because we felt he was managing his time well.

Was that a good decision? Over the years, his choice of career changed as did his choice of colleges—but he got the scholarship. So, all the work paid for his college education and paved the way for a successful self-disciplined life.

TIME MANAGEMENT AND KIDS

Although our basic philosophies may differ, I'm sure you agree it's important for children to learn to manage their time well. Let's run through the time management success formula as it pertains to kids.

Step 1: *Setting goals.*

No, I promise I'm not going to rehash this. If necessary, reread chapter 2, Goal Setting, then begin leading your children in the goal selection process.

Step 2: *Simplify their lives.*

Again, this needs no further discussion. Sit down with the child, take a hard look at all his time requirements and decide together what, if anything, needs to be dropped or restructured.

Step 3: *Planning for wise time use.*

Wouldn't it be wonderful if all your kids kept planning notebooks, jotting down all their assignments, scheduling blocks of time for reports and projects, and reminding you of their upcoming doctors' appointments? Yes, it *would* be wonderful, but don't hold your breath. If my family is any indicator of the norm, probably less than 20 percent of the world's children would be so inclined, and that may be a generous estimate. Still, having the children become independently responsible planners is the desired result, right? Don't throw your hands in the air and declare defeat—here's a program that will gradually lead your kids to that point.

For years we used planning sheets for each of the children. Divide an $8\frac{1}{2}'' \times 11''$ sheet of paper into four vertical columns: chores, assignments, activities and appointments, and things I want to do. Each category is broken down into daily squares so the whole page shows one week at a glance.

We kept the planning sheets in a section in our Family Organizer. You may discover some kids like to take these planning sheets to school for recording homework. A family wall calendar can be used

	Chores	Assignments	Activities & Appointments	Things I Want to Do
MONDAY				
TUESDAY				
WEDNESDAY				
THURSDAY				
FRIDAY				
SATURDAY				
SUNDAY				Name:

in place of the weekly planning sheets, too.

Sit down with the kids once a week (Sunday afternoon is a good time because it's the beginning of a new week) and have them fill out their sheets. The chores column holds a list of the household work they've agreed to do during the week (and I use the term "agreed" loosely). The assignment column is where they record any big or recurring school assignments. (Unless the sheets are taken to school, it will be impossible to record every single assignment they're given.) The activities and appointments section is where they note anything with a specific time attached to it. The things I want to do section will act as their motivation and reward. Be sure they have at least one thing each week to look forward to.

If you have children who can't read, you can fill out the charts using stickers or pictures (from magazines, coloring books or rubber stamps).

Make this weekly planning session a ritual. The first few weeks it'll be pretty easy because your own level of enthusiasm will be high and it will be something new and different for the kids, so they'll be fairly interested.

After the novelty wears off it may become a little harder; don't despair. Stick to it. You're just forming a new habit and once you're over the hump it'll become second nature for you and the kids.

Remember, *any* program will work if *you* work. Like any new habit you're trying to form, you need to start over and start over until it's well established. Programs don't fail or cease to work— people do. As a parent, this habit will cost you some time initially, but in the long haul you'll save a bundle.

As the children mature and show a desire for a more independent program, you're ready to move them along to a system that requires less parental guidance. When you feel a child is ready, you might want to have him start using a pocket calendar, assignment book or a complete planning notebook (similar to yours, but with sections helpful to him). If you select a calendar, usually a month-at-a-glance or a week-at-a-glance works best for kids; the books are thinner and less cumbersome. Encourage the child to use it at school to jot down homework when it's assigned or when something isn't completed during the allotted school time and must be finished at home. That way a quick check at the end of the day reminds the child what must come home.

Try using this weekly planning form, making whatever modifications you deem necessary. Then, as soon as the children are ready, encourage them to independently plan in advance, using a calendar. It's a lasting habit worth developing in children. Can you imagine what a great advantage they'll have entering adult life as planners?

Step 4: *Delegation.*
While the kids won't be doing much delegating (unless an older child is left in charge), they need to be responsive to being delegated to.

I know you have many questions: "What if the kids refuse to plan?" "How do I become a successful delegator?" "There's no way my fifteen-year-old is going to sit down and set goals. What then?"

(Remember, a detailed discussion about delegation is coming up in chapter 8. In chapter 9 we'll look at what to do when all else fails. This chapter may give you some answers.)

I think the real key, though, is your relationship with the child. If there's a general feeling of camaraderie between you, the kids will do just about anything you ask them to.

With younger children you have more control, and (at first) insisting the child sit down with you and plan his week is usually effective. However, as kids get older, it becomes increasingly difficult.

You may get your fourteen-year-old son to sit down and plan every week, but what do you do if he sticks his planning sheet in his drawer and forgets it? What if he ignores the family wall calendar? What then? Keep planning with him anyway. Your devotion to the cause has to outlast his indifference.

You can also take a "tough love" approach and let the child miss a few of his "Things I Want to Do" activities. If he forgets about it and doesn't plan far enough in advance to arrange a ride (or whatever), he may begin to feel the responsibility (and the need) to plan.

Granted, there's really no way you can force anyone to do something they don't want to do, and just trying often makes things worse. Your role as a parent is to set an example and encourage. Encouraging, however, doesn't mean badgering, fussing or excessive reminding. It means you have the tools (in this case, planning sheets, calendar and family organizer). It means you watch for moments of receptiveness and make yourself available to help.

The time management formula for kids, then, is essentially the same one we use, only it's a little less rigid and allows for some immaturity. Initially the system will be guided, directed and gently led by you or any other willing and available person, such as your spouse, an older child or other interested party.

If you find yourself falling into the immature category (as I often do), you, too, can begin your system the same way. Find someone— a spouse, a friend, Uncle Harry—anyone who will prompt (nag), guide (boss) and direct (force) you to do it!

Now, let's see what we can do to organize and help manage the five basic time demands placed on children.

HOUSEHOLD CHORES

In the next chapter we're going to delve into housework, so I won't go into specifics now. As far as time management for kids goes, the important thing to remember is that children need to know in advance what you've got planned for them.

I know I'm often guilty of piling on the work when I need it done, when I'm in the mood and when it happens to be convenient for me. No wonder the kids complain.

You know how frustrated you feel when you've got your head full of plans and ideas and someone all of a sudden imposes something on you? (When the boss dumps an urgent project on your desk, when out-of-town guests arrive a day early, when the phone rings and it's Chatty Cathy.) Well, kids feel the same way. Get them mentally prepared so they can work *their* head full of plans and ideas around the work you've assigned. Give the children the same courtesy you'd like to receive.

ASSIGNMENTS: THE RAW MATERIALS

Homework is necessary, and I know we need more of it. But it's a real pain, isn't it? Even kindergarteners have to paste and cut and color. First-graders bring home their stimulating reading books and word lists for you to listen to (at least thirty minutes every night). As far as I'm concerned, it goes downhill from there. The work gets harder, takes longer and causes a lot of family traffic jams. Homework is not going to go away until the kids do, so we'd best make the most of it.

There are several things you can do to make homework easier and more enjoyable for the kids and less of a burden for you.

As a parent, your role in the homework process is to:

1. Ask if they have any homework.
2. Show your interest in their work by providing them with the necessary raw materials.
3. Provide an area conducive to study.
4. Teach them how to break down large, tough assignments.
5. Use a landing/launch pad.

Before we proceed further, keep in mind that here's where the "cherry picking" comes in. You may choose to have a supply of paper and pencils and forget about the file I'm going to suggest. You may not have time to make up an outline for a big project or the space for a central homework area. The child, too, makes a difference. Some kids seem to need the extra discipline of forms and outlines; others don't. Just evaluate the needs of your family and choose accordingly.

A lot of these ideas, though, are one-shot deals. You and the kids make the initial time investment (while you're setting things up), then you sit back and enjoy the benefits. I'd rather *plan* the initial time outlay than be constantly interrupted by trips to the store for supplies, jaunts to the library for information, and problems caused by the frenzy of last-minute efforts.

With those cautions in place, let's get started.

First, be sure your home is well stocked with good reference materials. You need a dictionary, a current atlas and a set of encyclopedias geared to the child's age level. Secondhand stores are replete with cheap sets of encyclopedias. Even if the set doesn't match, it'll be adequate and inexpensive. As far as being outdated, I figure history won't change once it's history. If it's dead or over (Abe Lincoln, World War II) you have an accurate source. (Of course, you'll have to check out other sources for reports on computers, space shuttles, etc.) If you're on the "super highway," though, you'll have everything you need right on the computer.

Second, a subject file filled with pictures and articles is a good resource and usually adds to the quality of the work being done.

Here is a list of some useful subject headings for your file: alcohol and drug abuse, art, biology, clothing and textiles, ecology, energy, geography, history, literature, medicine, music, physical fitness, space, sports, transportation.

Keep your eyes open for colorful advertisements, particularly from travel agencies and book publishers; postcards; magazine and newspaper articles; materials gathered from museums and art galleries; maps; and anything else that grabs your attention.

Again, secondhand shops are havens for *National Geographic* magazines, *Reader's Digest*s and other magazines of varied interest. (I'm so proud of all those folks who had the courage to *share* their old magazines, aren't you?) I'm not recommending you cart all these periodicals home because they "might come in handy someday." But if you need information and pictures about Zimbabwe, let's say, a secondhand shop is a good place to get them.

Other resources to keep in mind are places like the American Dairy Council, Heart Association, travel agencies and government agencies (the Department of Alcohol, Tobacco and Firearms, Civil Defense, Department of Agriculture, etc.) and your local college extension office. Look through your phone book for agencies that deal with the subject in question. They have charts, posters, pictures and booklets that are yours for the asking. Sometimes a nominal fee is charged, but most of these things are free.

Due to storage and time limitations it's probably best to file away only those things you come by naturally. Don't go into hot pursuit of material unless it's needed for a specific project. Any leftovers, though, can be tucked away for safekeeping. (Another idea is to preview the curriculum at the beginning of the school year and develop the file accordingly.)

Along with reference books and a subject file, keep a stock of these supplies on hand: paper (ruled and unruled), pencils, pens, markers, colored pencils, crayons, erasers, glue, tape, stapler and staples, rulers, folders and a pencil sharpener. It's also helpful to stock up on poster board. Also, a few empty shoe boxes come in handy from time to time.

Nothing's more frustrating than last-minute trips to the store for these essential supplies. And it never fails—as soon as you get a child into the store he sees a silver and green marker that makes iridescent stripes and he absolutely, positively *has* to have that one for his map. And wouldn't it be great to get that five-compartment has-everything, does-everything notebook that (according to the child) functions much like a laptop computer? Save yourself some grief—inventory your school supplies as you do the groceries.

It's helpful to provide the children with a folder for each of their main subjects: reading, handwriting, arithmetic, science, etc. These help to keep their desks organized at school and give them a safe place for completed homework.

Systems and Storage

As far as the actual homework doing is concerned, that's pretty much up to you and what your family schedule dictates. Some families insist homework be done immediately after school. Others wait until after dinner. But whatever program you enlist, be consistent. Make homework part of the child's regular schedule so he gets used to an orderly routine.

The spot for doing homework should be conducive to study. Generally, at our house, homework is done in the kitchen while dinner is being prepared or while dishes are washed. It's nice for the child to have someone handy so he can ask a question or discuss insights he's gained from study.

If the kids do their homework in one central location (kitchen, den, family room, dining room, living room), you'll need only one set of supplies. But if everyone is banished to various parts of the house, they either have to chase around for the dictionary and a sharpened pencil, or you have to provide duplicate equipment.

Are radios usually blaring while homework is going on? That could present another problem: one person wants to listen to country while the other wants rock—so they can't work together in the same place. Sometimes there's teasing and arguing (or just talking and horsing around) going on. What then? Maybe the schoolkids can work in their bedrooms and keep the supplies stored central to both—in the linen closet perhaps. So if you have to separate the kids, keep all the home-work materials in one cache convenient to everyone.

Storage for your school supply repository need not be elaborate. Your reference file, if you have one, can be contained in an expanding, accordion-type file, or individual file folders can stand in a cardboard box. Many types of portable file containers made from cardboard, plastic or lightweight metal are available at office supply, discount or variety stores.

Your paper supplies can be stored in a portable file container; per-haps you have a spare drawer or shelf. In either case, keep the paper separated and neat in a dishpan or cardboard box. If your only empty space is on the floor or the wall, you can use covered baskets or under-the-bed storage on the floor, bicycle baskets (they're flat on one side, making them ideal for hanging), or hanging purse files for hanging wall storage. Don't forget the hanging space on the inside of cupboard and closet doors.

Cardboard shoe files provide you with nine little cubbyholes in which to stash your supplies. Pencils, pens, crayons, etc., can be kept in a drawer (compartmentalized with drawer dividers or small cardboard boxes), a shoe box, a cardboard shoe file or a lightweight tool or tackle box. (Look for plastic boxes so the kids will do minimum damage when they bang them into furniture and slide them across the kitchen counter.) Also, small parts cabinets made especially for screws, nuts, bolts and nails come in all sizes and lend themselves perfectly to storing school supplies. These cabinets stand on a shelf or are easily mounted on any vertical surface. It's best to store poster board in an art portfolio. These are available at art supply or craft stores. The portfolio keeps the poster board clean and flat.

If space is limited, see if you at least have room for a dictionary, some paper, pencils with erasers and a pencil sharpener; these nitty-gritty materials are the mainstays. Keeping supplies in reserve and handy will make homework time more pleasant for you and the kids.

Breaking Up Is Easy to Do

Special problems arise when the *big* one hits—the science project or the term paper (complete with footnotes, bibliography and title page). To a young child, especially, this can seem like a monumental, overwhelming task.

The first step is to sit down and break up. (Believe me, that's what I always feel like doing when someone brings home another big assignment.) Seriously, though, begin by breaking up the job into manageable portions.

Let's say your child has been assigned a report on another country. Here are the specifics: The report can be about any country, it must be 19 handwritten pages, and must also include a map, a flag, an original picture and a graph—all prepared by the student. The report must have a title page, table of contents and a bibliography of at least three different sources. The report is due April 16.

Start by asking the child what country he'd like to research. When that's decided, go on to the kinds of things he'd like to cover in the report. (You may need to lead this discussion if the child is in elementary school.)

Let's say the child decides to write a report about England. Through the remainder of your discussion you both decide to cover England's history, geography, sociology, political science and economy; an introduction and summary will be included. The last step in this initial planning session is to decide how many pages to allocate to each subject. Once this is done, I find it helpful to type up a work schedule for the child to follow:

1. Introduction, 1 full page. *Due Feb. 19*

2. History, 5 pages. *Due Feb. 26*
   Include a time line, the country's great leaders, magazine and newspaper articles (current history), ancient and modern maps.

3. Geography, 2 pages. *Due March 5*

   A. Location and size of the country
   B. Land regions (elevation and area and type of land—desert, grassland, etc.)

C. Natural features: rivers, lakes, waterfalls, mountain ranges, plants, animals

D. Climate

(This would be a good place to include the map)

Map—*Due March 5*

4. Sociology, 5 pages. *Due March 12*

This is the way the people live. Try to include something about each of the following:

A. Major religions

B. Education and schools

C. Major cities

D. Principal languages

E. Food and clothing

F. Architecture, painting, sculpture

G. Literature (legends, myths, famous writers)

H. Music and famous musicians—folk music, instruments and dance

I. Crafts, skills, occupations

J. Famous people: artists, poets, musicians, statesmen, rulers
   Consider adding pictures, biographies of famous people, music, recipes for food preparation, pictures of costumes, homes, holidays, etc. (Good place for your original picture.)
   Picture—*Due March 12*

5. Political Science, 1 page. *Due March 19*

Write about the kind of government the country has. How it compares to our government, the good and bad things about this type of government. What is the relationship of this country to the United States? Does it belong to the United Nations?

Consider Using:

A. A diagram of the government structure

B. Picture, flags, emblems, posters

C. News articles
   (Good place for your flag.)
   Flag—*Due March 19*

6. Economy, 2 pages. *Due March 26*

Include:

A. Natural resources of the country and uses made of them

B. The ways in which most people make their livings

    C. Compared to our state, are the people rich or poor?
    D. Major industries: Farming, mining, fishing, etc.
    E. Exports and imports
    F. Transportation and communication—what kinds do they have?
    G. Currency used. Compare to the American dollar
    H. Technology: What kind and how advanced?
       Consider using charts and graphs, comparison maps, news articles, science reports, coins. (Good place for your graph.) Graph—*Due March 26*

7. Summary, 3 pages. *Due April 5*

8. Rough draft. *Due April 7*

9. Final draft. *Due April 16*

After the outline is ready, sit down with the child again and, working backwards from the deadline (April 16), fill in minideadlines. (If you're afraid the child might be overwhelmed by the content of such an outline, type each section on a separate sheet.)

I know this takes some time initially, but now the child is on his own, secure in the knowledge he can handle it. The job is broken down and feasible. Anyone can write a one-page introduction. And five pages about the country's history isn't impossible. The only other thing the child will need from you is support in the form of making sure minideadlines are met and possibly an occasional ride to the library. As far as I'm concerned the initial time outlay is well worth it.

Since reports on other countries are such common assignments, please use this outline as more than an example. When someone comes home and says he's got to do such a report, pull out this book and use the outline! Of course, you'll need to alter a few things, e.g., number of pages, date due, specific requirements (maps, pictures, flags, etc.), but most of the work is already done for you. Better yet, take the outline to school and suggest the teacher provide the kids with a similar guide. The sixth-grade teachers at our school do this on a regular basis—which is evidenced by the quality of work the kids turn in.

As the child advances in age and skill he'll be able to do his own schedule outline. I can't overemphasize how important it is to learn this skill and to use it! Believe me, I'm using this same technique to write this book. Your child will use the work schedule outline throughout his life.

The outline I gave you is an example of a major project, so it's quite detailed. However, use this same idea for all extra projects no matter their size. Sit down with the child and start a brainstorming session: What are the requirements for the assignment? When is the report due? What do you want to research? What topics sound interesting? What things do you think you should cover? What type of extras do you want to include: maps, artwork, experiments, interviews, models, posters, an arty report cover? The outline can be as elaborate or as simple as the assignment requires.

Homework: Wrap-Up

For years I've wallowed in a never-ending stream of schoolwork, library books, permission slips, lunch money, bookbags, artwork, school calendars, and messages from the principal. This junk is always stacked, stuffed and piled in the kitchen as if attracted there by a strong magnet.

Here's what we did that cleared off the kitchen counter for good! We gave each one of the kids an in and out basket. You need one for every school-age child. Any container or portion of a bookshelf will work. We use vegetable bins because they're narrow and they don't take up a lot of space. We keep these bins behind closed doors on a low cupboard shelf for easy access. They're so important—they remove so much clutter—I'd gladly put away a whole set of dishes just to make room for them.

The kids come home from school, take all the papers out of their backpacks and toss everything into their bins. If they've received mail or magazines during the day they're waiting for them in their bins. If I have to sign permission slips, report cards, send money to school, send oatmeal boxes or egg cartons to school those things are put into their bins—not on the counter to remind them to take the things to school. Everything gets tossed inside the bin and is ready to launch the child to school without last-minute searches and without forgetting things.

In order to keep these working, you have to clean these bins out about once a month because old spelling tests and corrected math papers will sift to the bottom of the container. You will uncover treasures, though—cards from Grandma, photographs, old report cards, creative stories they have written. Whenever we find something "historical" (something meaningful we want to keep forever) those things are placed in another location where they are held until they're put into scrapbooks.

You may live in a tiny bungalow and may not *have* an extra cupboard or shelf to use for landing/launch pads, but you can use book bags or tote bags for the same purpose. They can hang on a peg, nail or hook in the child's room, in the coat closet or on the back of a door somewhere. Perhaps you have some unused floor space for a crock or covered basket. Maybe you have an end table or a nightstand with a spare drawer. Don't give up your search until you find a handy spot. This system will save you too much confusion to ignore it; I'd go so far as to say that this idea is *not* optional—it's necessary!

APPOINTMENTS AND ACTIVITIES

The appointments and activities column is where any activity (with a time attached to it) is recorded, e.g., lessons, practices, meetings, appointments. With the kids' activities and appointments noted on their planning sheets, *you* don't always have to nag and remind them about upcoming obligations. Whenever they come to you with a request to go somewhere or do something, tell them to check their planning sheets to see if they have to be somewhere else.

Again, this is a matter of simplifying and planning. It's helpful to be aware at least a week in advance of what's coming up so meals can be planned and scheduled, jobs traded if necessary, and transportation provided.

If you're doing a lot of chauffeuring and have waiting time, take along projects to work on: reading material, correspondence, bills to pay, needlework, motivational tapes, manicure equipment, business work, craft projects, remodeling ideas or plans for rotating your crops.

Carla Hassel, author of *You Can Be a Super Quilter,* has a gorgeous quilt she pieced together strictly during waiting time. I'm crocheting a doily the same way. Dallin Oaks, former president of Brigham Young University, is a voracious reader who often reads while waiting for a red light to change.

If you find yourself waiting during your child's guitar lessons every week, check out the neighborhood. Are you close to a market, a dry cleaner, a library, secondhand shop, a friend's house, shoe repair shop, bakery, pharmacy? In other words, is there anything in the immediate area that could help you accomplish an errand or two, move you closer to a goal, or occupy your time productively?

Since we spend so much time in the car, we've found it helpful to have a "car organizer." This is just a plastic school (or pencil) box that slides under the front seat of the car. In the container we keep: a zip-type plastic bag (it comes in handy for many things), a few pieces of paper and an envelope, stamps, scratch pad, comb, tape, scissors, pen, mending kit (in case a button falls off or a seam rips), plastic bandages, wet wipes, rubber bands, aspirin, emergency change for a phone call or a toll, tissue. Now, if you want to use a larger container or carry more things you can also include things like emery boards, screwdriver, can opener, extra pantyhose, disposable diaper, etc. If you have young children, diapers and pins, extra cans of formula and a small box of crackers are additional conveniences to consider. Just include anything you've ever wished for when you were away from home. This car organizer will really clean out your purse. Most women keep a lot of extra supplies in their purses because the things might come in handy. But, with everything in the car organizer you'll have the security of knowing what you need is just as close as the car.

THINGS I WANT TO DO

I can't imagine enjoying my life if I weren't able to do a lot of things I just want to do; these activities are necessary and can make living worthwhile. Be sure, too, your kids aren't locked into a rigid time management regimen that provides little or no escape.

When we registered our oldest child in seventh grade, he was still only eleven years old; the guidance counselor handed me a current list of college entrance requirements and probable future requirements. In today's rat race world of whirring computers, international competition and pressure to achieve, our kids hardly have the chance to be kids any more!

Don't misunderstand, I'm not opposed to looking ahead to college entrance or generally nudging children along, but I think we need to let them be kids, too. The "things I want to do" portion of a child's life is important. We just need to keep a check on it so it doesn't tip the scale.

Kids need a good balance between the five areas: homework, housework, activities, appointments and things I want to do. Your function is much like a weigh station on interstate highways: just as the truck pulls in for periodic weighings, your child's time demands need routine checks and balances.

CHAPTER FIVE

Scheme Cleaning

Today's assignment:

Straighten up the house	Fix dinner
Fix breakfast	Clean up the kitchen
Help get the kids ready for school	Wash a few loads of laundry
Get ready for work	Fold and put away laundry
Pack lunches	Vacuum traffic areas
Make beds	Dust furniture
Clean the bathroom	Empty trash
Wash dishes	Iron
Straighten up the kitchen	Paperwork

Tomorrow's assignment:

Straighten up the house	Fix dinner
Fix breakfast	Clean up the kitchen
Help get the kids ready for school	Wash a few loads of laundry
Get ready for work	Fold and put away laundry
Pack lunches	Vacuum traffic areas
Make beds	Dust furniture
Clean the bathroom	Empty trash
Wash dishes	Iron
Straighten up the kitchen	Paperwork

Yes, all the things you've heard about housework are true: it's like popping corn without a lid; it's like running in place; it's like stringing pearls without having a knot on the end of the string. It's like always going to practice and never getting to play in the game. And, when you get finished, it's time to start over. Yes, we get up and do today what we didn't even want to do yesterday.

Granted, housework is a loathsome job, but I'm afraid inept cleaning methods have made it worse. Not until you're able to keep housework under control will it become agreeable to you.

Basically, we make two mistakes:

1. We don't use enough work simplification techniques.
2. We don't schedule well enough.

And while I'm aware of these two pitfalls and though I try to simplify the work and schedule my time, I realize that I, too, can still sharpen my skills. There's always room for improvement.

Now, I won't promise after reading this chapter you're going to await cleaning day with eager anticipation. But I can promise you'll feel like the hundreds who've read *Confessions of an Organized Homemaker* and have written me to say: "Now I have more time to do everything else I have to do, without worrying about my housework. I feel so much better leaving my house, and feel even better knowing that when I return my house is clean and organized.

Here's my favorite comment from a reader: "I have never been compelled to write to the author of a book before, but I've also never had a book change my life.

"I was expecting my second child and feeling totally out of control. I had given up my job, which didn't pay me a lot but was very fulfilling. My house was always a wreck, which drove me nuts. I used to freak out entirely when people came to the house without calling first. Then they had to give me at least two hours while my husband and I frantically picked up and hid most of the mess.

"I found housework thankless and a general waste of time—I used to say 'creative people are never tidy.' I was forever doing crafts and other things I felt were more rewarding than laundry, dishes, feeding three dogs, vacuuming, etc. . . .

"Then I bought your book—I knew there was no way I was going to keep my sanity and get any sense of self-worth going down the road I was on. I knew I could get organized. Actually I love to put things in order but the problem was keeping things that way.

"It's been a little over a month now and I still feel like at least I have a handle on the house no matter how bad it gets. I had a friend I hadn't seen in six months call me the other day to say she was on her way up to see me. Imagine my complete surprise when I leisurely picked up my living room and entry area in half an hour and sat waiting for her with tea!"

I couldn't have said it better. You can experience those same feelings by following six basic work simplification techniques, the same techniques used by these delighted readers.

MAKE IT EASY ON YOURSELF

Work simplification methods apply to all areas of your life from fixing breakfast to preparing a fiscal-year-ending financial statement. These six guidelines are simple and logical:

1. Think before you act.
2. Discard and sort.
3. Group.
4. Be motion-minded.
5. Accrue your benefits.
6. Preventive maintenance.

In my first book I devoted a lot of space to these techniques. For our purposes, let's see how they apply specifically to housework.

THINK BEFORE YOU ACT

Thinking before you act implies two things: First, you need to think before doing anything—even a routine task. Second, in the broader sense, it means to plan and schedule your work. Let's explore these two principles.

In his book *Executive Housekeeping: The Business of Managing Your Home* (William Morrow), Auren Uris suggests using the word "why": "Why is it necessary? Why in that place? Why at that time? Why by that person? Why in this manner?"

Every time you set off on an expedition to get the mop, a box of Tide, a wooden spoon or the vacuum, ask yourself, "Why?" Most of our actions are habitual, not deliberately chosen as they should be (and *will* be once you begin using work simplification techniques).

A while back I started taking a class on Wednesday mornings. It was an awkward day for me, but the only day the class was offered, so I made the best of it. Every Wednesday I'd get an early start to tidy up the house and do the laundry before the class started at 10 A.M. It's no easy matter to finish an entire laundry for seven people—including diapers—before 10 A.M., but I worked like a fool, knowing when I got home I wouldn't feel like doing anything.

Wednesday mornings became so hectic I almost decided to drop the class. But "why?" put everything into proper perspective. Why was Wednesday a mess? Mainly because I did the laundry on Wednesday and I was having a hard time getting everything finished before I left for class.

The next logical question was, "Why do you wash on Wednesday?" The only reason I could think of was that years ago I made an arbitrary decision to wash on Wednesday. I had always washed on Wednesday. There's where I discovered my error. I didn't have a good reason for using Wednesday as laundry day. It was perfectly all right to change the day and open up Wednesday for more useful and productive pursuits.

Habit is comfortable; we feel secure keeping everything at status quo. It feels safe, but it isn't! When you notice yourself walking around your house not getting much done, ask yourself "why?" When you're in the midst of confusion, ask yourself "why?" "Why" will tell you if a job is necessary—and then let you know if your methods can be improved.

At first, questioning your routine behavior will seem too self-conscious, and feel ponderous—but stick with it. Soon it will become an instinctive procedure that will make work simplification an ongoing process.

As my Wednesday morning story points out, as your circumstances and lifestyle undergo changes, so must your ways and means of doing things. Don't assume once everything is running smoothly you can slack off.

Start right now, today! Ask yourself "why?" and begin to think before you act. As a parent, I've discovered work simplification leads to greater family cooperation because tasks are both more convenient and quicker to accomplish—two marvelous incentives.

SCHEDULES: YOUR GOAL MINE

Everyone needs to write down a housekeeping schedule even if they're not going to follow it! Slobs need schedules so they'll know they have to start; they have to do something. (Besides, nagging is quieter on paper.) Perfectionists need schedules so they'll know when to stop. There are more important things in life than housework and perfectionists forget that.

Life is too short to spend it washing the water softener and the inside of the dishwasher. And who cares if the cup handles are facing in the same direction or the furnace vents are scrubbed and sanitized once a week?

A person who can't follow a schedule needs one, too. At first he uses it as a guide—a list to pick and choose from. Or the schedule can be followed for an hour or so. The point is simply to direct your activities so you're in the driver's seat instead of under the wheels.

One of the big problems with housework is that it's never done. You can work for hours and hours and never feel like you've accomplished anything. But a schedule eliminates those feelings of frustration by giving you a stopping point. The work may not be finished, but *you* are. Monday's work can be completed. Tuesday's work can be done—and so on. Sure, there may be other areas that need your attention, but that's scheduled for another day. You have a point at which you can say, "I'm finished!"

Finishing is a technique espoused by many time management experts. Finishing adds to your energy level, aids your concentration, and accelerates feelings of success, motivation and personal satisfaction. Completing today's scheduled items helps you concentrate on the things you *have* done rather than on the things you haven't.

I believe the reason housework has a bad reputation is because most of us don't schedule it. We never get that "I'm finished" feeling. Soon we're overcome with emotions destructive to our spirit and our energy. We decide what we're doing is boring, unfulfilling and beneath us, when in fact we ourselves have made it that way. No wonder we have trouble getting the rest of the family to cooperate.

Schedules keep things on track so certain areas aren't polished too often and others aren't neglected too long. A home that's clean and well managed offers added leisure for all to enjoy.

A house that's overdone, remember, is just as destructive as one that's neglected. If you only allow people to sit, stand or walk in the roped-off area, you're creating a place that people leave when they want to enjoy themselves. Home should be a tidy, comfortable place: a place where you want to be and a place where other people want to be; a place where everyone feels warm and welcomed. Let's see how you can create just such a place.

STANDARDS VS. SCHEDULES

Schedules fail for many reasons. Too often we try to keep up with other's standards: "Oh, the Joneses are shaking their throw rugs. We better shake ours, too, only we'll shake ours harder and longer!"

And of course there's the awful prospect, "What if someone should drop by!" Horror of horrors! Wouldn't it be a shame if they discovered that you live in a house—not a museum? Somewhere along the line we arrived at the thriving misconception that the house should be cleaner for visitors than it is for the family who lives there.

Another reason for schedule burnout is that we don't keep asking "why?" as our lives change. If you start working the swing shift, have a baby or move in with relatives, you need to rethink and redo your schedule. Just as your life is constantly changing, so must your schedule be revised.

Schedules often fail because we overprogram, thinking we can do more on any given day than we actually can. Or we schedule as if we're mortally afraid of dirt: "Clean between blender buttons four times a week. Remove all crumbs from toaster Monday, Wednesday and Friday. Eat out as often as possible. Clean bedrails, stored folding chairs and window tracks twice weekly." You'll agree, with *this* approach, that giving up is better than giving in.

Let's figure out a realistic, workable schedule and see if we can't encourage (and successfully recruit) some help.

Basically, there are only five things you need be concerned with:

1. General pickup (including bedmaking)
2. Laundry
3. Meals
4. Dishes
5. Bathrooms

If you're worried about folks dropping over you might want to add a sixth item to your list: the entry area.

If you and your recruits can keep up on these five or six areas, you've taken care of the most essential home management tasks. If you're holding down a job in addition to your domestic duties, these five or six assignments are probably all you'll have time for.

If you're feeling swamped and overwhelmed, is it because you have visions of grandma doing the family wash every Monday, hanging freshly starched and ironed curtains up to a sparkling kitchen window, and doing spring and fall housecleaning with a vengeance? (Our kids' grandma washes the outside of her mobile home with Formula 409.) It's hard to compete with a role model like that.

It's wise to remember you're busier than your parents or grandparents and houses are basically cleaner than they were years ago. We have powerful equipment to suck dirt off the floor. There are few coal furnaces, more air conditioners, paved roads, carpets, cleaning agents and state-of-the-art, ergonomically correct cleaning tools. We live in a time when new and improved, one-step, one-stop, no-wax, giant-sized products are widely available and samples are sent free through the mail. Yet, with all these luxuries, do you keep at it, picking and flicking dust and dirt, moving things a little closer to the center, and lowering the blinds to exactly the same distance from the sill?

Maybe that's why you're feeling swamped. Perhaps you should relax your standards just a little. Use some selected neglect. Decide what you'll do well (those five or six areas) and choose things to ease up on.

Then again, you might be overwhelmed because there's so much to do that you don't know where to start. The job is *so* big, it's paralyzing. You *can't* start. The best thing to do at this point is to sit down and make a list of everything that needs to be done. Just making the list will instantly help you to feel better because everything on the list is in your brain reminding, criticizing and harping on you when you're trying to go to sleep, concentrate on a project at work or read the newspaper.

Look at the list and choose one thing to work on. That one thing is your goal. Work at it everyday until it's done. Maybe you can only devote five minutes a day to the project. That's okay. If you keep chipping away at the task, it will be done.

Completely finish the job you've selected. Don't do a little bit here and a little over there. Focus your attention on your chosen goal and finish it. Then go back to the list and choose another project. (Remember to maintain the area you just completed.)

Yes, this can be slow. It took me six months to get on top of things after I "hit bottom." But it's the only way to make progress without being overwhelmed.

THIS ONE'S FOR YOU

OK. I'll stop preaching and start helping. What's called for is a housekeeping schedule tailor-made for you: a schedule that takes into consideration your family size, home size, the amount of time you spend at home, how much help you can uncover, your energy level and your individual value system.

It's an easy, sure-fire method. All you need to do is to survey every room in your house, indicating everything you think needs to be done to clean each room. Then decide how often each job should be done and who should (or could) be responsible for the job. (In *Confessions of an Organized Homemaker* there is a Schedule-Maker form that makes this process much easier.)

Keeping Up Down Under

Occasionally, your house will require a little "down under" attention. While spring and fall housecleaning may be a thing of the past, it's still necessary from time to time to clean drapes, carpets and furniture, to wash walls and windows, to fix up, paint and repair. With the pace of today's typical lifestyle it seems impossible to come up with blocks of time large enough to make even a dent in these jobs, let alone complete them. Many of us do nothing, waiting for the perfect situation to present itself—and then we'll get busy.

If you feel the need to dig in, but don't have an expanse of time available, all you do is to break the job into bite-sized pieces. If you can scrounge up at least one half-hour or hour a day and dig into one room, you should be able to complete a room a week. Although this may not be the ideal way to deep-clean, it's better than doing nothing. It sure beats spending your two-week vacation on all fours sorting, scrubbing, stripping and screaming.

If you can afford hired help, so much the better. You can forget the burdened-down feelings that accompany big cleaning jobs, and the process will be infinitely quicker.

That wraps up our discussion of the first work simplification technique—think before you act. Think about what you're doing and how you're doing it and look for easier and quicker ways to accomplish every job. Next, plan and schedule your housekeeping chores—a vital step in successfully navigating your life.

CHAPTER SIX

Surviving Slob Syndrome

Do you have places in your home that look like a garage sale in progress? Do you have drawers filled with broken cup handles, dead batteries (or are they still charged?), sunglasses, rope, check stubs, spilled fingernail polish, belt buckles and a Santa soap dish? (This same drawer usually contains *one* drawer divider—evidence that you tried to get organized, but it just didn't stay that way.)

Do you find yourself piling things in corners or closets because there's no place else to put them? Do you have to move things to discover what's under, behind or next to them? Don't despair! Have I got a chapter for you!

Let's get to the bottom of this mess. Now that you've mastered the first work simplification technique (think before you act), we can delve into the second: discard and sort.

SLOB SYNDROME: ITS CAUSES AND CURES

A slob is defined as anyone who's messier than you are. A slob saves things he can't use, freeze, recycle, repair or fit into again. A slob plops items down at the point of last use, and thinks that organized people are just too lazy to look for things.

There are many reasons for slob syndrome. Sometimes well-meaning parents continually wait on their children and follow them around the house picking up after them. The child grows up expecting others to take care of him and never changes his childhood patterns.

Conversely, children can learn to tolerate a mess if that's what they always experience at home. Again, they bring their habitually messy environment along into their adult lives.

Some people revolt against a childhood home that was so immaculate it became uncomfortable. Still others rebel against a particular chore; one woman told me she would never as long as she lived dust the platform under her stationary rocker: that had always been her job as a child and enough was enough.

Freud would suggest more serious, deep-rooted causes for slob syndrome. One popular belief is low self-esteem: The slob creates an environment that reinforces his poor self-image.

Seething anger is another cause uncovered by therapists; the fury manifests itself in the form of obscene messiness.

Teenagers can use their bedrooms and belongings as a means of declaring independence from Mom and Dad. This can be a temporary stage, and probably we shouldn't get hysterical when clothes are hung on the floor; CDs, Happy Meal toys and designer jeans are piled on top of the dresser; and basketballs, sleeping bags and paperbacks are shoved under the bed. This *can* become a way of life, but most kids outgrow it with proper help and encouragement (what this chapter is all about).

For example, my mother could hardly believe I wrote a book on home management. When I was a teenager, she'd have to heap my clothes and other miscellaneous debris in front of the bedroom door or on top of my bed—feeling sure I'd take the hint and put it all away. Basically, my plan of attack was to step over the pile or roll it up neatly in my bedspread when I went to bed.

So cheer up. If you find yourself sitting in a welter of wet towels, bumper stickers and stained plastic tablecloths, remember this grim situation may be a transient one: Even a hopelessly messy teenager can repent and become a well-organized adult.

But what if *you're* the culprit? Suppose *you're* the messy teenager who never transformed. No matter who's afflicted with slob syndrome—you, the kids or your spouse—I've got an offer you can't refuse. You can put an end to this endless squalor. I'm going to show you not only how to get rid of clutter, but how to prevent clutter's recurrence.

Admitting Your Guilt

Have you ever noticed that every treatise on clutter discusses in depth throwing away, selling or donating things to charity? No wonder you're frightened! That stuff those experts are talking about is part of your life.

Unfortunately I, too, am going to mention the trash, but I solemnly swear on a stack of decomposing *Saturday Evening Post*s that you won't have to throw everything away. Duchess of the dumpster that I am, even *I* have an assortment of totally worthless junk. For example,

I have a threadbare afghan (crocheted by my grandmother) that no one could get me to part with. I have my set of china doll dishes, outdated college textbooks, a 1978 Montgomery Ward's Fall and Winter catalog and umpteen unfinished Christmas decorations.

But even so, I'm usually not surrounded by clutter. Here's why. The dictionary defines clutter as a "confused collection; hence, crowded confusion." You see, a collection isn't clutter until it becomes crowded and confused. It's then the experts make a mad dash for the wastebasket. I can go through a closet, cupboard, drawer or entire room in minutes ruthlessly throwing stuff away, and earmarking things for charity without a second thought. But, while this process is second nature to me, I know it causes excruciating pain for others.

So here I offer a proven method to help you unclutter your house. With this modus operandi, I hope to ensnare even the most ardent pack rat.

And you know who you are. If you've got a fistful of keys you can't identify, cookie sheets that look like they were used by Mr. Goodwrench, old eyeglasses, balding snow tires, tangles of wire, bicycle fenders and worthless souvenirs (like that vial of sand from the Painted Desert), be forewarned—I'm out to get you. Never mind what Aunt Betsy will say when she doesn't see her mosaic candelabra displayed on your mantel. (With all the junk, she probably couldn't see it anyway.) Stay with me, faint-hearted reader—I'll make a believer out of you, yet!

Even if you personally are not a junkmonger, read on. You need to understand those who are and learn how to deal with them. Maybe you can teach them to become clutter-free!

The great philosopher Aristotle said that all human behavior is motivated by at least one of these seven elements: chance, nature, compulsion, habit, reason, passion and desire. There they are: the seven reasons we hang onto stuff.

Chance: "It might come in handy someday."
Nature: "I'll be able to wear it again when I lose weight."
Compulsion: "I lived through the Depression."
Habit: "I'm just a saver."
Reason: (Here's where we go into high gear.)
    1. "It's too good to get rid of."
    2. "As soon as I throw it out, I'll wish I had it."
    3. "I'll fix it some day."
    4. "It's somebody else's junk."

Passion: "I received it as a gift."

Desire: "I wouldn't get rid of that if my life depended on it!"

Smart cookie, that Aristotle. Did you recognize yourself? Is your behavior motivated by any of these seven elements? Facing up to your reasons is important, because it's the first step to a clutter-free environment. Perhaps now you'll become painfully aware of the many times you actually rattled off one of these phrases, rationalizing your reason for saving something. Now you can catch yourself and think twice, thus changing your automatic behavior into deliberate behavior. Theoretically, this will slow up new accumulations while you deal with the old ones.

CLUTTER FREE

To get started here's what you need: three boxes (or large plastic bags) and a wastebasket. The boxes are marked: "to give away or sell," "put away," "don't know." These four containers are vital to the success of your project because they'll keep you from putting off this demanding and disagreeable job.

Since you're prone to clutter it's safe to assume you're also in the habit of procrastinating. ("I'll just put this oil filter here for now until I decide what to do with it." "Before I de-junk this room, I'll have to clean out the closet.")

Here's how the four-container ploy keeps you going. One box or bag will hold things you definitely want to give away or sell. The "put away" container holds things that belong in another room. Ah-ha! There's the trap. How many times when you discover something that belongs in another room do you stop what you're doing to return it to its rightful place? (You're procrastinating.) Then, when you get to *that* place, you say, "While I'm in here I better straighten this shelf or dust off this spot before I put it down." Or you walk past the TV and notice that the "Guiding Hospital" is on. As you sit down you wonder if Jeremy is finally going to tell Susan the truth: that he has webbed feet.

Procrastination is cloaked in many disguises. So be aware of all the strategies you use to get away from the unpleasant situation.

The "don't know" container is the most important one. Procrastination takes on another form here. Making lengthy decisions and fondling each article makes the job more painful. This container helps you speed up the whole process.

The fourth receptacle is, of course, the wastebasket. Its use will become increasingly apparent as you go along. Discarding frees up space, and just think—you'll never have to pick up that stuff again!

These four containers are the tools—the real secrets for a successful purging of closets, counters, cupboards, drawers and shelves. These containers will speed up the work, keep you from getting sidetracked and organize your maneuvers. Best of all, you don't need a large block of time to accomplish this. Get the boxes and start sorting. Work as long as you can, even if it's only for ten to fifteen minutes. Whenever you have a little spare time, go back to the sorting project. Try to do something every day, if possible. Of course, this isn't the ideal way to get the job done but, even if you don't have much time, you'll still be able to tackle the job.

Maybe you're a little skeptical. I don't expect you to attack the mayhem with all the fervor of a religious army, waving your trashbag as a flag in battle, but I do expect you to start.

Clutter is a parasite. It receives food and shelter at your expense and multiplies faster than fruit flies around a ripe banana. Junk lies at the root of so many problems, from marital discord to government waste, that it needs to be taken seriously. It is truly hazardous to your health. In a day when everyone is talking about stress, clutter ranks right up there as one of the chief causes.

OK. You've got the equipment, but how do you decide what stays and what goes?

First, survey your surroundings. Your decisions will depend to a large degree on the amount of storage space you have available. Obviously, if you live in a mobile home or a tiny brownstone in lower Manhattan, you won't be able to hang onto as much as someone who has a full basement and a two-car garage.

Keep your eyes open for wasted space: walls; above or behind doors; under, behind or in-between furniture; under stairs; empty drawers or shelves. Is there a place to install or set up shelves? Is there empty wall space where you could house a credenza, cupboard or end table? Storage will be covered in detail later; for now, get a rough idea of your space limitations.

Your financial situation is another consideration. Rented storage units can alleviate space problems and allow you to stash to your heart's content. But even storing at home can cost you.

I have a creative friend who can pick something out of the garbage and make it into a masterpiece. She saves everything, but you've never seen a neater, more orderly home. Sherrill gets away with this because she has a lot of room. She has a huge storage area that houses, among other things, over sixty boxes of Christmas decorations. She also has the funds to make the system functional. She recently spent several hundred dollars on 180 large cardboard cartons and metal free-standing shelves. Everyone in the world should have the opportunity to see Sherrill's storage room! I guarantee she could charge for tours.

Do you understand the point? Sherrill can save anything she wants because she has the space and the money to make the space work. You and I may not be as fortunate, so we have to pare down our belongings to a workable few.

Once you've set your space and fund limitations, you're ready to begin. Think small and start with one room, one drawer or one shelf in your refrigerator. But before you lay your hands on anything, determine the function of the room or area in which you're working. "The bedroom closet shelf will be used only for bed linens, hats and out-of-reach medicines." "The rec room will be used for TV, toys, games and eating. We are not going to use it for repotting plants, woodworking or playing dodgeball." "This shelf in the refrigerator will be used only for leftovers." These parameters will guide you in the sorting process. Knowing the function of an area enables you to make quicker and more accurate decisions regarding what goes and what stays.

Your Clutter Quiz

Now it's time to reach out and touch something. Give each item a hard, fast look. How long has it been since you used it? If you answer "I use it quite frequently," then ask yourself if it contributes in some way to the newly assigned function of the area. If "yes" it stays; if "no" put it in the container of things to put away.

However, if you realize you haven't used this article for a year or more, it needs reevaluating. Have you been looking for it? Did you remember you had it? If not, try to convince yourself to get rid of it. (Failing your best efforts, put it in the "I don't know" box.)

Does this item have sentimental or monetary value—Grandma's tatted doilies, a 1952 Mickey Mantle baseball card? Here's where we really get bogged down. What do you do with your bronzed baby shoes, the porcelain bud vase you received as a wedding gift, the bullfighter painted on black velvet (that your brother expects to see hanging in your new log home) and the photographs of trees, rocks and waterfalls the kids took during your last vacation? If you cannot resolve the keep/go conflict quickly, don't waste time—just pack all this stuff into the "I don't know" box. (Things of obvious monetary value such as jewelry, coins, antiques, first editions, etc., should be dealt with separately for safeguarding.)

Here are some guidelines to help you take a stand on these delicate issues:

1. A thing is either good or it isn't good. Don't judge it on the basis of whether it's old or new.
2. Keep your value system in mind. (If you want a completely coordinated, well-decorated home, you'll opt for packing the bullfighter over your brother's feelings.)
3. Suit your own tastes and those of your family. What's in vogue doesn't matter (unless that's your preference).
4. Can you keep the love and get rid of the object of that love? (Why waste space storing a hideous picture you know you'll never hang?)

Even with all this sound logic and crisp advice, I'm still going to keep my grandmother's afghan (my value system) and you're probably going to keep the nut cups from your grandmother's eightieth birthday party. That's OK. I promised you wouldn't have to eliminate everything. When you come across those heartrending things you can't live with and you can't live without, put them in the "put away" box.

Next, ask yourself if you have duplicates. If so, do you need so many, e.g., six paring knives, four brushed felt hats, three electric power drills, four sets of everyday dishes?

Particularly in the kitchen you run into the problem of sets: nesting bowls and casserole dishes, matching pans and glassware. Do you use all the members of any given set? Perhaps you never use a certain bowl or casserole because it's too big or too small, and you never use your sherbet glasses or Dutch oven. Don't feel compelled to store these unused things in potentially functional space just because they're part of a set.

Clutter Checklist

Let's break down the system into a more usable form:

To give away or sell:

- Anything you haven't used for one year or more.
- Clothes that don't fit or look nice on you.
- Things you dislike and don't want—but that are too good to throw away.
- Things you have no current use for (or need of) even though they might come in handy some day.

- Things you didn't remember you had.
- Things you haven't missed, and haven't been looking for.
- Unused parts of sets.
- Sentimental objects you have the courage to part with.

To put away:

- Things that belong in another room or area of your home.
- Things of obvious monetary value.
- Sentimental belongings you just can't part with.
- Things to be stored—seasonal or seldom-used items removed from needed functional workspace.

I don't know:

- Any item that causes a conflict in your mind. (You can think of reasons why you should keep it and reasons why you shouldn't.)

To throw away or recycle:

- Any unrepairable object (things even charitable organizations don't want).
- Worn-out clothing.
- Any unnecessary paper (including newspapers and magazines).

Now, what to do with all this paraphernalia?

To Give Away or Sell

Call Goodwill, the Salvation Army, the Veterans (VFW), your church or hospital charity; they're eager to take these things off your hands. Their programs provide jobs and means whereby people can provide for themselves and their families inexpensively. Aren't you proud of yourself for helping such a worthy cause! In addition, your donations are tax deductible.

As added encouragement to help you finish the job quickly, arrange with the charity to pick up your castoffs *before* you begin. Then you'll have a deadline and goal to work toward.

And you know what? If you ever wish for something after it's gone, these thrift stores are wonderful places to buy things cheap. You'll be amazed at the wonderful things people give away.

If you decide to have a garage sale, think big—you'll have better results. Tell your friends about your plans and encourage them to join you. The larger your sale, the more business you'll attract.

A sale is a great motivator for kids. They'll get rid of twice as much if they know they can keep the proceeds. (A few rules may be needed here: No selling the television, your school shoes, your coin collection or your little brother.)

Also, consider the option of a flea market or a secondhand shop. In the case of the flea market, you usually pay a small fee up front and sell your wares on the organizer's premises. Secondhand shops will usually sell things on consignment and pay you a percentage of the sale price of each item. (You get paid after the item sells.)

Think about people who would welcome your largesse. Could the boy next door use the pants your son has outgrown? Would Elmer like your collection of science fiction paperbacks? Marilyn does a lot of entertaining; maybe she'd like those snack sets. Sometimes, if you give things to people you care about (especially if they appreciate your contribution), it makes it easier to let go.

I still remember fondly those days when we would get a box in the mail from Aunt Nelda. She lived far away, but we knew she was thinking of us because as soon as she was finished with something—clothes, shoes, purses, jewelry, anything—she sent it off to us. It seems like every time our family gets together someone says, "Remember how much fun it was to get a box from Aunt Nelda?" Her simple act has blessed us twice: then, the joy of discovery; now, a cherished memory.

To Put Away

If you're left with a large box of misplaced articles, you may want to work on this box piecemeal fashion. Determine to put away a few items a day or put things away for fifteen or thirty minutes a day. If the items belong in an area that also needs sprucing up, just put it away in the general vicinity. This box may contain several items that need to be stored in an out-of-the-way place—things such as seasonal clothes, canning equipment, sentimental keepsakes you're not going to display, etc. These items should be categorized, packed in labeled cartons and stored in a dead space area (or areas) of your home. (A storage system is detailed in *Confessions of an Organized Homemaker.*)

Interior decorators suggest one way to reduce clutter is to group your collections: displayed as an arrangement they become art instead of clutter.

To illustrate my point, think of the word "clutter," then think of the word "cluster." When I think of a cluster I think of diamonds clustered together on a brooch, mounds of curly leaves cascading on a trailing vine, and a group of friends and family clustered around the fire on a chilly winter evening. A cluster has a pleasing connotation. Maybe you can make a cluster out of some of your clutter.

I know a hat collector who made a charming wall grouping from his collection; standing in his corner is a brass hat rack displaying still more of his haberdashery.

Another friend took his train sets out of storage and built a miniature city for the train to skirt around. He now has a room devoted to his electric train collection and other railroad memorabilia.

My basket collection graces tables, fireplaces, corners, walls and tops of cupboards.

If you've got a collection of anything, from stamps to firearms, look for organizations relating to your hobby. Subscribe to their newsletters and magazines. You'll pick up a lot of good storage hints.

I Don't Know

Here you have a box of miscellaneous goods, things you can't decide whether to keep or to part with. Close up the top of the box, put the date on it, and stick it somewhere out of the way. (The more out of the way the better.) Now, the objects in this box will do one of two things:

1. They will age and die a natural death, or
2. They will earn a rightful place in your home.

More than likely that box of stuff will sit untouched for months or years—proving its value to you. In the unlikely event you need or want something out of that box, you'll have to risk body and soul to get to it and retrieve the specific item you're after. Whatever you unearth, then, truly belongs in your home. It deserves to belong.

What could be easier? A system that makes decisions for you. How can you beat that?

And here's the kicker. When the date on the box has passed the one-year mark, take the easy way out. Arrange for a charitable organization to pick it up or deliver it yourself—sight unseen. No peeking, even though you reason, "Just in case." Your curiosity could be your undoing, so proceed with caution.

After storing her boxes of "I don't knows" for months, one client of mine pulled them out, convinced she could live without her hoard. She was so positive, she put all the stuff on large tables and invited her daughters and friends to take whatever they wanted. You guessed it— a lot of the junk never made it out the front door. It seems absence made the heart grow fonder.

Don't make it harder on yourself. The box has decided for you.

Now that you're familiar with the basic system, you can decide whether to get the kids involved. From my experience it works best for me to be involved with the project from start to finish. (I doubt the kids would do any better by themselves. Like most children, they've been known to check the trash before the garbage collector comes.)

There have been times, though, I've tackled the kids' rooms alone and broken a few hearts . . . like the time I threw away the satin binding that had disintegrated off someone's security blanket. Our son hadn't slept with that blanket for years, but he sobbed for hours.

Now, I apply the Golden Rule: I wouldn't want them going through my things, deciding what stays and what goes, so I give them equal rights. (I *do* reason with them, though, and encourage them to eliminate as much as possible.)

Removing clutter is therapeutic. The more you get rid of, the lighter your spirits. Though right now it may be impossible for you to toss out even one old lipstick, a single bleach bottle or a rusted key, you too may learn to enjoy it. (And you thought getting rid of clutter was grindingly monotonous!)

BECOMING A CLUTTER CONTROL OFFICER

After all your hard work, you'll want to sit back and relax, enjoying your airy surroundings. Unfortunately, it's not going to stay that way. Clutter is like weeds—it keeps cropping up. But regular "weeding" keeps it under control. Here are some ideas to make the job easier.

Don Aslett (author of *Is There Life After Housework?*, Betterway Books) has another helpful household book, *Clutter's Last Stand*. Whenever you need a good shot of motivation to get things under control, here's a great reference to turn to. It's a real upper in book form.

Another preventive is the errand drawer (or box, or shelf, or sack, or something). If you leave things sitting around so you won't forget to do something about them, then you need an errand drawer. Here's where I put the Matchbox cars we need to return to a neighbor boy, material we have to photocopy, the stove drip pan we must return to the store, the caster that broke off the living room chair. Whenever we go somewhere, I take a quick peek into the errand drawer to see if there's something else I can do to make my trip more productive. (Some people have told me they keep the errand box in the trunk of the car.)

Hesitantly, I mention the "for-now" spot. This can be a box, a bag, a drawer or a corner where you put things that collect during the day:

toys, shoes, business cards, magazines, whatever. This can be a useful tool if it's not abused. The way to keep it effective is to make sure— positively, absolutely sure—that everything inside the for-now spot is put away at *least* three times a week. (Daily would be better.)

For example, someone leaves his coat hanging on the doorknob and you ask him to please hang it up. He says he'll do it as soon as he's off the phone. Naturally, he forgets and the coat stays where it hangs. Now, multiply that episode times the number of people in your household and the number of misplaced items and you're out of control fast.

If you want a straight house and unless your children are scrupulously well-trained, you have to resort to nagging, screaming or following them around to pick up after them. But the for-now spot can prevent all that. Take the coat, drop it in the box (or whatever), and make it a habit that everyone pulls out his possessions and puts them away before bed.

Here's a variation for toys. (This is especially handy if you have an upstairs and a downstairs.) When the kids finish playing with a toy, instead of making them put it away, have them toss it in a laundry basket, wastebasket or box. As miscellaneous toys are discovered throughout the house during the day, you also do the same. Before bed (before a story is better), take the collection to the toy storage area, where everyone helps put the toys back in their proper places. This sure takes the pressure off you continually checking up to make sure toys are put back.

You can keep the yard junk-free by providing a large covered trash can in which the kids can toss their outdoor toys.

Be aware of other "for-now" spots you can use. If someone is always throwing car keys, change, ticket stubs and business cards on top of the dresser or refrigerator, set a basket on the spot and at least conceal the rubble. For now is OK if you don't let it become forever!

The in and out baskets discussed earlier are marvelous clutter reducers, too. They're convenient and keep an enormous amount of material under wraps.

A quick and easy system for incoming and outgoing mail is helpful for retarding clutter. Have a convenient basket or other container to hold incoming and outgoing mail. Some have further success using a two-basket method—one for mail requiring action (bills, magazine subscriptions, letters to answer) and another for information (magazines, announcements, sale notices).

Paper clutter should be dealt with frequently. Whenever something comes into your home that's of no current interest to anyone, get rid of it—even if it might come in handy some day.

One last idea for keeping clutter within respectable limits: If you have stairs in your house you know what a nuisance it can be to constantly chase up and down returning things (or getting other people to do it). Have a spot upstairs and a spot downstairs to put things that need a ride up or down. Let the family members in on your plan and tell them to grab a handful whenever they're making the trip.

Tips for Avoiding Clutter

1. Beware of labor-saving devices. Some require more labor (assembling, cleaning, disassembling) than they ever save. The more you have, the more you have to take care of and store.

2. Don't buy anything unless you know exactly where you're going to put it.

3. Don't buy anything because someone else has one and they love it. Although thousands of people may have and love widgets, that's no guarantee you will, too. Borrow the gadget and talk to the owner of one to discover all the pluses and minuses of ownership. Visit a few secondhand stores and thrift shops. If you see numerous "kitchen wizards" or "dandy do-all tools," that should be a hint these appliances are not all they're cracked up to be.

4. Don't accept others' castoffs and hand-me-downs if you honestly can't use them (or don't want them).

5. If you're planning to celebrate a birthday or anniversary that represents a milestone, ask friends to send sealed donations to your favorite charity instead of gifts. It's a lot more satisfying than receiving gifts you'd never use.

6. Keep a recycling box handy in which you immediately dump all items to get rid of.

Clutter can be eliminated, or at least reduced to an acceptable level. Above all, remember once it's under control it won't stay that way. But, as quickly as you and your family master and maintain this clutter-abatement policy, you'll break through to discover the bonus of extra time and the joy of organized living.

CHAPTER SEVEN

Finding a Place for Everything

Does anyone in your house go to the city dump and bring home more stuff than he (or she) threw away? ("Hey! This motor will be super for John's go-cart! Can you believe it? Someone threw away this perfectly good radiator! And look here—I can use this lawn mower body as a cart to push the garbage cans out to the street! This is great. I'm going to go to the dump more often!")

Our kids have stashed and stored things like a dead praying mantis, empty Chap Stick cases, rocks, feathers, Honeycomb bike reflectors, Cap'n Crunch treasure boxes and homemade baseball cards.

I love to comb through garage sales and secondhand shops. One of the clerks at a thrift store I frequent once said to me, "You drop it off at the back door (i.e., donations) and bring it out the front door!" Sad, but true.

I suppose there's a little pack rat in all of us. In any case, you can unclutter and de-junk all day and still be faced with storing things that never should have made it through the front door. No matter how much you get rid of, there are certain things to keep and storage decisions to make.

To help you make the best choices for how and where to put things, I'm about to reveal the inner workings of the next two work simplification techniques: grouping and motion-mindedness.

Now that you've thought first (work simplification technique number one), and discarded and sorted (technique number two), you're ready for a carefully designed storage program that gives everything in your house a well-defined, well-confined place. Grouping and motion-mindedness (techniques three and four) will show you the way.

In this chapter you'll find some general storage rules to guide you in setting up your personal storage system. You will also discover the best way to store anything that is brought into your home.

Good storage procedures are necessary if you want to be able to find things when you need them instead of waiting until they show up. Giving everything a definite place reduces clutter and increases cooperation among the ranks.

At the outset, most parents complain there's no use organizing. "I can put these combs in the bathroom in this very spot and in two days, they'll completely disappear." If you, too, share the concern that you'll spend weeks organizing and the kids will spend seconds destroying the whole project, I know how you feel. I've seen our kids move through the house like a detachment of Sherman tanks, leveling everything in their path. In five minutes the house can go from totally awesome to awesomely totalled. And that's exactly why I extol the virtues of having a place for everything.

When there's a well-defined place for each object (down to the very last hairpin), it's much easier to rebuild after the "war." You rest assured when there's an underlying order behind the closed closets, cupboards and drawers. When things have a designated nook, cranny or container, it's easy to quickly put them back. A storage program that has been maintained reinforces itself. Everyone knows exactly where things belong and they experience the satisfaction of grabbing whatever they want without raising dust or pulling muscles.

RULES OF ORDER

1. *Convenience.* All useful items should be stored conveniently. (Sometimes, of course, with small children it's dangerous to store things as conveniently as you'd like but you can still follow the basic guidelines.)

Frequently, this is where we make our first mistake. For example: "Where are the scissors?" "I left them in the bathroom and forgot to put them back." If the scissors keep showing up in the bathroom, it sounds like you need to keep an extra pair of scissors there.

Store things where people use them. Sometimes this means duplicating certain commodities, but it only makes good sense. If you store things where they're used, even if they're not put away at least they're in the room where they belong.

Always store things at or near the point of first use. The ice bag should be stored close to the freezer; the jumper cables, car wash and fast food coupons should be in the car; the cold cereals, snacks and other foods served directly from container to dish should be stored close to those dishes. After a bath, do you streak through your house running for clean underwear? Store it at the point of first use—in the bathroom.

Convenience is further served if you store things with motions in mind. Things used once a week or more often should be given one-motion storage. That means you can open a door or drawer, reach in and grab the object with one motion, and quickly put it back with one motion. Things used less often than once a week can be stored on a higher or lower shelf and given two- or three-motion storage, depending on frequency of use.

One-motion storage is the key to getting the kids to put things back. It's easier for you to put things away, too. When something takes the least extra bit of effort to put away, it's put down at the point of last use with the promise it'll be put away when time permits.

That's why the outdoor Christmas lights are still in the rain gutter come spring. That's why the large platters and serving dishes are stacked on the counter for days after the party. That's why stored clothing doesn't fit the child by the time you get it out of storage.

Young or old, male or female, we all hate extra motions. As we mature, with luck, we can work around this idiosyncracy. But children aren't as apt to do that, so one-motion storage is the key to getting cooperation.

If the lid were taken off every clothes hamper, clothes would be deposited. If toys could be tossed effortlessly into containers, they would be. If only clothing didn't have to be folded and hung, it would be put away!

2. *Divide and multiply.* Use drawer dividers everywhere and watch your space multiply. This is the way to give everything a well-defined, well-confined place.

Drawer dividers come in many different sizes. You can find them in discount or variety stores, hardware stores, department stores and large supermarkets. They're made of plastic, heavy vinyl or vinyl-coated steel. As soon as you acquaint yourself with the array of sizes, start using your imagination. In addition to buying something specifically labeled "drawer dividers" or "organizers," you can use anything that's square or rectangular in shape and hollow: cardboard boxes, ice cube bins, four-sided napkin holders, liners for planters, dishpans, cat litter pans, baskets, cutlery trays, cosmetic trays, desk trays, etc.

These loose drawer dividers are useful for many things and are far superior, I feel, to built-ins. They can change with you as various possessions come and go. They can be moved from one house to another, so you can take your organized system with you.

Use drawer dividers everywhere: in kitchen drawers, under sinks, on shelves (not only to divide and separate items, but to serve as slide-out trays so several things can be handled as one unit.) Use them in bathroom drawers and bedroom drawers to separate socks, underwear, pantyhose. Use drawer dividers to sort and categorize toys, office supplies, gardening supplies, automotive needs, plumbing and hardware material.

When using these bins, categorize everything generally. If the system is too exacting, things will be increasingly harder to put away. The rule (especially with children) is: The urge to play is greater than the urge to put away! Even as adults, we want to use something with a greater sense of urgency than when we want to return it to its place.

For example, our kids have a large dishpan filled with animals. To find a little dog, they have to sift through the dishpan to get it. But when it's time to put it back, they can toss it in without a thought.

Jim and I, though we're not plumbers, have a dishpan filled with plumbing supplies: copper tubing, Teflon tape, joint sealer, a box of faucet washers and so on. It takes a few seconds longer to find the box of washers than it does to toss it back into the container when we're finished.

The point is, when you have a choice, make things slightly easier to put away than they are to find.

3. *Label.* Labeling is an important part of a good storage program. Containers should be labeled with either pictures or words so everyone knows the category of things contained therein.

Some people have found it helpful to label individual drawer dividers so everyone will know which space is for the measuring spoons and which space is for the potato peeler. Sometimes it helps to label the insides of dressers so children know which space is for their socks or shirts. Don't overlook labeling. Because it eliminates any doubts about where an item belongs, it's more important than you may think.

Oftentimes it's useful to label individual items. For example, we have identical pairs of scissors and when a pair is discovered out of place we can't tell if they belong in the kitchen, in my desk, in Jim's desk or in the family room. So each pair is labeled and we can see at a glance where it belongs.

Color-coding can help, too. The black combs can be for the upstairs bathroom, colored ones for downstairs. The toothbrushes with a red dot (made with fingernail polish) go in the upstairs bathroom, the unmarked ones go downstairs. Yellow pencils go in the kitchen, colored pencils in the family room.

Some people even color-code their kids. Let's say Jimmy's color is red. He'd have red towels, a red toothbrush, a red comb, a red bathroom cup, a red thread sewed to the toes of his socks, and so on. Other possessions could be marked with a dollop of red nail polish or a red self-adhesive signal dot.

I'm sure you get the idea. Label everything: the roll of transparent tape, the bin that holds the Legos, the box of electrical supplies, the container that holds the clips for the electric rollers.

FIGURING IT OUT

OK. You've got everything organized. Things are stored conveniently in well-labeled containers. Then someone brings home a stuffed buffalo head, a rock collection, an old weathervane, waders for fishing, a large wooden cable spool and a new-fangled food processor (complete with forty-three attachments that do everything but baby sit). What do you do with all this stuff? Chances are you won't stumble across an article entitled "1,001 Ways to Store a Stuffed Buffalo Head," so you've got to get creative and discover for yourself those 1,001 ways. (Well, two or three, maybe.)

No matter the size of your dwelling, you have only four alternatives when it comes to storing things: shelf, floor, hanging or drawer.

When someone presents yet another bit of paraphernalia you've got to find a place for, mentally run down the list of storage alternatives (unless like the buffalo head the storage alternative is obvious— hanging) and decide what would work best for you.

Delving Into Shelving

Do you have any shelf space available? (With all the de-junking you've just done, you've probably got plenty!) If you've got empty wall space you have potential shelf space. Don't forget the spaces over or behind doors. If you've got at least a three-inch clearance behind a door, you've got room for some shallow (great for one-motion storage) shelves that won't be seen when the door is open. There are shelves made from vinyl-coated steel that hang on walls or over the back of a door. Inexpensive metal shelving (generally gray) is widely available. (These are usually found in three- to eight-shelf units.) Track and bracket shelving is another possibility, as well as the old standby, cement blocks and boards.

Do you have space enough for a freestanding bookcase? If you don't like the looks of open shelving, consider the possibility of mounting shutters to the bookcase.

Look up under the sinks. There's a lot of room under there for a shelf or two. And above your existing closet shelf there's probably room for another.

Shelves are a wonderful storage alternative. If they're not too deep, they're a boon to convenient, one-motion storage.

I Bet It's on the Floor

The kids are well aware of the merits of floor space: there's a floor in every room and they're *so* convenient. Gone are the days when folks gasped with horror if something was discovered under a piece of furniture. The floor is a wonderful place to keep things and it's beginning to come into its own.

Look under, behind and in between beds, couches, desks and other large pieces of furniture. Box, bag or stand up your infrequently used things and store them out of sight.

Covered baskets can hold and hide unsightly items and decorate your home at the same time. Open crocks and baskets can hold blankets, afghans, fruits, vegetables, yarn, utensils, wood, diapers—you name it. A three-gallon can will hold thirty pounds of dry food. Painted and topped with a pillow, it becomes a useful and decorative stool.

If you're cramped for space, start looking at your floor space creatively instead of just checking for holes in the carpet and dustballs in the corners.

Hanging Around

Certain items seem to lend themselves to hanging storage (the buffalo head, garden tools, mops and brooms, fishing waders, punching bags, hoses, ladders and so on). Those objects will be fairly obvious to you.

But for people who are low on storage space, hanging storage is not only a luxury, it's a necessity.

If you've got empty wall or ceiling space (and who doesn't), you've got room to start hanging. (Don't forget about hanging space on the backs of doors and inside cupboard doors.)

You can hang up just about anything. If it's got a handle, drill a hole through the end and hang it up on a nail. Failing that, hang it on a wall-mounted clip.

Up under a sink is wasted storage area where you can hang a pail filled with extra bathroom or kitchen supplies, clean rags, food items (if pests are not a concern), pet food or light bulbs. The pail can be used as a small tool kit or first-aid kit. Your imagination is the only thing standing between you and progress. While this idea is helpful for finding unused storage space, if you have young children, safety precautions need to be taken. Install child safety latches for lower cupboards. Or, can you lock the cupboard with a padlock or bicycle lock? Perhaps you'll just decide to store everything high for a while.

Kitchen tools, gadgets, baskets, et al, can hang decoratively on a wall or attached to a colorful grid. Tiered wire baskets can hold anything from beauty supplies to onions.

Baskets mounted on a wall are stylish receptacles for incoming or outgoing mail, plants, dried flowers, or the contents of someone's purse or pocket.

Awkward things like vacuum attachments, accessory items for the food processor, out-of-season snow gear, extra rolls of wallpaper, large carpet scraps—all sorts of things you'd never dream of hanging up—can be placed in drawstring bags, tote bags or heavy plastic bags with handles, and hung out of the way.

You can purchase specialty devices made for hanging bicycles, power tools, heavy lawn equipment, skis, fishing poles and golf clubs. Hanging pocketed organizers (shoe bags and purse files) provide space for cleaning and toiletry items, aluminum foil, file folders, schoolbooks and, of course, shoes and purses.

So when I say you can hang up anything, I *mean* it! You will find, however, if you're forced to use a great deal of hanging storage, that it can be slightly inconvenient at times. Rummaging through a tote bag to find what you need is somewhat short of one-motion storage. But if these items are seldom used or if hanging storage is your only alternative, it can be perfectly satisfactory.

Open a Drawer

The other storage option is the drawer. It's handy for many things and it's easily shut, keeping an unsightly mess out of sight.

If you have a number of drawers available, don't let conventional drawer storage ideas waste your space. Anything you can store on a shelf you can put in a drawer, providing the object isn't too large. It might go against the grain to store books, shoes, food, dishes, paper products, toys or whatever in a drawer, but if you've got drawer space, why not? Don't inhibit yourself.

Drawers are easy to come by. There are many inexpensive heavy cardboard models, and the drawers come in a wide variety of sizes.

We have a four-drawer fiberboard chest that has small drawers just the right size to hold thirty-four cassette tapes, fifty-four CDs, fifteen videos or hundreds of baseball cards. I'd hate to imagine my life without that little chest.

There are styles well suited for clothes or file folders. Check an office supply store or variety store and discover for yourself all the possibilities.

Inexpensive chests of drawers can be purchased unfinished, or look through your neighborhood secondhand shop, garage sales, flea markets or check the want ads. Plastic drawer units in various sizes are available at discount stores and home improvement centers. You'll find stackable drawers, drawers on casters (you can move them around easily) and drawers you can mount under a cupboard or shelf. If you have wall and floor space, you have room for drawers.

Furniture That Stores

If you're in the market for furniture, shop with storage potential in mind. If you live in an apartment and are forbidden to pound, mount, or glue anything to the walls, freestanding furniture is your only hope.

Look for shelves and cabinets that climb the walls. Wide, low furniture might look great, but it wastes space. Think high and eat up those squandered areas of useful space.

Look out for things that only serve one purpose. Never buy an end table that's merely a tabletop on four legs; an end table should house shelves or drawers. (Sometimes your personal taste in furniture has to take a back seat to your need for storage.)

Flat-topped trunks are great for storage and can serve as an extra end table or coffee table. Sofas or chairs can house beds. Armoires are expensive but can come to the rescue if you're low on closet space; metal wardrobe chests are considerably less expensive and can fill the same need.

Ruffles skirting a couch, chair or crib can hide what's stashed underneath. There are types of dining room tables that fold up against a wall, taking very little room, yet they add a decorative touch. Wooden or plastic crates can hold magazines, towels, toys or books.

My Contention With Convention

Frequently we stereotype storage areas and fail to get the most out of our space. If you've got empty shelves in your bedroom or family room, let's say, there's no rule that says you can't store extra laundry aids, power tools, surplus food or grass seed on them. The storage rules I mentioned earlier (convenience, storing at the point of first use, etc.) are important and should be considered whenever feasible, but sometimes it's not architecturally possible to store everything exactly where it should be.

If you find yourself in that position, implement the rules only for those items you use all the time. If necessary, break conventional standards and store things (neatly and well labeled) in unusual places. Then stand back and be proud of your creativity.

After setting up your storage system, give it a chance to work. You may not feel comfortable with it until it becomes a habit, but stick with it long enough to reap the rewards. If after six weeks or so things still don't seem right, rework your arrangement.

Continually put things back where they belong so others will learn the exact spot assigned to each object. Repetition is important in all facets of learning.

Troubleshooter's Guide

Make a note of things frequently misplaced or missing. Do they belong in a specific place? Is that place conveniently located? Is the item stored where it's used? Is it hard to get to or hard to put away? Is the object grouped with the things it's most often used with? Are you employing the best storage alternative? Does this item need to be duplicated? Does the object (or it's designated place) need to be labeled?

Whether you're having trouble keeping track of combs, pencils, scissors, transparent tape—anything—re-read the troubleshooter's guide. I guarantee you'll discover the cause of your problem and be led to a workable solution.

Maybe now you can see why grouping and motion-mindedness are considered work simplification techniques. Just imagine how much simpler your life would be if everything had a well-defined, well-confined place.

You're only one step away from reaching this plateau. All you have to do is *do it*.

CHAPTER EIGHT

Delegate or Abdicate

Anyone stupid enough to enter this bedroom must have friends among the paramedics," I mumbled to myself as I tripped over the catcher's mask and chest protector that were lying in the doorway. Aghast, I stood back to soak in the gut-wrenching scene. I felt like a member of a SWAT team called in to quell a major riot—only to realize I had arrived too late.

The kitchen strainer (which someone had used for a butterfly net) was hanging on the doorknob. Schuyler's first doll, bereft of hair (it fell prey to a five-year-old with electric poodle groomers), was casually perched on a pile of Sega cartridges. I noticed someone was conducting the "does your chewing gum lose its flavor on the bedpost overnight" experiment. Football jerseys, gym shoes and sweat socks were strewn amid the rubble. (That accounted for the faint stench of "locker room" greeting me when I first entered the devastation.) A half-eaten bowl of cooked cereal of a consistency you could set fence posts in was stashed under the bed.

"No wonder they started naming hurricanes after boys!" With only one daughter, my experience is somewhat limited, but I understand girls are no better.

This disgusting description leads me to the fifth work simplification technique, accrued benefits.

First, what are accrued benefits? They are simply investments that grow and pay rich dividends in return. In the kitchen an accrued benefit is tripling a recipe and freezing two portions for later. You make one investment that pays back thrice.

Recently, I heard a professional housekeeper describe the virtues of cleaning your toilet with a fizzing denture cleaning tablet. "Just toss one in," she said, "let it sit, brush the bowl just a little, and flush. You'll get about forty fizzing flushes for $1.49." Too bad this expert didn't know about accrued benefits. Why, you could throw your teeth in there and get two jobs done in the same amount of time.

Around the house accrued benefits are often in progress. The washer, dishwasher and garbage disposal are humming while someone is scrubbing the floor. Someone empties the trash while others clean the bathroom and make up a bed. Several things are being done during one investment of time.

Obviously, all this congenial cooperation doesn't happen automatically. In fact, psychiatrists, psychologists, pediatricians and concerned parents everywhere are trying to unlock the mystery of getting the kids to help around the house—the greatest accrued benefit of all.

If I knew a sure-fire, no-fail method, I would be a millionaire, at least. But, like others before me, I can only offer suggestions and relate successful experiences I've had. I know certain things that work well, and I'll share them with you. But ultimately the responsibility is left to you.

I've seen families who triumph in this area and I've seen others struggle. I know one woman, the mother of eleven children, whose home is run as efficiently as General Motors. She related her philosophy for raising such a cooperative family: "Children do what they're trained to do." This family alliance reflects her skill as a trainer.

The secret is *you.* Are you willing to teach, to train, to delegate, to follow through and above all to set an example? Successful parents are the ones willing to put in the time to follow through with a delegation program. That means you must stop acting on impulse—asking for help only when you need it—and start requesting and expecting consistent orderly behavior. Following through also means that once an assignment is given, you take the time to see it's done and done well. The program doesn't matter—you do.

MAKING A MOLEHILL OUT OF A MOUNTAIN

If only it were that easy: Stop doing that and start doing this. I confess I've been a problem delegator (I frequently asked for help only when I needed it). And I know why I had a hard time delegating. Here's a list of my well-rationalized reasons:

1. It's easier to do it myself.
2. I get the job done the way I want it done, if I do it myself.
3. I don't have time to work at the kids' speed.
4. I don't have time to train the help.
5. Actually, I don't mind doing the housework.
6. I hate to nag. (Jim Jr.'s terse reprisal still haunts: "Mom, being mean is your hobby.")

While the children were young, I subscribed to all those theories whole-heartedly, but now that they're older, I resent it when they expect me to take care of their every whim. Somewhere along the line I developed the reputation for indestructibility, and now I'm paying the price. It only took a few eye-opening experiences, however, for me to see the error of my ways. (Like the night I stayed up and got the kitchen shiny and clean so I wouldn't have to wake up to a mess. Next morning there were dirty dishes scattered around the counter; cereal, cracker and chip boxes standing at attention; and nacho cheese riveted to several dinner plates.) If your children are still young, learn from my mistakes and start training them now!

I am infinitely busier now than I was five years ago, and I desperately *need* the kids' help. Perhaps I should have more noble reasons for delegating, such as increasing their ability to be responsible, building self-esteem and self-confidence, teaching the necessary skills and helping them use their time better. Yes, those are the right reasons and they merit further consideration, but the plain truth is I need their help—and so do you.

What are the elements for successful delegation? Here's an inventory:

- Discussion
- Eliminating busywork
- Finding the best person
- No dumping
- Tools
- Training
- Consistency
- Follow through
- Avoiding upward delegation
- Rewards

DISCUSSION

The first step is to have a discussion. This can be a family meeting or a one-on-one experience. This is a discussion, remember, not just a "telling." Begin by letting the child know you need his help.

A good friend of ours, a mother of seven, vividly demonstrated to her family how necessary their help was to her.

Everyone gathered in the living room; each person was handed one piece of bread. When Mom gave the signal, everyone broke the bread into little pieces and dropped it on the floor. When all the bread was broken and tossed aside, she asked one of the kids to pick up every tiny piece. The family timed the child and noted how long it took for one person to pick up all the bread.

Then the bread was thrown on the floor again—only this time everyone helped pick it up. Again, the procedure was timed and noted; there was a great reduction in the time. This demonstration clearly effected a change in the family's thinking. Even the smallest youngster was able to grasp the idea of cooperation demonstrated with this visual aid.

During your discussion, find out what types of things each child enjoys doing. (Steven and Jim love to cook, Brian loves to baby-sit, and Jeff likes to clean anything if he can use a squirt bottle.)

Get the kids' ideas. Do they want the same jobs for a week or a month? When should the work be done, before or after school? Also encourage the kids to make up a reward list—things they'd like for a job well done. Discuss, too, what disciplinary action should be taken if jobs are neglected (no TV, being grounded, no car or phone privileges). With everything clearly established (what the kids will do, what they can expect when they do it and what they can expect if they don't do it), they can be totally responsible for their actions. Your job is to see that the rewards and consequences are put in force.

If the children are involved from the beginning, they'll feel more like members of the team instead of just water boys. A good, two-way discussion will nourish a spirit of family unity.

Decide with each child what quality of work is acceptable. (No water spots on the chrome, only trophies left on the top of the dresser, beds smooth but hospital corners not necessary, pants folded on creases and hung up after church.) How will the bedroom look when it's clean? Will the dresser tops be cleared? What will the garden look like after it's weeded? Will all the tools be put away? Agreeing on these standards up front will eliminate a lot of excuses (I didn't know I was supposed to, you didn't say, etc.) down the road.

Next, agree on a deadline. Remember, though you're in control, to be fair. You want them to cooperate; so must you. Work out a deadline agreeable to both of you. When the work is completed, ask for feedback. Get ideas as to how the job went. Are there ways to make it easier and quicker? What went wrong?

Communicate, don't complicate. Whenever you're delegating anything, remember that asking is better than telling. Asking sends a positive message to the delegatee. It lets him know that you're open to suggestions, willing to listen to possible conflicts. While the doing of the job may not be subject to negotiation, perhaps the how and when are. Asking keeps the relationship in better shape, which always makes delegation an easier and more cooperative venture.

ELIMINATING BUSYWORK

When the group has decided what needs to be done, recheck the list. Are there any jobs to eliminate? (Scrubbing the basement, digging dandelions, bleaching the whitewall tires.) If possible, consider the feasibility of outside hired help to ease the workload. Don't make up things for the kids to do just because "it'll be good for them." Eliminate all busywork.

FINDING THE BEST PERSON

Select the best person to do the job. At our house we frequently think of the oldest child when a job needs to be done. (Or we pick on the child going through the most cooperative stage!)

An effective method is to think of the youngest child first. Often he is the most willing, but usually by the time you get around to giving him a job, there's not much of a selection. (Even a little sprout can put his diaper in the diaper pail or garbage can.) There's a lot a small child can do if you revamp.

If you have a handicapped child, you may want to consider him first, as well. Sometimes we make handicaps worse by overcompensating. Give him a chance to be as much as he can be.

When deciding who'll do what, take into consideration the child's physical limitations and his time schedule, as well as his interests. If you need the laundry sorted every morning before school, don't delegate that job to the child who has band practice at 7 A.M. This is common sense, but because it's so obvious it's an easy point to overlook.

No Dumping

Be careful not to dump your own distasteful jobs onto the kids. We repeatedly ask them to do the things we just can't bear ourselves. This sends out the message that work is loathsome and something to be avoided. The kids pick up these messages fast enough on their own.

My mother is my best friend in the whole world and I love her dearly, but to this day I can still remember thinking (when asked to do the dishes or dust the furniture), "If she didn't want to do this stuff, why did she get married in the first place?" I always felt like I was doing my mother's work.

So be aware that your kids probably feel the same way. These smoldering thoughts didn't bother my mother one bit: She kept right on delegating. Today, I'm grateful.

Try a trade-off. If you hate shopping or cooking, let's say, consider trading someone once-a-week bedroom cleaning for the week's shopping or fixing Sunday dinner.

With younger children it helps to trade jobs back and forth once in a while. (I'll make your bed and you make mine. I'll do one of your jobs and you do one of mine.) This way the child feels more like a citizen instead of a subject. (Under supervision, the children can occasionally trade jobs among themselves. Sometimes this will spark lagging interest.)

With all these things in mind, then, it's time to decide who's going to do what. This information will be transferred to the housecleaning schedule we talked about earlier. Also, if the child is using the time management sheet described earlier, check that and keep the child's other activities in view while you're assigning. Just remember, the child's age, ability, likes, dislikes and time demands should all be considered.

By the time a child is fourteen he should be able to do everything you can do. (Wouldn't that be a blissful state?) However, while your fourteen-year-old may be bathing and dressing himself, he may not be making his bed every day, returning dishes to the kitchen or taking out the trash. Sometimes with older children you have to start from scratch.

Back to Basics

Take a look at the following skill chart. It's broken down into four main areas: hygiene, clothes, food and basic housekeeping. In each category, determine where your child is right now and begin to move him down the list as age, skill and maturity increase. If your fourteen-year-old is still at the top of the list, you should be able to move him along rather quickly. A younger child will require more time.

Hygiene

Bathe and wash hands	Wash hair
Brush teeth	Comb hair
Floss teeth	Set/style hair

Clothes

Put clothes in the hamper	Operate laundry equipment
Dress himself	Simple mending (needle and
Put away and hang up clothing	thread)

Select coordinated outfits
Sort laundry

Complex mending (sewing machine)
Ironing

Food

Feed himself
Knows where basic foods (bread, milk, fruit, peanut butter and jelly, cereal) are kept
Prepare basic foods (sandwiches, cereal)

Prepare simple meals
Plan menus (shopping list and grocery shopping)
Prepare complicated meals

Basic Housekeeping Skills

Pick up (toys, clothes, trash, etc.)
Empty trash baskets; trash disposal
Make beds
Bring dishes to kitchen (This leads naturally into table setting, clearing the table, doing dishes, loading dishwasher, etc.)

Dust
Vacuum
Wash floors and windows
Operate appliances

Not included on this list are certain general items you may deem necessary as you go along. The older child should know how to lock/unlock the house, where extra house and car keys are located, where medications are kept and for what purpose they should be used and whom they are for, how to get to the doctor's office or hospital, how to use basic tools (hammer, pliers, screwdriver, plunger, etc.), how to replace a fuse or operate a circuit breaker, replace light bulbs, etc.

The list should include everything *you* know how to do—from changing a tire to balancing the checkbook. With a little imagination, you can come up with all sorts of interesting jobs.

The reason for variety is important—not only to improve skills and build self-confidence, but to alleviate boredom and to keep the kids somewhat interested. We tend to keep the best dishwasher in the kitchen, the best mower in the yard, and the best baby-sitter in the nursery. If you suspect monotony or boredom, give the child more responsibility.

Remember, your first area of consideration should be the five or six essentials: general pickup (including bedmaking), laundry, meals, dishes, bathrooms and entry areas (optional). This is where you need the most help, so focus on these six routine tasks.

TOOLS AND TRAINING

Here's an obvious little step often taken for granted, yet it's probably the real key to successful delegation. When someone has the training to do a job, he proceeds confidently, knowing the result will be a success. He knows he won't have to waste time because of inept fumblings and mishaps; he doesn't complain or feel morose when asked to do the job. Thus you get a higher-quality performance with fewer hassles, less screaming and infrequent tears. The proper tools are necessary for the same reasons.

Every one of us looks for the easy way out. If something is inconvenient (or takes more than one motion) we seem to put it off. Each motion added to a job makes it psychologically more difficult. Children are the same way, so if you're going to ask for their help, make it easier on them. They tend to make a mess in the kitchen, for example, because most young children are too short for the work facilities. Provide a safe, sturdy step stool for them to stand on.

Be sure the things they need to use and put away are within easy reach. How would you like to climb on top of the counter every time you wanted a drink, or every time you had to get the dishes to set the table? You'd balk, and so do the kids.

Supply tools that the kids can grasp and use with small hands. Provide anything that will make it easier for the child to succeed (small garden tools, brooms, a low mirror, coat hooks, low closet rods, lightweight equipment). Most equipment is made for use by adults and yet we become dissatisfied when a less-than-adult job is done. So be sure the tool matches the child's ability and size.

Make your children's chores as easy—and as much fun—as possible and you'll be amazed at the results. If I give our kids a spray bottle filled with colored liquid, a mop, and a pail of water, they'll clean anything! The last time Jeffrey mopped the kitchen floor, it looked like a rescue mission for transient goldfish. I just dare melted ice cream, baby mush or clumps of mud to stick to a floor like that! (He didn't think drying the floor was quite so much fun.)

Quilts or comforters make bed-making much easier. Low closet rods, a generous portion of hooks, low drawers, categorized toy bins and step stools are helpful.

And there are other helpful tools. First, you need a manual that teaches the specifics of how to clean windows, carpets, woodwork, walls, etc. Don Aslett, in his book *Is There Life After Housework?*, not only details this necessary information, he tells you how to do it fast and cheap! For example, you can find out how to clean an entire bathroom in a few minutes using just one cleaning agent. Imagine the cooperation you could extract from your family (and yourself) if cleaning were made "fast and easy." Pick up this book—you'll be glad you did.

Another good timesaving device is my cleaning cart system. In *Confessions of an Organized Homemaker* there's a picture and description of a compartmentalized cart I use that enables me to move around every room in a circle. Everything you need is contained in the cart and you never chase back and forth to deposit laundry, trash, misplaced articles or to grab cleaning supplies and rags.

I like that television commercial that advertises a power paint roller. The paint travels up a tube directly into the brush roller so you never have to use a roller pan. The announcer proclaims, "Why should you spend hours painting a pan instead of painting the wall?"

Think about it. We all spend hours cleaning house, and much of that time is spent jogging around to retrieve and deposit things. This cleaning cart stops you dead in your tracks.

A variation on the cart idea (great for the kids) is to use two boxes or laundry baskets and a paper sack. Kids can take these into the room they're cleaning and use one box to hold soiled laundry, one box to hold things that belong in another room, and the bag to hold all the trash. Anything that speeds up a job will make it more palatable for everyone—try it and see.

An intangible but necessary tool is convenience and lots of it. I've observed that inconvenience is the biggest single cause of trouble in parent/child working relationships. If you practice the storage and motion principles found in the preceding chapter, you'll be one giant step closer to your goal of organized living with kids.

To reiterate: When items are placed conveniently, they're stored where people use them, they're labeled, they're stored with motions in mind and they're slightly harder to find than they are to put away. When things are put back exactly where they belong at least several times a week, you begin to experience the reality of organized living.

Four Steps to Effective Job Training

Before the actual training begins, break down the job into bite-sized pieces. "Clean your room" is a series of little tasks that add up to a greater accomplishment: make bed, pick up toys, put away books, pick up clothes, straighten dresser, dust, vacuum. All of these things together equal "clean your room."

Listing each specific job (either with pictures or words) so the child knows what's expected eliminates communication gaps.

Once the job is divided into all its component parts, the first step is to show the child how a job is done. You may want to do this a few times before the child actually begins helping.

Work slowly so the child can see exactly what you're doing. Explain your reasons for doing certain things. ("I only squirt a little glass cleaner on the mirror so it won't streak and smear." "I tuck in the covers so they won't fall out while you're sleeping and it makes the bed look neater.")

Always teach the child to do the biggest thing first. (Make the bed, clear the table, straighten the counter.) That way a large area of the room is completed, the whole place looks better and the child (and you) feel immediate success.

The second step is to have the child do the job with you. Again, you may want to stay at this level for a week or so if it's a daily job.

Many parents complain kids don't put things back where they belong. One reason could be that things are stored inconveniently, but another reason for this universal problem is that the parent hasn't worked with the child long enough for him to learn exactly where things belong. Working with the child long enough usually takes care of the problem.

The third step is to have the child do the job alone, under your supervision. Generously praise every single thing (no matter how minuscule) the child did right. If correction is necessary, make it very tactful and sandwich it in between two positive comments.

Constructive criticism is well received when it's camouflaged in questions like: How do you think your room looks? What could you do to make your bed look better?

After a time you're ready for step four—independence day. This is when you leave the child to his work. If you've mutually agreed on an acceptable standard of quality, the child will know when the job has been done right. Even so, don't forget to inspect.

As the child increases in skill, he needs to be encouraged to use whatever method he feels comfortable with as long as the end result meets your agreed standard of quality. For example, you may show the child how to wash windows with a clean rag. Later, however, the child decides he can do a better job with a squeegee. The method should not be dictated—only the result (as long as the method isn't wasteful or otherwise unacceptable).

Too many restrictions inhibit growth, creativity and interest. Remember, if you want a completely controlled environment, prison is a nice place.

CONSISTENCY

Once the child is on his own, insist on consistency. If necessary, interrupt the child from playing (or whatever he's doing) and require him to complete an assignment or spruce it up if it was done unsatisfactorily.

Some parents awaken a sleeping child or bring a child home from school to complete unfinished chores. (As for me, I have one child who'd leave everything undone just so he'd be pulled out of school. As for sleeping, I'm so grateful when one certain child is asleep, I wouldn't wake him up unless the house were on fire.)

Not only is it important to encourage consistency in children, we as parents need a large measure of it ourselves. When we pick up after them one day and expect them to do it the next, we're sending a mixed message and giving them the definite impression that their help isn't that important or necessary. No matter what your behavior is, you're teaching habits. If you're not teaching good ones, you're teaching bad ones. If you aren't teaching them to pick up after themselves, you're teaching them to leave their belongings scattered. In addition to that, the children are learning to tolerate a mess.

Do It Daily

Part of being consistent is to give home management attention every day. And you may recognize "preventive maintenance" as the final work simplification technique. To refresh your memory, the others are: think before you act, discard and sort, group, be motion-minded and use accrued benefits.

Protests sound when someone is forced into a pigsty with the firm command, "Clean up your room!" The child (and you, too, for that matter) dreads the lengthy, toiling process. He tends to dawdle, knowing the job will take so long he can't watch his favorite show or visit his best friend. So why hurry? The day is lost anyway. Your frequent countering with, "If you hurry, it'll only take a little while," doesn't make an impression.

Imagine how much better the situation would be if the child had given his home management attention every day. Five or ten minutes a day is a lot easier dose to swallow than two hours on Saturday.

You know yourself that once something is organized and orderly, it only takes a few seconds or minutes a day to keep it that way. It takes hours to completely redo. Nothing stays organized. People keep things organized and when people don't, they have to start over. That revolting thought should remain in your mind long enough for you to develop the "preventive maintenance" habit.

We try to put things back where they belong once a day. Whenever I open a drawer or cupboard and see something out of place I take one second and put it back where it belongs. Things out of place can be put in the "for-now" spot or immediately assigned for disposition. Constant reinforcement is necessary for everyone to learn exactly where things belong. (This system is effective only after everything in your home is given a well-defined, well-confined place.)

The general maintenance theme has another application. Aside from daily routine upkeep, there's long-term home maintenance to consider. A well-maintained home saves large amounts of time and money. If you take care of what you have, you won't have to continually replace toys, furniture, tools, garden equipment and appliances. You eliminate extra paint and wallpaper jobs and too-frequent deep-cleaning sessions. Preventive maintenance is the final work-simplification technique.

I know one wealthy man who attributes his success to taking care of his possessions: He claims that his savings accumulate because he seldom has to replace things. One simple procedure he advocates is reading the instruction manuals that come with various appliances.

My friend Sherrill is a great believer in the maintenance principle. She keeps small jars or cans of paint handy to touch up chips in the paint. Using bits of sponge or disposable foam paintbrushes, she makes touching up part of her weekly cleaning routine. (When she uses oil-based paint, she freezes the paintbrushes and has no cleanup. After a quick thaw, the brushes are ready to go again!)

Maintenance—both the long-term and the do-it-daily variety—can eliminate wasted time and money and extra work for everybody!

FOLLOW THROUGH

Above all, remember the kids "do what you inspect, not what you expect." Come to think of it, I guess we do, too. Otherwise, why are we plagued by those ubiquitous stickers on new merchandise: Inspected by No. 2? Why does a brusque salesman suddenly become congenial and submissive when you ask his name?

Management has long known that when you put your name on something you do a better job. When you know someone will actually see what you've done, knowing you're responsible for the product, you always give a little bit extra, right? Kids, too. That's why you must inspect, not just expect.

AVOIDING UPWARD DELEGATION

This is where the real headaches start. "Why do *I* have to do all the work around here?" "I forgot." "I can't!" "Ugh!" "I didn't make the mess." "Oh, Brother!" "It's not my turn!" Sigh! Moan! Groan!

No wonder we figure it's easier to do it ourselves.

But *now* is the time to get tough with yourself, and above all, hang in there. These plaintive cries are cleverly disguised attempts at upward delegation—and unfortunately they often work. We feel sorry or come to the rescue "just this once" and pretty soon the kids have us right where they want us—behind the sink, under the bed retrieving lost shoes and running through the house picking up after them.

Our oldest son was skilled at the fine art of upward delegation. His primary tactic was to ask a *lot* of questions: "How big do I cut these chunks of cheese? How long will it take to melt? Do I have to put anything else in it?" You don't have to be a Ph.D. to cut up and melt cheese for nachos. But even at fourteen years old Jim would ask the questions. He knew if he interrupted me often enough, I'd decide it was easier to do it myself.

For me, the best solution has been to offer a few words of encouragement and then leave the room. This way I eliminate myself from the game. This also works well when I'm tempted to take over a job. Sometimes it grates on my nerves to watch a child grapple with a potato peeler, straighten a crooked bedspread, laboriously fold the laundry or vacuum awkwardly. Whenever it's not a safety hazard, I leave the room. That way I don't give in to those feelings of superiority ("I can do it better and faster") or pity ("He *is* so little. He's doing the best he can. He'd love for me to help"). Watch out for upward delegation and be prepared for it.

While I automatically assume all whining, fussing, fumbling and languor are attempts to get me to do the job, occasionally these problems are signals that the child has not been trained properly. Had Jim been seven years old and not made nachos several times before, his questions would have been acceptable. So, determine the cause of the kids' protests. If they've been trained and you've seen them be successful in the given area, you may well assume the problem is upward delegation. If not, more quality training is required.

I remember my own attempts at upward delegation. "Mom, I'm ironing more wrinkles into these clothes than I'm ironing out of them!"

"Dad, I'm just getting too many streaks on these windows." "I know I'm burning the white sauce!" "I don't know how to do it."

Too bad for me—I was number six in the family and my parents knew all the tricks. Without question they'd always say, "You're doing just fine." Or, "You'll figure it out." End of discussion. I learned how to iron, wash windows, cook and solve most problems all by myself— thanks to two wise parents who made upward delegation impossible.

REWARDS—HOW TO JUMP-START YOUR FAMILY

Credit the kids' accounts. Be sure to catch them in the act of doing something right. Most of us only mention the things that bug us, right? What's called for is a large measure of positive reinforcement: praise, compliments, pats on the back. We've all been the victim of "do it right and no one remembers, but do it wrong and no one forgets." Let's not be guilty of doling out the same.

To some folks, discovering how to motivate yourself and others is the mystery of the ages. If we could unlock those powers there'd be no end to what we could accomplish.

Here are a few of the tricks I have learned from some super self-motivators. Choose and use the ones that fill you with the exciting feeling of motivation. Then, teach them to your family.

- Have a deadline. This works much better if you absolutely *have* to meet it. And that happens when you get other people involved. (You're having a dinner party Friday night, so the house *has* to be cleaned. The publisher is expecting the manuscript by May 1, so you *have* to keep writing. The garden club is touring your yard this weekend so you *have* to start weeding.) Some of the most successful self-starters I know deliberately schedule things that will get them up and moving.

- Change the environment. Sometimes a slight change in your surroundings is all you need to spur you on. If you're often working in a dreary area, see what you can do to make that workspace more attractive and inviting.

Rearranging the furniture, hanging a new painting, or redecorating can often help renew your dedication to any task. These methods are especially effective with children.

Maybe a major improvement is needed, such as more efficient equipment (a frost-free refrigerator, a computer with a bigger hard-drive, a new table saw). Perhaps your dread of a task is brought on by outdated gear.

You may decide to completely move the job. Make the bedroom into a workroom. With a little remodeling, you can set up a kitchen in the family room or a laundry area in the bathroom. Remember, your house should be stimulating and functional. The better it serves your needs, the more motivated you'll become.

• Use telephones, alarms and early appointments to help you get up in the morning. Have an early-rising friend call you every morning at a specified time. (This works better if you have to trot to the kitchen to answer the phone.)

An alarm works well if you have to get out of bed to turn it off. If you're a stubborn case, don't rely on a clock radio; sometimes the music will soothe you right back to sleep. Select a blaring, buzzing, ringing alarm—and put it across the room.

Whenever you have the option, schedule your appointments early—again, forcing you to arise early.

• Use a reward system. I have a list of things I love to do; whenever I need motivation to get going, I check the list and choose my reward. (When I finish this book I can begin working on several unfinished craft projects.) This reward list can contain simple things like a hot bath, an hour with a favorite magazine, an afternoon at the flea market or elaborate things like a catered party, a vacation or a new house. Whenever you feel even a little excited about something, write down the cause of your excitement. Pretty soon you'll have a lengthy and varied reward list to choose from.

• Ask yourself, "How long is it really going to take?" I used to hate to change sheets, so I decided to time myself to see if it took as long as I thought it did. After clocking myself at two minutes, I decided it was no big deal and I've never dreaded the job since. I did the same thing with emptying the dishwasher, reading a storybook, putting away the laundry, changing a tire and washing the kitchen windows. Each job, I discovered, can be accomplished in five minutes or less and now is not quite as loathsome.

• Just start. Tell yourself you will just start the job and work for only five minutes. At the end of five minutes, if you don't feel like continuing, don't, but chances are you will. Clear the table, set a bouquet of flowers in the center, and soon you'll want the whole room to look equally inviting. Sharpen your pencil, start a pot of water boiling, throw the towels in the washer—just start and watch the magic begin.

• Finish! Remember that finishing what you start is a wonderful source of motivation. It says, "Look what I've accomplished!" It builds self-confidence and the feeling of "What can I conquer next?"

Motivators Especially for Kids

• Try money, the great motivator. Steven was flipping through one of my reference books and asked me what it was. I said, "It's a book that tells how to get your kids to work." Steven said, "Oh, I already know how to do that. Just give 'em five bucks!" (Out of the mouths of babes, I guess.) Erma Bombeck confesses that she paid her kids to breathe.

There is, however, some controversy as to whether to pay children for working around the house. Some say an allowance should be paid to children only for extra jobs, not for daily, personal upkeep. Others insist that money should be earned from outside sources, since household duties are a basic responsibility.

Whatever your conviction, you must admit that money is motivating, and earning it provides the child with money management experiences that will prepare him for adulthood. Regular allowances or paydays help children learn how to budget, plan and save. Decide with a child what his allowance must cover (lunches, clothes, lessons, gifts?) and then come up with an agreeable figure. The fixed sum should be enough for the child to enjoy, but not enough to help him get into trouble. Allowances won't work if they're not consistent, so be sure you can fit the agreed upon amount into *your* budget.

• Alternatives to money. Perhaps your salary fluctuates or you find yourself occasionally low on funds or unemployed. When that happens, allowances are frequently the first bills to go unpaid. Another problem with allowances is you've got to remember to have the right amount of change come payday. After a hard week's work the child is discouraged when you say, "Sorry, I only have a twenty."

Here are a few ideas to help you get around the problem, yet still allow you to meet your obligations.

Make up a sample check and photocopy a stack. Then write out paychecks on allowance day. When the child decides to make a purchase, he cashes his checks at the bank—which is, of course, you. This can be an elaborate learning experience if you have the time and care to take it that far. You can provide each child with a check register and have him record each earned check as a deposit. When he cashes it in, it's recorded just as you'd record a check written against your account.

Rather than the check idea, you can use play money, which will also eventually be cashed by you, the banker. A variation of this idea is that the child earns his salary in play money. He not only cashes it in when he needs it, he uses his play money to pay you for services rendered:

It'll cost him $1 for a ride to and from the movies. You could charge him $5 for pizzas to serve during the slumber party. Replacing the library book he lost will cost $8 (or whatever the book actually cost you).

Coupons are another alternative. Make your own, or cut various cents-off coupons from magazines and distribute them on payday or when a job has been especially well done. Again, you pay the child the face value of the coupon (i.e., 25¢ off shampoo means you owe the child 25¢). Again, these will be cashed by you when several are collected.

Perhaps regular rewards of money are totally out of the question. What then? Instead of working for monetary gain, maybe a desirable activity or other treat would work. How about an afternoon of swimming, a slumber party, arts and crafts, a trip to the children's museum, an ice cream cone, a carrot cake or fruit leather? Help your kids make up a reward list like the one described for you and have them decide what they're going to work for.

• Charts, posters and other visual incentives can be helpful in motivating children to work. They allow kids to plan ahead, knowing what's expected of them. The children also see the work is divided fairly and that everyone's cooperation is necessary for family success.

The big disadvantage, I feel, is that they lose interest unless the charts and posters are frequently changed. Just as your nose becomes accustomed to your perfume or aftershave, your eyes don't really see what they're accustomed to. Charts et al. only attract attention and pique interest for a short time; as soon as the novelty wears off, it's time for a new poster. This can be enormously time-consuming unless you give the job to one of the kids.

• Lists. You've probably guessed by now that I'm a list maker and that this is my favorite method. It takes very little preparation on my part and allows me some inconsistency. (With some types of charts you have to be sure all assignment cards are in place every single morning.)

You can use lists in different ways. For example, by using the time management chart for kids (page 43) you can sit down once a week and fill in the child's weekly assignments. Or you can give the kids a list of jobs to do every day.

Even though our children each had weekly chore assignments there were days when I needed extra help. At those times, I'd run through the house and list specific things for each child to do (each child had a separate list). Then I'd pass them out, though I did get them mentally prepared. "Don't make any immediate plans, I'm making up a list."

With all the children scurrying around, the house looked better in no time. (Also, by dividing everything equally, everyone's list was usually brief. That kept complaining to a minimum.)

When I'd say, "Steven and Jeff, go pick up your room," they'd be fighting within thirty seconds. "Mom, Steven isn't doing anything." "Jeff, quit putting your books on my bed." "Mom, Steven still isn't doing anything." And every disagreement (no matter the cause) was punctuated with at least one "I'm telling!"

The list method works everything out. Instead of listing "clean your room," one child's list might say:

— Put your dirty clothes in hamper.
— Pick up books.
— Put away action figures.
— Put tapes away.

Another child's list might say:

— Put your dirty clothes in hamper.
— Pick up baby's blocks.
— Put away Legos.
— Put away stuffed animals.

With only four things on each list further confrontations are avoided, and when all eight things are finished, the room is clean.

Writing up the lists takes only a few minutes and it's well worth the time. If a child can't read, assign an older child to read the list to him.

I think everyone should be a list maker and list user. It seems to nurture good planning habits that make life much easier. The list users I know are the kind of people who read and follow directions, study instruction manuals and approach things methodically. In my opinion, it's one of the best habits you can develop in your children.

• Ten jobs for $1. When the boys were younger we experienced an enormous amount of sibling rivalry. Being the same sex seemed to generate a general feeling of competition. The four-year-old was old enough to know that he got less money than his eight-year-old brother, the older brother resented the fact that he had more jobs than the younger brother. This led to all sorts of bickering.

So we instituted "Ten Jobs for a Dollar." This replaced our previous allowance system. Here's how it worked. I kept an index card in the kitchen that had the three boys' names on it. Every time they did a job, they got a check mark by their name. Everyone who had ten checks by Saturday afternoon got their dollar. If they had nine checks, they got nothing. Points did not carry over from one week to the next.

This idea works well if it's used in addition to the children's regular daily chores. It can also be altered as to the numbers of jobs and amount of money. Because it takes no forethought or advance preparation, it's ideal for a working parent to implement.

The system worked because a job for the four-year-old was "empty the trash" and a job for the six-year-old was "straighten the toy closet." Even though the size of each job varied depending on the age of the child, in the child's mind, everyone had to do ten jobs. And you never saw more eager workers come Saturday morning—the day I needed the most help.

Another reason I liked the system was because of its spontaneity. Whenever I needed help, I'd call out, "Who wants to earn a job?" I'd usually have three little volunteers ready and waiting.

• Before is the best motivator of all. Before a story, before play, before eating or before anything always brings forth an eager response. But before bed is the real winner!

I've seen our kids shovel snow before bed, clean the basement, straighten their dressers and place the Legos in descending-size order (with all the little bumps facing the same direction). Before bed they suddenly remember all the extra-credit assignments they could do, stories they could write, multiplication tables they could memorize. Yes, mention the word "bed" and you'll have a work crew comparable to the staff at the White House.

One last thought about motivating kids. Get them mentally prepared. Let them know that work time, bedtime, church (or whatever) is coming up. That way you'll experience half the resentment, resistance and wrangling.

That's why a weekly planning session is so important. The kids know from the outset what to expect and they have a chance to accept it and take part in the planning. If you're going to spring something on them like a chore, a nap or ending a phone conversation, let them know a few minutes before the deadline. It's only common courtesy.

Delegating enables you to plan more effectively, helps relieve the pressure of too much to do, and it's a great way to train your staff! But the real payoff is that delegating gives you the time you need for personal development. Follow the steps and climb the ladder to freedom!

CHAPTER NINE

When All Else Fails

In *The Working Woman's Guide,* Alice Skelsey says, "Discipline is really more a way of life than a series of isolated responses as they come up. A consistent response to discipline situations takes up less of your energies and creates much less turmoil than reacting, often overreacting, in sporadic attempts to establish laws and order in the home."

Janet's Yellow Sink

Jim and I have an interior decorator friend, an experienced professional who takes great pride in her career. Recently she took us on a tour of her gorgeous home, which reflects her talent. Just before we left, Janet voiced her dismay over the yellow sink in her kitchen. "What yellow sink?" I thought. Janet's kitchen made me feel like I was in a tiny village in the south of France. The pink wallpaper, the wooden cupboards, the abundant baskets and plants, the green trees outside peeking through shuttered windows—all combined to created that warm country French illusion. I certainly didn't notice a yellow sink.

Janet went on to explain that the yellow sink would be replaced as soon as her budget would allow. For now, she would close her eyes to it and pretend it wasn't there.

Janet is a professional with high standards regarding design. For that reason, I know how hard it must have been for her to overlook that yellow sink. But she did it—and taught me a good lesson in the meantime.

We all have yellow sinks, as it were. Maybe your yellow sink is a spouse who saves every tiny scrap of paper. Maybe you've got a teenager who won't clean his room and refuses to let you do it. Maybe your spouse leaves books and papers scattered across the kitchen counter. What if someone just won't cooperate, despite your best efforts? What do you do? How do you maintain your sanity?

Many of the suggestions in this book (storing things conveniently, planning, eliminating clutter, setting up a housekeeping schedule) will streamline your workload and relieve a lot of your pressing problems.

With young children it's easy to mold their habits and shape their behavior using the delegation principles you've just learned. Start while they're still young.

As kids get older it's difficult (and sometimes impossible) to get them to cooperate. If you encounter an occasional hopeless case (and this could include your spouse), the following general suggestions might help:

• The first alternative (with kids anyway) is to try discipline. Put in force those actions you agreed upon in your family discussion. Are there privileges you can take away? Can you incur the logical consequences of the misbehavior? For instance, if you're too tired to work you must take a nap or go to bed for the night. Your chores will be waiting for you. If you don't get your clothes in the washer, they will not be washed. (Even a little child can understand this one. When there are no clothes to wear, he can't go outside and play or go to the park.) These are not ultimatums, but simple outcomes for chosen behavior. If you need help with discipline here are some sources:

Parent Effectiveness Training, Thomas Gordon. (Peter H. Wyden).
The Good Kid Book, Howard Norman Sloane. (New American Library).
Children: The Challenge, Rudolf Dreikurs. (Duell, Sloan and Pearce).

• Can you compromise? For example, we have a drawer in our kitchen designated as a minioffice center. I like that drawer to be just perfect—paper clips here, pencils there and so on. Every night Jim comes home and tosses receipts, keys, change, his watch, phone messages, bills and business cards in the drawer and ruins the order. I used to run myself ragged running up and down stairs carrying this stuff to his desk—and complaining got me nowhere. So I compromised. I took out a small local phone book that was in the drawer (I stored it with our other phone books) and filled the empty space with a drawer divider. Jim still tosses his junk in the drawer, but it's contained in the divider and the drawer still looks tidy. (When the divider gets too full, one of us manages to put the contents on Jim's desk.) With this compromise, we're both happier: I got a neat drawer and Jim got the convenience he wanted.

Don't forget those trade-offs we talked about. ("I'll mow the lawn if you'll do the dishes; I'll do the dusting if you'll play with the baby; I'll get the car serviced if you'll defrost the freezer.")

• Have you tried bragging, praise and appreciation? Be quick to express your appreciation for any help you receive—especially when a job is well done. Also, be generous with your praise.

One night I happened to walk into the boys' bedroom and noticed how well-made-up Brian's bed looked—a real miracle. I wanted to tell him what a great job he'd done (before I forgot) but he was spending the night at a friend's house. So I gave him a call and said, "I just wanted you to know what a good job you did on your bed!" He said, "Is that all you called for?" "That's it," I said. He seemed pleasantly surprised, and since that time I've had a great little bedmaker.

Whenever you have a chance, brag just a little. (Be sure the child or your spouse can hear you, too.) "This kid is the best eater you've ever seen! He'll eat anything!" "I think I've taken out the trash once in the whole fifteen years we've been married. I never even mention it. Every Thursday morning, Jim's out there putting the cans by the curb!"

Brag, praise and sincerely express your appreciation to your kids, to your spouse or to anyone who gives you a hand with your responsibilities. Oh, I know—everything isn't *your* responsibility and maybe you feel you shouldn't have to appreciate it when someone does a routine task. Appreciate it anyway. Even the tiniest bit of cooperation contributes to the family's well-being and fosters a sense of unity, love and peace. And who knows—by setting this example you may soon be getting a few pats on the back, too!

• Failing all of the above, do it yourself. If something is driving you crazy and you can't stand it for another minute, do it yourself. But do it quietly—no hollering, nagging or acting the martyr. This is *your* quirk, remember.

Sometimes this can get you in trouble, so proceed with caution. If your actions start causing contention you better back off. (Jim got a little testy when I kept moving his papers, because he wanted them handy when he left for work.)

You may argue, "Why should *I* have to give in? Whose rights are more important, anyway?" Sometimes I say to myself that since I'm the one who wants things a certain way then I'm the one who's going to care enough to do it that way. When you're cleaning up after someone (especially a spouse) just keep saying, "I'm doing this for *me*." That will keep you from feeling like a martyr.

I like to think in terms of relationships rather than rights. You can

fight this out to the death of your marriage (or the parent/child relationship) if you want to, but is a neat mini-office drawer really worth it?

CHANGING WHAT YOU CAN CHANGE

When I make bread on a cold, dry day, sometimes the dough sits on
the counter and doesn't rise very fast. So I put the bowl of dough on
top of the refrigerator where it's nice and warm. Before long the dough
is puffing up and ready to bake.

What made the difference? I changed the atmosphere by placing the
dough in a warmer spot—a place where the yeast was more likely to
grow. I didn't pull the dough up, yank it or stretch it trying to make it
bigger and fluffier; I just changed the atmosphere and the dough rose
all by itself.

As a home manager, I think that's my main job—to create a climate
conducive to change. I can't make people change, but I can do a lot
to create the right environment should they want to.

If you keep a feeling of love in your home, people are much more
likely to meet you halfway. But nagging, harping and bickering close
the very doors you're trying to open.

One woman told me she had married a definite male chauvinist.
He heartily espoused the theory that women should be home baking
brownies.

She said, "Over the years I made some changes in him with a lot of
cheer and heavy use of the word 'we.' " When faced with a difficult
situation (like dinner guests on Saturday night) she would tell her husband all the things that needed to be done, then choose several and
say, "This is what I can do." She left the conversation open-ended so
he, in turn, could voice what his contribution would be. She would
also remind him to pick up the cleaning or the groceries "since you'll
be in the area anyway."

This subtle, no-nag approach worked for her and just might work
in your situation, too, regardless of whether you're dealing with an
adult or a child. (One woman tried a blunter approach. She told her
husband, "I'm so glad we're going to share the housework fifty-fifty.
I've handled it for the last five years. Now it's your turn.")

Jim makes up an index card of things he has to do every day and
carries it in his pocket. Occasionally I'll add a few things to his list:
While you're in the city, can you pick up the book illustrations? Will
you mail these letters for me when you pick up the mail?

Remember, this is a two-way street. You have to contribute as well
as take. Display your willingness to work things out. (What can I do to

help you? I've got to run some errands today; do you need anything?)

Don't expect more from the kids (or your spouse) than you expect from yourself. If you're in the habit of sleeping late, operating without a schedule and dropping your clothes on the floor, how can you honestly expect the rest of the family to do better?

Also, try to understand their moods will not always match yours. You probably have ambitious days as well as lazy days, and the others do, too. Sensing their mood swings will help you capitalize on their good days.

If you're a tidy person living with a slob, or vice versa, you may have to come to grips with your situation as Janet did with her yellow sink. Sometimes it's necessary to accept things as they are and quit struggling against them. Why waste your energy when you can direct it in loftier pursuits?

Try to concentrate on the areas you do have control over. Your clothes closet and dresser can be well organized. Think about the efficient work centers you've set up in the kitchen or basement. Enjoy the organized rhythm of your home office. In other words, throw yourself wholeheartedly into the things you *can* change, and try to accept those you can't. Everyone will be happier in the long run.

What if it's just too late? Is your marriage crumbling? Are the children totally out of control? While the advice in this book will help, you may need to consider family counseling. Call your family doctor and get a referral to a psychologist or a psychiatrist who specializes in family problems. If you live near a university, that can be a good source to check as well. If money is a problem, contact your local mental health center; they usually charge according to your ability to pay.

When our piano gets out of tune, we don't throw it away—we call in the piano tuner. I hope you'd do the same. If you're married, don't throw that relationship away and don't give up on the kids. Maybe all you need is a tune-up!

To recap the past few chapters, we've looked at a six-step work simplification program to help you manage housework—the glutton of your time.

1. Plan
2. Eliminate clutter
3. Group
4. Use motion-minded storage
5. Accrue your benefits (with a lot of delegation)
6. Preventive Maintenance

When the inevitable snags come up along the way, look over this work simplification list to discover what went wrong. Where did the breakdown occur? Reread any sections you're having trouble with and look for ways to overcome any problems.

People under pressure are more likely to experience job burnout. Home management is a lifework: The reason all other jobs and occupations exist is to enable you to make a home. You cannot afford to get discouraged. The way to insure a long, prosperous career is to eliminate pressure from your life. The program you've just studied will do that for you if you'll only use it.

It is my hope you will feel (to some small degree, at least) the peace, love and security that come into your home when things are organized and orderly.

CHAPTER TEN

Wash and (S)Wear

E
vidently, Isaac Newton didn't spend much time at the Laundromat. I mean, it doesn't take a genius to refute the law of gravity:
anyone who's discovered socks hanging from a hemline
knows that static cling is stronger than the force accelerating
us toward the center of the earth.

Static cling, the super glue of the laundry industry. Manufacturers
are searching for clues, cures and treatments with all the fervor of mad
scientists. They've given us liquid fabric softeners (you know, the ones
we forget to put into the final rinse) and dryer sheets (the ones sucked
into the lint trap after the first tumble). They've given us sprays that
smell like rubber cement and anti–static cling detergents. Yes, industry
knows how much we hate static cling and they're out to do something
about it.

So if you've been all the way to Tide country and still suffer the ill
effects of static cling, tattletale gray, unmatched socks, "after you
wash" stains, shrunken and puckered clothing (when they say "dry
clean only" they *mean* it!), ring around the collar and mountains of
laundry, I guess it's safe to suppose you have the washday blues. Spend
a few minutes learning how to manage your family's laundry and you'll
be in the pink in no time.

LOCATING THE LAUNDRY

If you're lucky enough to have your own equipment, you've probably
got the washer and dryer in the spot they *have* to be (where the hook-
ups are) instead of where they should or could be. But just in case
you're building or remodeling your existing structure, let's examine
some possibilities.

A laundry area can be set up in a corner of the kitchen or bath, in a
separate room, closet or niche in a wall. A washer and dryer can be
placed behind louvered doors in a family room, in a garage or carport,

in a passageway between bedroom and bath, in the basement or under a kitchen counter (so the countertop can be used for meal preparation or folding clothes). Space under a stairway can be turned into a laundry if water pipes are handy.

If you're cramped for space, there are compacts, portables and stacking laundry equipment that fit into small places. If you opt for standard machines, front loaders help you gain counter space in tight areas.

In a small house or apartment, you can arrange a laundry area in a spacious closet. You don't need to vent an electric closet dryer if you attach a special lint trap. (However, if the dryer is unvented, it should stand four inches away from the back wall.)

In a standard closet, a dryer can be bolted to the top of a front-loading washer. There are units made especially for this purpose; the machines are flat-topped, with front-mounted controls that make them easy to reach and operate. (Be sure to keep the closet door open during drying cycles so the front air intake isn't blocked.)

Of course, the ideal is to have a separate laundry/utility room large enough to house sewing, ironing and hobby areas. That way you can close the door when something is in progress you haven't had time to finish and don't want to put away.

If you live in a warm climate and have your washer and dryer installed in your carport or garage, it's helpful to put a plastic tablecloth in front of the machines to catch any clean wet clothes that might fall out while being transferred from washer to dryer. When the laundry is completed, fold the tablecloth wrong side out to keep the top clean.

You've Got What It Takes

Following is a list of equipment and supplies to keep in mind when you're planning a laundry center. Even if you take your clothes to the Laundromat, you have to arrange an area to store the supplies and organize the laundry. Read through the list and choose the ideas that fit your situation.

• If you have the space, it helps to have something to sort the clothes in: cardboard boxes or laundry baskets (one for each category—whites, darks, special handling), wire drawer units (for sorting or storing), tall plastic wastebaskets or hampers, drawstring bags or pillowcases. Having a place for each washload eliminates an enormous amount of clutter. Aside from the fact that the laundry constantly interrupts you, it also looks generally disorderly. So keep as much of it as possible under wraps. Also, these sorting containers can store folded clean clothes and keep them intact while you distribute them.

• A bulletin board furnishes ample space for a stain removal guide, safety pins (to fasten buckles and drawstrings before washing), small scissors and several needles threaded with basic colors (or clear nylon thread) so you can do quick mending jobs before the clothes are laundered. You can also tack up special-care instructions or clothing receipts for specific garments. (If a machine-washable garment falls apart, fades excessively or shrinks after a few washings, you'll be glad you saved the receipt.)

• If the directions for operating your machines are not permanently printed inside the lid, write up a set of instructions on an index card. Slip the card into a protective plastic sleeve (or have it laminated) and tape it to the control panel so everyone will know how to operate the equipment safely and correctly. Include the amount of detergent, bleach or other additives, the water level and temperature, and drying times for various loads. Also, most manufacturers recommend adding the detergent to the water before adding the clothes so it will dissolve and emulsify. If you do not have a bleach dispenser, the bleach should not be added until the machine has been agitating for about five minutes.

• For spot-cleaning jobs, have a dish detergent bottle (with a pop-up lid) filled with bleach or other cleaning liquid. When only a tiny area needs to be treated, this bottle helps you make a direct hit. (Be sure to clearly label the bottle so no one mistakes it for dishwashing soap.) Small embroidery hoops are good for isolating the area that needs to be treated.

• For presoaking, keep a plastic pail stored by the sink, laundry tub, bathtub or shower. Fill it with water, presoak detergent, and the soiled clothing. Should anyone need to use the sink, tub or shower, it's easy to remove the pail.

• Everyone needs a small can or plastic container close to the washer where you toss all the things you find in pockets or in the bottom of the washer after a cycle (buttons, change, screws, etc.). More than likely, when you're looking for a matching button, change for the parking meter, or the screw that fell out of the doorknob, you'll find it quickly just by checking the can.

• You'll also need a small trash basket to hold the lint from the lint traps, the washed wads of paper, pieces of food impervious to water, and the gum wrappers you discover in the bottom of the drum. (Wouldn't it be great if everyone emptied their own pockets?)

• A zippered mesh bag is great for holding nylon stockings, small baby items or socks. (In the case of socks, just toss a load of socks into the mesh bag. At the end of the washing/drying cycles, pull out the bag and all the socks are together.)

• A beverage can opener or razor knife helps you rip into heavy detergent boxes.

• Have a spot where you can immediately hang up items as they come from the dryer. A tension rod mounted in a doorway is convenient and easily removed (and remounted) after every laundry session. A towel bar attached under any high horizontal surface is another possibility. (If you're tall and working in an unfinished area of your home, the towel bar can be placed on a ceiling stud.)

• A floor-to-ceiling (tension spring) plant pole is another idea. It has hooks for hanging plants to effectively hold a lot of clothing. A bracket

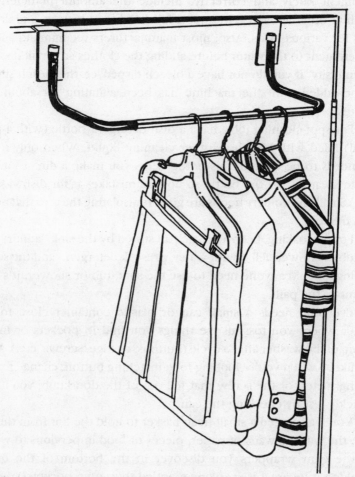

Provide extra hanging storage space wherever you need it by using an over-the-door rod.

mounted on a wall track can be a sturdy "arm" for holding freshly dried clothes. And there are racks that hang over a door.

• A chain hung around the neck of a wooden coat hanger has many links in which to place clothes hangers. The coat hanger can be hung from a cupboard knob or from a nail or hook in the wall or ceiling and it's easy to carry from room to room as you put the clothes away.

• Perhaps you need a place to hang drip-dries or clothing not suitable for the dryer. Folding dryer racks are widely available and can stand in the bathtub, out in the yard, in the basement, garage or on the back porch. When they're not in use, they fold up and require little storage space. A three-arm towel rack can be mounted to a wall or inside a cupboard door; these are perfect for plastic pants, bibs and other small items.

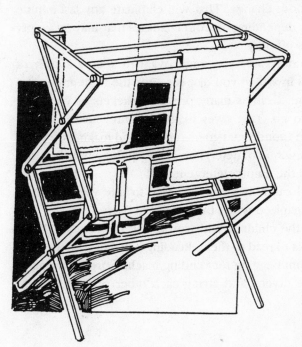

A fold-up laundry rack holds plenty of nondryer items, yet takes up little room when not in use.

Use shower space for drying. Slip a rubber band around the neck of the shower head to hold hangers tightly in place. Another idea is to mount a second shower rod that hangs directly over the middle of the tub; when the shower curtain is closed, the rod is completely out of view. (Using a tension bar will eliminate any installation.)

• Have a place where you can fold the clothes. If you don't have counter or table space available, keep a card table nearby, and fold it up and store it when it's not in use.

• Even if there's not room by your washer and dryer for ironing equipment, find a small area where this chore can be performed. You'll need space for the iron and ironing board. (Ironing board caddies that hold the iron, ironing board, spray starch, water, etc., are available; these units can be mounted on a wall or the back of a door.) You'll also need a place to hang clothing. In addition to the hanging ideas mentioned above, small freestanding clothes hanging racks made especially for ironing are available. These, too, fold up after use. You'll also need a basket or box to hold folded clothes waiting to be ironed or put away and a spot to store a container of distilled water. (Using a clean plastic ketchup dispenser is a simple way to fill the iron with distilled water.)

• If you frequent the Laundromat, you'll also need a can or jar in which to toss your loose change. That will eliminate any last-minute groveling for coins or depending on coin changers that may be empty when the attendant is off duty.

• Also, in your laundry area you might want to keep a supply of plastic sandwich bags in which you dispense just the right amount of detergent for one load. Grab as many premade packets as you need when you're ready to go. This saves lugging around heavy opened boxes and jugs. (Some Laundromat-goers recommend making up packets when you buy a new box of detergent. Make up the whole box and drop the packets into the empty detergent box.)

• A plastic carryall caddy is a handy device to tote your supplies, plus it keeps them organized when they're not in use.

• If you're taking the children with you to the Laundromat, bring along a few storybooks to read to them. Reading helps to pass the time and keeps the kids from begging for vending machine treats, trying to dry themselves in the dryers, and giving each other rides in laundry carts.

THE MAIN EVENT

Now that your work area is in order, it's time to schedule the main event—laundry days. How often you do the laundry basically depends on three things: how many clothes you have, your disposition, and your time schedule. If everyone in the family has enough clothes to get them through a week, you'll be able to get by with a single weekly wash (if you can stand spending a whole day washing). Personally, I'd rather spend a day touring a post-war tractor factory in the former Soviet Union than to spend it doing laundry.

However, here are two more factors to consider. The laundry is terribly interrupting and can be awfully messy—what with piles of dirty clothes, stacks of folded clothes placed wherever space will allow (usually on the bed), spilled detergent granules, wads of dryer fuzz and single socks waiting for mates. So there are advantages to the once-a-week laundry session. You have six days free of laundry clutter and nagging interruptions (changing loads, sorting, folding, etc.). You have only one "get ready" and one "cleanup" per week, thus you save some time.

If you do your laundry at the Laundromat, it would pay you to beef up the family's clothing supply and make the trip just once a week. Eight loads take only slightly longer than three loads, so it makes sense to make the most out of every jaunt to the Laundromat. (I know a single woman who has a wardrobe with more pieces than a Monopoly game. She does her laundry once a month!)

Though I hate to do laundry, I do like to be in charge of it—so I've chosen to keep that job for myself. However, it's helpful to have an assistant to help sort, fold and put away the clothes. I schedule three laundry sessions a week. That way I have four days a week when I don't have to worry about it and I'm freed from the mess and the interruptions. Also, washing this frequently, I never have to spend a long time at it.

It works best for me to put all the clothes away, because then I don't have the added clutter of individual piles of clothing sitting around waiting for the kids to put them away. I straighten drawers as I go—everything is constantly maintained and seldom needs a complete redoing. It only takes me five minutes to put away all the laundry—even though there are seven of us—so I figure, "What's the big deal?"

You, however, may not feel that way, or have the time to handle the whole system. Some families have each person do his own laundry. Each person has a scheduled day a week when he does his personal washing. Can you imagine the time you'd save? If that sounds like an impossible order, how about just getting everyone to put away his own clothes? Many people have told me that they have a dishpan for each person in the family. The clothes are folded and put into the tubs. Each person retrieves his container from the laundry area and puts away his clothes.

I know of one fifteen-year-old whose job it is to do the laundry for his whole family—nine people! That's a big chore, but he's done it for three years and handles it beautifully.

So when you schedule your laundry, keep in mind your disposition, how many clothes everyone has, and the amount of time you want to spend per laundry session. Then choose a specific day (or days) to do the laundry. Waiting until you need something or doing it on a casual basis is courting disaster. Plan specifically so you can work other activities and time demands around it.

At our house, it's a matter of course that the washing is done on Monday, Wednesday and Friday. Everyone is well aware of the schedule and plans accordingly. ("If I wear this blouse today, it won't be clean for the dance Thursday.")

When trying to come up with a workable personalized system, remember when you wash frequently you can get by with fewer clothes; thus, you'll need less storage space.

Take Up a Collection

Even if your kids have the aim of William Tell, it's likely they'll have little success getting their clothes tossed in the hamper. Here I offer several ideas to increase the likelihood the clothes will, at least, be *touching* the hamper.

We have hampers everywhere—in each bedroom and in each bathroom. (The clothes may not be in the hampers, but at least they're piled around them in one general area!) Because of all the soiled dishcloths, towels and rags that accumulate in the kitchen, that's another logical place for a hamper or laundry bag.

Soiled clothing can be deposited in any container—a regular hamper, a box (covered with contact paper or wallpaper), a tall plastic wastebasket, a heavy vinyl garbage can, pillowcases (these can be tacked to the inside of a closet door), or a laundry or drawstring bag. (Hang these on a door or over a hanger in the closet.) Also, a bag can be fashioned to hang conveniently over a hanger; a side opening instead of a drawstring makes it easier to use.

If someone in the family is a roofer, a mechanic, works on an oil rig or spends his time on the back forty, you'll need a separate hamper in which to deposit heavily soiled items. That will keep the worst dirt, grease and oil isolated.

If you happen to be the lucky owner of a laundry chute, you can use an old playpen to catch the clothes, and if it's mounted on casters you can roll it right to your laundry equipment.

Post your laundry schedule on the family calendar. If you're using several hampers around the house, have each person bring his hamper to the laundry area on washday. That'll save you (or whomever) from making the rounds.

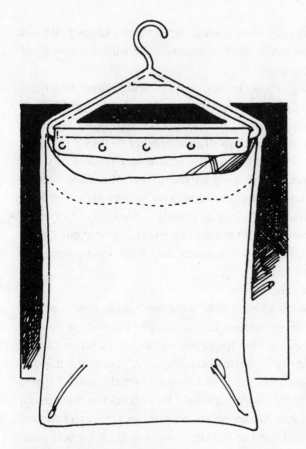

A hanging clothes
hamper made from a
wooden coat hanger and
a pillowcase is handy and
inconspicuous.

SORTING IT ALL OUT

Sorting clothes bogs down the whole laundry process, so we need to
look for shortcuts. This group of simple maintenance procedures will
save you a lot of time in the long run.

Sort by fabric, color and soil. This automatically segregates lint pro-
ducers and extra-dirty things from the rest of the wash. It also makes it
possible for you to wash and dry each piece at the correct temperature.

Have an impromptu treasure hunt and search through pockets. This
keeps you from washing and drying facial tissues, chewing gum, felt
markers, toys, important papers and crayons. It takes some time, but
occasionally it pays off when you discover loose change!

Repair snags, mend seams, hems and loose buttons before washing.
After washing, the repair will take longer. The agitation of the washing
machine will cause tears to fray, seams and torn hems to open further.
Even if you've just lost a button, it's easier and quicker to sew it back
on when you can still see exactly where it was sewn on before. After
washing, the exact button placement is harder to determine. A stitch

in time really does save nine. (Using clear nylon thread keeps you from having to change colors while you're mending. This thread is also good for sewing on scout badges.)

Also before washing, close hooks, zippers and Velcro fasteners. (Velcro will snag other clothes if left open.) Turn things inside out if they pick up lint or fade. Remove pins, ornaments, removable shoulder pads and fragile trimmings. Pin drawstrings together so they won't pull through the opening. Pin buckles to the inside of a pocket or other reinforced area to prevent clanking in the dryer. Thread shoelaces through buttonholes and tie them loosely. Also tie any sashes or long attached belts. (Removable belts can be placed in pockets or in a mesh bag.) To keep long fringe from tangling, tie every six or eight tassels together at the end with string. Treat stains, necklines, knees, cuffs and seats of children's clothing.

Now, for some real time-savers.

There are lots of ways to save time handling socks. Everyone can mate his own before he puts them in the hamper by using a colored rubber band (red is for Jim, blue for Brian, and so on), a safety pin, or a sock mater. (That is a small plastic disc with an "X" cut in the middle. The socks are pulled through the X and thrown into the wash.) If you decide to mate socks before washing (and a lot of folks use this system religiously) keep a stock of rubber bands, pins or discs by each hamper. Some parents return unturned or unmated socks to their owners as is.

If you've still got young ones around, train them early. Teach them how to take off their socks right: pull socks down to just below the heel, grasp by the toes, pull off, and shake a little. That way, socks aren't turned inside out. Two more ideas to consider: Have a separate sock hamper or use a mesh bag and wash all the socks in a particular load as one unit. Better yet, have a separate mesh bag for each person.

Coding clothes can also save time. Use colors, initials or *X*s (one *X* is the firstborn, two *X*s the second child and so on. When the clothes are handed down, it's a simple matter to add another *X*.) Use permanent felt markers or special laundry markers to mark neck tags, labels or the insides of pockets. Coding can speed up the whole laundry.

If you think you can pull it off, get your family members to sort their own clothes. (Of course, sorting the laundry is a good job to delegate to one of the kids.) If you have a central depository for soiled apparel, you could use three or four labeled hampers or bins and the clothes will be sorted and ready when it's time to wash. If the kids deliver their clothes to the wash area on laundry days, have three or four boxes handy for them to sort their clothes into. (If you have a large hamper, perhaps you could compartmentalize it in some way using three pillow-cases or Masonite dividers.)

Sorting clothes the night before a scheduled washday is the fastest way I know to get a head start in the morning—a real boon to the working parent. If the laundry is sorted and ready when I get up in the morning, the job is completed much earlier. There's always enough time during busy morning hours to throw a load into the washer, but there's not always enough time to sort. (After the clothes are sorted and before you hop into bed, toss a load of towels or jeans in the washer and start the machine. They can sit all night without harmful effects and the dryer will eliminate wrinkles.)

If you didn't sort the night before and wake up wishing you had, here's a quick way to get started: Dump all the laundry in a big heap in front of the machines. Quickly pull out a load of towels, sheets or jeans. (They're easy to spot and there aren't many pieces in each load.) Start the machine and continue sorting (or feed the kids, or whatever). Get the machines going as quickly as possible. Don't let them sit there watching you sort clothes for thirty minutes.

THIS IS THE WAY WE WASH OUR CLOTHES

Now that the laundry is sorted, here are a few tips for washing and drying.

First, avoid buying clothes that require special handling (hand-washables, shrinkage-prone clothes, fussy-detailed clothing requiring a lot of ironing, etc.). It's easier to teach the kids how to do the laundry if they don't have to learn the fine points of hand washing, delicate cycles, "dry flat," "do not wring," "rinse in cold water only." Unless you've got more time than most of us, you'll want to gradually get a wash-and-wear wardrobe. As things need replacing get the easy-care items. Whenever possible, choose clothes that are durable, shrink-resistant, colorfast and wrinkle-resistant. (Overloading and rinsing in hot water can also produce wrinkles.)

Read labels on garments and cleaning aids and follow directions. Measure your detergents and other additives precisely for optimum results; keep a measuring cup right inside the box. If you buy detergent in the largest size possible you're forced to measure because the box is too cumbersome to pour. (Be sure to have two measuring cups— one for dry additives and one for liquids.)

When you start the laundry, wash in the same order you'll put it away. Here's what I mean: At our house the underwear, socks and pajamas are kept in the top dresser drawer. The second drawer holds shirts and tops; jeans and pants are in the third drawer. So when I do the wash, I wash jeans first. When they come out of the dryer, I fold them and begin a pile for each person. Next I wash the shirts and tops. They're folded and placed on top of the jeans and pants. Next come the white clothes. Likewise, they're folded and placed on top. The clothes are all ready to put away and I've used a minimum of space because there's only one pile for each person.

Now for a bunch of my favorite washday hints:

• When you're washing an article that shouldn't be dried in the dryer, put a signal on top of your washer—a feather duster, a small stuffed animal, a hammer—anything that will attract your attention and remind you that there's a nondryer item inside. Or keep a few colored clothespins by each hamper. The clothespins can be snapped onto an item that's stained or needing special care and serve as a signal to the person doing laundry.

• If you're always forgetting to wash your robe, a blanket or a throw rug, write a note to yourself and drop it in the clothes hamper.

• If you're so far behind with the laundry (more than five loads) that you're beginning to despair, head to a nearby Laundromat. In an hour and a half (as opposed to three hours it'd take to do five loads at home) you can be finished! This is a quick fix to get you back on track fast. It's also a good way to catch up after a vacation.

• Rotate washing bedding so laundry doesn't get bogged down as it would if you were to wash all the sheets on Friday. If the kids know when their day is, they can pull their sheets off and cart them to the laundry area.

• Keep your appliances healthy by reading instruction manuals and following the directions. Keep track of the dates you performed regular maintenance (remove agitator and clean, run vinegar through a cycle, vacuum dryer vent, etc.).

• Spin-dry hand-washables and lay flat to dry. Place the article on a towel and lay it on the kitchen counter, on top of the dryer, or better yet, buy a rack (made especially for this purpose) that fits over the bathtub.

• Don't string long things like sheets around the agitator. Instead, grasp the sheet in the center and fold into an "S" shape, then place it around the basket.

• If garment care tags aren't sewn inside an article of clothing, save the hang tags that come with it. (You may have to mark the tags to help you remember which article of clothing they came with.) File these instructions in a recipe-card box, behind tabbed dividers labeled with the owner's name, and keep this in the laundry area. Be sure to have a tab marked "household items" (curtains, throw rugs, blankets, etc.).

• At better Laundromat facilities some attendants will (for a price) fold and hang your laundry when the cycle is over.

• Launder all seasonal clothing before storing so stains and soil won't be permanently set in.

• Stuff toys, dolls, dustmop heads, etc., inside an old nylon stocking. This will protect the article (especially dolls' hair) and will keep the lint trapped inside.

• After removing excess hair from combs and brushes, toss them in the washer with a batch of towels. Cellulose sponges can also be freshened and cleaned in the washer.

IT'S DRYING TIME AGAIN

Dryers are wonderful inventions and they can save a lot of time if they're used properly.

Three easy tricks will help you get the most out of your dryer:

1. Clean the lint trap after every cycle.
2. Don't overload it.
3. Remove clothes promptly.

Trying to iron wrinkles, wrinkled permanent press especially, is as much fun as a speech on the foreign trade deficit. Oh, sure, you can always toss the clothes back into the dryer with a damp towel to release the wrinkles, but that doesn't always work. Save yourself as much time as possible and get to the dryer as quickly as it turns off. If necessary, use a separate timer with a loud bell to signal when the load is finished.

Removing lint will enable the dryer to run more efficiently, drying the clothes in the least possible time.

Be sure to turn off all your equipment when you leave home. I know it's tempting to let the machines finish the work while you're gone, but you never know when a water valve won't shut off or a wire will ignite. (Listen to the voice of experience. One day I decided to take my chances and came home to a flooded basement.)

Here are a few quick tips:

• Use the dryer to dust draperies, bedspreads, blankets and slipcovers. Just pop them in along with a damp towel for fifteen minutes. You can also fluff shag rugs and sofa pillows this way. (Before you toss the draperies in the dryer, run a piece of masking tape over the drapery hooks. That way you won't have the extra work of removing and replacing them.)

• If you know in advance which articles of clothing you're going to iron, stop the dryer and pull out those things while they're still slightly damp and iron them (if time permits). If you're going to do the ironing later, carefully hang or fold those pieces to avoid further wrinkling. Always iron important things first in case you don't have time to complete the whole project in one block of time.

• If your dryer doesn't have an automatic cool-down cycle, turn the dryer heat to "air fluff" or "no heat" at the end of the drying time. This will reduce wrinkling.

• If you pull something from the dryer that's covered with lint, brush the garment with a clean, damp cellulose sponge. If you take something out of the washer that's covered with lint, put the item into the dryer with a yard or two of nylon net. The abrasive net will brush the lint off the article.

• If you're hanging clothes on a clothesline, a hanging plant pot is a good weatherproof container for clothespins. If it rains, the water comes out of the drainage holes in the bottom of the pot. An over-the-shoulder bag is another good clothespin tote. You can "wear" it while you're hanging clothes and the pins are easy to grab. Attaching a length of chain to the clothesline provides individual links in which to hang clothing on hangers; this will keep the wind from blowing them off and keep the hangers from sliding together.

The End of the Line

Now it's time to fold and put away the clothes. If you follow some of the above advice (color-coding, removing clothes promptly, etc.), folding and putting away the laundry will be a snap!

Never put anything away if it needs repairing. Have a separate mending box or assign each person to handle his own.

When the laundry is finished, you're apt to find single, mateless socks. This happens for several reasons:

1. Static cling—someone will discover a lump in the leg of his pants and unveil the missing sock.
2. The house isn't as orderly as it should be. Chances are the sock is under the couch, wet and soggy in the bottom of a boot, or behind the bathroom door.

3. The sock was so badly worn the owner threw it away, leaving the other sock mateless.

To avoid making room for your developing sock collection, hold onto strays no longer than one month. After that, get rid of them.

When folding clothes, consider folding sets as one unit (pajama tops and bottoms, top and bottom sheets, matching outfits). Just fold pieces separately and tuck one inside the other to form a packet. Stack folded clothing into the laundry baskets in the reverse order in which you're going to put them away. (If you go into the bathroom first, put the towels on top of the load.) This is just common sense, but it sure saves time and steps.

In this chapter you've read a number of ideas that may seem small and individually insignificant. But as soon as you start using a few of them, especially one or two from each category (i.e., collecting, sorting, washing, drying, folding and putting away), possibly for the first time in your laundry career, you'll be managing the washing with the precision of finely meshed gears. Step out of the vicious laundry cycle. Try some new ideas instead of wallowing in the mire of old comfortable habits. Then stand back and watch those washday blues gurgle down the drain.

CHAPTER ELEVEN

How to Become a Food Processor

I don't know who's responsible. Maybe it's television (I suspect the Waltons) or riveting literature from the past (perhaps *Little Women*), though it could simply be my nagging conscience. But whenever I think of "a family meal," certain images are conjured up in my mind. I see a father sitting at the head of a dinner table (covered with a tablecloth). Polite, soft-spoken children are eating everything on their plates, their napkins are neatly in place on their laps. Quiet conversation ensues and everyone says "May I pleased be excused?" when the meal is over.

This imagery certainly doesn't come from my own experience, yet it seems to be a subconscious standard by which I measure the quality of our family mealtimes.

"Your dinner is in the microwave. I have to pick up the Cub Scouts." You leave a note on the refrigerator that dinner is in the fridge. There's a message from Dad on the answering machine that he'll be late for dinner. Children are capping their teeth and fingertips with pitted olives, flipping cream cheese with their carrot sticks, and someone is gargling his milk. There are frequent (and dramatic) protests: "Oh, sick!" "What is this garbage?" "What *else* are we having?" At this point it is best to retort: "Take it or leave it. Like or lump it. Eat it or wear it!"

One Saturday afternoon I happened to mention to one of the kids that I had already made Sunday's dinner. He said, "What is it?" I said, "Swiss steak." He said, "Is that the barfy-looking stuff in the refrigerator?" Basically, I think it's safe to say the kids regard all home cooking as inferior to McDonald's, Pizza Hut or KFC. Home cooking, they suppose, is what you have to eat when you're too poor to eat out every night.

As I see it, the family meal problem is threefold. First, there's kitchen management (organizing kitchen space in order to streamline preparation and speed up work). Second, we have the problem of food management (inventory, menu planning, shopping and preparation). Last, and probably the most difficult, is the issue of kids and food (getting them to eat it as well as serving an actual meal when the family calendar looks like the flight plan at O'Hare Field).

Let's take it one step at a time and discover whether successful family meal management is, in fact, possible. (In *Confessions of an Organized Homemaker,* seventy pages of material are devoted to these very problems. You might want to refer to them in addition to what I'll cover here. Also, you'll learn to organize the refrigerator, the utility closet and the junk drawer!)

Menu Planning Made Easy

If you're busy, you need menu planning. If you don't know what you're going to fix for dinner, how will anyone know what they can do to help? With your menus planned in advance, you can dovetail your operations, plan leftovers, delegate effectively and work ahead of yourself.

Let's say your week's menus are as follows:

Monday: Swiss steak, peas, baked potatoes
Tuesday: ham, potato salad, broccoli spears
Wednesday: chicken and rice, asparagus tips, vegetable gelatin salad
Thursday: stir-fried beef, rice, Chinese corn soup
Friday: scalloped potatoes and ham

Now, let's see "dovetailing" in action.

Monday: When preparing vegetables for the Swiss steak, chop up a few extra to be used in Wednesday's gelatin salad. (Leftover peas will also be used.) Also, chop extra celery for Tuesday's potato salad and Thursday's stir-fried beef. (Keep sliced vegetables in an airtight container to keep them crisp and prevent vitamin loss.) Cut up the flank steak for the stir-fried beef and quickly brown it just before you brown the Swiss steak. Refrigerate until needed. Bake extra potatoes to use in Tuesday's potato salad. While the Swiss steak and potatoes are baking, bake the chicken that will be cut up and used for Wednesday's chicken and rice.

Tuesday: With the potatoes all ready for potato salad, it's easy to toss the salad together while the ham is heating and the broccoli is steaming. Be sure to plan enough leftover ham for scalloped potatoes and ham later in the week.

Wednesday: The chicken is already cooked, boned and cut up. The vegetables are ready to add to the gelatin. All you need to do is set the salad, cook the rice (make extra for Thursday's stir-fried beef, rice cereal for breakfast, or rice pudding), steam the asparagus and assemble the chicken-and-rice casserole.

Thursday: With the rice, meat and sliced celery prepared, all that's left is to assemble ingredients and quickly stir-fry beef and vegetables. Heat soup and rice.

Whenever you have time during the week, make up a batch of muffins. Put the batter into muffin tins lined with foil baking cups and freeze. Once they're frozen, remove the unbaked muffins (foil and all) from the muffin tins and keep them frozen in a resealable plastic bag. When you want muffins, do not thaw. Place them in a muffin tin and bake as directed for a few minutes longer than originally required. This is an especially good time-saver at breakfast time.

Are you beginning to see what a little planning can do? By concentrating your activities you've eliminated several "get ready" and "clean-up" jobs. For example, in our sample menus, if you prepared each meal individually you'd have to chop celery four times. By dovetailing, we did it once. You'd prepare potatoes and rice twice each; with dovetailing, we did it once. You'd brown meat twice; with dovetailing, we did it once. Those figures tell me that I can cut my work in half! I'm all for that. How about you?

To get the most from your dovetailing efforts, be sure you have your meal plans written out so you can "see" exactly what needs to be done. Remember those work simplification techniques? Think before you act is the key here.

Now, you can drop a few more clean-up jobs from your list by working ahead of yourself. Monday night, while cleaning up dinner, mix up the potato salad. Tuesday night, set the gelatin salad. Wednesday night, mix the corn soup. You can clean up these preparations right along with dinner dishes.

With the meals well underway it's simple for the first one home in the evening to put the finishing touches on the dinner preparations. You may have to assign this job—post it on the family calendar or on the child's weekly planning sheet. Or this could be one child's full-time responsibility. (Be sure to leave menus and instructions posted in an obvious spot!)

Menu planning and dovetailing operations enable you to bunch your saved time into a useful portion. Plan your menus for a week, two weeks, a year; or just list several meals and have all the ingredients on hand. Every morning choose and prepare whichever meal fits your mood and your schedule. If you use a rotating schedule for your menus (as outlined in *Confessions I*), set up a dovetailing system to go along with it. That way, you'll have everything down to a science and get your meals prepared in record time!

Meals can be planned around hectic schedules, too. On busy days, crank up the Crock-Pot and let it simmer all day, or whip up some hot soup and sandwiches. Bake some potatoes and top them with a quick, nutritious stuffing. (Cut a hot spud in half, fill it with cheese, close it back up, wrap it in a napkin and eat it on the run!) Cook up a batch of omelets and serve fillings buffet style.

Food cannot nourish if it isn't eaten. With menu planning and your calendar working together, everyone will be assured a nutritious meal even on the busiest days.

Menu planning can also prevent the scourge of leftovers (you know, those things you save so you can throw them out later). You should never have leftovers unless they're planned. Use leftovers for lunches or as the fixings for an upcoming dinner, e.g., leftover pork can be used for barbecued pork, etc. Leftovers clutter up the refrigerator, anyway. If you're frequently discarding leftovers, start planning them—or prepare smaller servings to begin with.

Menu planning is a fundamental skill far too important to disregard. With your meals planned you can clearly outline what you want your recruits to do. They can start chopping the vegetables, boning the chicken, peeling the potatoes, tossing the salad. Before long your fledglings will become veteran cooks who can put together a whole meal on their own.

Delegating kitchen detail is easy if you follow the steps in chapter 8. The most important aspect of the routine is training. Work with the kids long enough so they feel competent. Be sure they're in the kitchen through the whole meal preparation so they learn all aspects of the job—including where things should be put away.

Do you ever stop to think about how much of your time is spent planning, preparing and cleaning up meals? Just imagine how many extra minutes or hours you could snatch for your own personal development if you turned over some (or all) of the K.P. duty to the kids. (Does that sound unfair? It shouldn't, because this is good personal development for the kids, too!)

Without written menus you're always thinking about what to fix for dinner. And when you finally decide you'll probably have to run to the store at 5 P.M. (or stop on your way home from work) to pick up a few things. (Sound familiar?) Do you see what that does to your time?

You are deciding what to fix for dinner. *You* are running to the store. *You* are bringing home the food and the responsibility of putting it together. If your menus had been planned, someone else could have done something to help.

GROSS IS A FIVE-LETTER WORD

"Hey, Brian! Is that your head or did they learn how to grow hair on a meatball?" Ahhh. The peace and tranquility we enjoy when the family gathers around the table. What camaraderie, what unspeakable joy. (And if you believe that, you've got a loose lid on your cookie jar.)

How do you get the kids to get along at the table? How do you get them to try new foods? How do you fix something everyone likes? How do you feed people who aren't home? Mealtime can be a real hassle; no wonder we head for the Burger Barn. No complaints, everyone's happy. No dishes, no time investment.

With the vast amount of information now readily available regarding nutrition, we're more aware of what we feed our bodies. My problem is that I learned too late: Some bad habits are already well entrenched in our kids. How can we reteach them? It's not easy, believe me, but here are a few suggestions:

Start by reading labels. By now, you know the main culprits are cholesterol, fat, sodium, sugar, additives and excessive calories. Avoid buying products high in any of these ingredients.

Discuss nutrition with your kids. Talk about TV commercials and let the kids know that a company's main motivation is to make money— even if they have to resort to half-truths.

Use fewer convenience foods and mixes. Make your own mixes or make foods from scratch. That way you control the quality. Keep good food handy and convenient: cleaned vegetables that can be crunched raw, shelled nuts, fruits, hunks of low-fat cheese and so on. Don't have junk food in the house and the kids will eat less of it.

If you're an exerciser, encourage your kids to participate. When our little girl was only eighteen months old, whenever we'd say, "Check your pulse," she'd put her little finger on her neck. Physical fitness was already a part of her life. Kids are never too young to get involved. (Remember the power and influence of example.)

All this advice is well and good, but there are still going to be kids (mine included) who'd rather go through a coronary bypass than eat anything green. The older I get, the more convinced I am that kids will be good eaters if they're trained to be good eaters. I've seen too many families where the kids eat everything and I know it's the result of their training.

Our kids are not in that group; my sister's kids are. She has eight children (good eaters, every one of them). One day my mom was going to visit them, so she called my sister and said, "Debbie, I'd like to bring the kids a little treat. What would they like?" (Mother never calls to ask me. She knows she can bring *anything* loaded with sugar or other goo and the kids will just appreciate her to death.) Well, not so with Debbie. (Are you ready for this?) Debbie said, "If only you could bring them some brussels sprouts. They'd really like that!" Brussels sprouts! I nearly gag every time I recall that conversation.

There's a reason why Debbie's kids are good eaters. They rarely have junk food because they've been taught from infancy the value of good nutrition. Also, rules were set and followed through. ("If you're too full to eat, you're too full to have another bite of food until our next meal.")

Other successful parents have used and followed through with rules like: If you don't eat it for dinner, you have to eat it cold for breakfast. (One of our kids stayed overnight at this house, and I couldn't believe the things he ate. The thought of cold peas and chicken a la king for breakfast convinced him.)

Here's another: You have to stay at the table until your plate is clean. (I tried that once and come morning I had to break up camp to serve breakfast.) Or, "No dessert until you finish your broccoli."

I discovered another family whose kids were all good eaters. I asked the mother what her secret was. First of all, she admitted that she liked most everything and the kids had followed her good example. Also, when they were old enough to sit at the table, she'd put the serving bowl of vegetables in front of her plate and say they were all for her. The children weren't allowed to have even one morsel. Over and over they watched Mother savor each bite. (She did this for several meals.) Then, when the big day came and she shared her vegetables with the kids, they loved them because they *thought* they would.

My kids are past the rules stage at this point. I can only reason, bribe and hope they'll outgrow their fussiness as I did. I've had success with a few of these ideas, though:

- Have a new food party. Once a month or so, when trying a new recipe, set out the candles and make a big deal of dinner. Place a small wrapped gift by each plate with instructions to open after the plate is clean.

- Another thing that often works is to have the children prepare the meal (or be heavily involved in the cookery). They will almost without exception eat what they prepare.

Once, when we were going through a picky-eater stage with one of our kids, I put this idea to the test. Jimmy and I sat down and looked through a stack of recipes. He picked out one that he thought sounded good and it was easy enough for him to help prepare. (He was only six.) The recipe he chose surprised me—it was a cold salad with tuna fish, grated carrots (lots of 'em) and chopped onions. I never dreamed he'd eat it, but we got busy and mixed it up. With obvious delight, Jimmy served his meal to the family and, of course, gobbled down a generous portion himself.

This may not work every time, but it sure increases the odds the child will eat the meal!

• Enlist the aid of a friend. Our kids have learned to like a lot of things by eating at a friend's house. Things they'd never even consider tasting at home, they gobble up somewhere else "because it would be *rude* not to."

• If the child is in charge of a small garden plot, chances are he'll eat his crops!

• Mix up your meals occasionally. Sometimes it's fun to have grilled hamburgers and corn on the cob for breakfast and French toast for dinner.

• Make your meals interesting and versatile. How about creamed dried beef over wheat toast for breakfast, or bran muffins? Maybe green eggs and ham on St. Patrick's Day? How about a foil dinner (wrap meat and veggies in heavy-duty aluminum foil and roast over hot coals or bake in the oven), kabobs or a meal in a bowl once in a while? Eggnog and oatmeal molasses cookies for breakfast? Why not?

• Maybe alternate mealtimes would be helpful, especially if family scheduling is a problem. One family I know of decided to eat dinner shortly after school. The kids were always starving after school anyway and this was a good way to capitalize on their hunger. Of course, the working parent had to eat later, but she enjoyed a bedtime snack together with the family before they went to sleep.

• Another alternative is to make lunch dinner, and dinner lunch. Get it? If the kids are having a hot lunch at school and you're eating lunch out every day, why not have a more standard lunch-type meal for dinner? (Soup, chili, sandwiches, salads, etc.) These types of meals are also easier to serve if you have people eating at different hours.

• When you discover a new recipe the family enjoys, don't wait too long to serve it again. Otherwise, the kids will forget how much they enjoyed it and they'll have to go through the fear and trepidation of trying something new again.

- For extremely picky eaters, once more, menu planning can help. Let's say we're having spaghetti on Tuesday night and Jimmy hates spaghetti. So I make a few extra chicken enchiladas Monday night (Jimmy likes them) and serve him leftovers on Tuesday. I rely heavily on menu planning and leftovers with our kids; it helps to offer enough variety so everyone will have a well-balanced meal and still enjoy it.

- Give each child a piece of paper and tell him to write down three things he hates to eat. Gather the lists and tell the kids they won't be required to eat any of their listed foods; any other food, though, is fair game.

- Use self-adhesive signal dots to warn the family of foods that are off-limits. A red dot means "stop" (that cake is for the new neighbors, that tomato juice is for Wednesday's manicotti). A green dot means "go," you're free to help yourself. These little dots (available at office supply stores) are inexpensive and you get quite a few in each package. (Don't forget to tell the baby-sitter what the dots mean!)

- Have a set mealtime and serve whoever is there—even if it's only you. Be consistent with this. I heard of a woman who tamed her whole family that way. Every evening at 6 P.M. she'd sit down to the table and enjoy her dinner. Gradually, other family members wanted to experience the same comfortable atmosphere and they began to join her. (If this doesn't work, try the opposite approach. Every morning find out what the family schedule is and decide together what time dinner will be served that night.)

- Direct family conversations by deciding in advance what to discuss or by asking leading questions. (Current events; a funny thing happened on the way to work this morning; I have a problem with one of my employees—how would you handle it?)

Mealtime isn't the time to get after someone for using all the gas in the car, for *not* fixing the leaky faucet or for spending too much time in the bathroom. For more pacific mealtimes, strictly enforce the rule that all complaints are to be in writing.

All of us are busy and despite our best efforts to integrate schedules and mealtimes, I'm afraid the family dinner is becoming a vanishing species. So, when you do manage to pull it off, make the most of it! These mealtime ideas will help you keep the mood light and conducive to digestion—providing everyone isn't madly gulping to make it to the soccer game on time!

CHAPTER TWELVE

Curing Bedroom Bedlam

The organized bedroom. If that isn't a contradiction in terms, I don't know what is! It takes nothing short of genius to organize a bedroom without the aid of large machinery, a working knowledge of explosives or suicidal bravado. If you find yourself belly-up and bandaged after a trip to the bedroom, if you frequently wish for military assistance, if any bedroom in your home makes anyone within reach nauseated, you've come to the right place.

The problems with bedrooms (particularly those belonging to kids) are many and varied. Lack of convenient storage, too many things (as opposed to not enough space), poor clothing management and uncooperative roommates are the general malefactors.

For example, while taking a survey of teenagers, I asked what kinds of things were crowding them out of their bedrooms. Here's a sampling of the most common responses: clothes (old clothes, worn-out clothes, too-small clothes, too-large clothes), extra bedding, letters, things to put into a scrapbook (some day), too much furniture, books and magazines, stuffed animals, dolls, models and other projects (finished and in progress), souvenirs, hair curlers, makeup, school supplies, jewelry, posters, CDs and tapes, shoes, dirty dishes (I love that one), exercise equipment, skis, boots, empty boxes (another great answer), gym bags and Christmas decorations. (Oddly enough several kids complained about this one. One girl, though, delicately wrote, "Holiday crap!")

Not to be outdone, another participant responded this way: "My mother keeps old mattresses in my room, as well as one sweeper, and one tremendous garbage can." Old mattresses? Holiday decorations? Empty boxes? Skis? No wonder bedrooms are always a mess!

I'll swallow hard before I say this, but I think parents are largely to blame for much of this devastation. We don't keep each and every one of our possessions in *our* bedrooms, yet we expect the kids to keep everything in theirs. We wouldn't dream of letting the neighbors see our collection of old mattresses leaning up against our bedroom wall, no sir! We put them in our son's bedroom so *his* friends can see them.

COLLECT YOUR THOUGHTS

The first step, once again, is to think before you act. Whether it's your bedroom or the child's in question, decide specifically what the room will be used for. Consider the following guidelines.

Every person on this earth could live in a smaller, more compact area if he learned the importance of one central location: one central location for toys, books, eating, study, coats, hats, boots and so on. When you have books or toys, for example, stored in more than one location, you have the added expense (in space and money) of duplicating storage facilities. You have wasted motions when things are returned to various places instead of being delivered quickly to one spot.

Another big problem with storing things in more than one place is that no one but the owner can put away certain things. If I pick up a paperback, I don't know whose it is or where it belongs. If a child is assigned a room to clean, he won't know where certain things belong unless he knows who owns them. "Is this Jeff's G.I. Joe or Steven's?"

So think carefully and seriously before you assign individual belongings to that person's room. (If you have only one child or never experience any of these problems, this is a section you can neglect!)

A bedroom should function primarily as such. In bedrooms we keep clothes, shoes, junk drawers (for treasures like tiny motel soaps, trinkets from Happy Meals, key rings that glow in the dark, gum ball jewelry and bicycle license plates), and magazine files (to hold "important papers" like homemade baseball cards, notes from friends, pictures of Winnie-the-Pooh, old *Nickelodeon* magazines and unmailed fan letters to Cal Ripken Jr.). Also in the bedrooms we have kept storybooks (used at bedtime); boom boxes, tapes and CDs and sports card collections. All other possessions (books, toys, sports gear, hats, coats, etc.) are stored elsewhere.

I know this policy can cause certain conflicts with the child's right to ownership, especially if the kids are accustomed to having all their toys in their own rooms. But if the bedroom walls are closing in and you think you'd like to try this approach, now would be a good time for one of those family discussions. Explain your rationale for putting certain possessions elsewhere. Then listen to the kids' ideas and concerns. A good brainstorming session should bring about a meeting of the minds.

Tell them you'll do this on a trial basis and see how it works. If they're involved in the planning and rearranging, they'll be much more enthusiastic. Once they see how much easier it is to keep their rooms clean, you'll have a family of converts.

First of all, when something is brand new (a toy, game, book, etc.) we let the child keep it in his room for a while. However, after the newness has worn off, the item goes into the mainstream of family life and is stored in the central storage location. When the child is no longer particular about who uses a certain toy, you can feel certain it's ready for the central storage spot.

There are, of course, certain toys the kids *never* want to share (e.g., a security blanket, a special doll, the chemistry set, the stuffed dog your daughter's boyfriend gave to her). These treasured items are better off stored in the bedrooms rather than the central storage location.

You may also run into the child who considers everything a special, no-share, always-ask-for-permission toy. Our kids have tried that a few times, but I held my ground. I explained we didn't have room to keep everything in separate rooms and certain toys were all going to be stored together. Now that they're all used to the idea, it's an accepted routine. (They've also learned how much faster it is to clean things up when most of the toys go in one spot.)

What about privacy? Privacy is necessary and should be a closely guarded right, but too much privacy gets kids into trouble. When one of our kids has too much privacy, he's lighting matches, trading away his brother's prized baseball cards or outside playing "balance beam" on our second-story deck railing!

Now that you've determined the purpose of the bedroom, you'll know what stays and what goes when you and the kids begin step number two—discard and sort. (Refer back to chapter 4, "Surviving Slob Syndrome," to refresh your memory if the finer points of "discard and sort" have failed you.)

THE TROUBLE WITH CLOTHES

Let's zero in on the target areas. Most bedroom congestion begins with too many clothes. If you followed the steps outlined in the slob chapter, you'll have your wardrobe pared down to what you wear. Here are some more ideas to keep you on the right course:

• Don't buy clothes that aren't needed, even if you can get them for a marvelous price.

• Don't buy things (for the kids, especially) they don't like. We had a pair of blue-and-white checked pants that became part of the family. They have been owned (and hated) by every boy in our family and we never saw those pants in the line of duty. Getting rid of them was sort of like giving away the dog. Those pants have become part of our family history—something someone brings up at every family gathering.

So save yourself a lot of space and don't bring it home if someone dislikes it. That doesn't mean the kids shouldn't be guided toward good taste or encouraged to run around in army fatigues, checkerboard haircuts and Levis with bleached-out polka dots; but I know from experience you're wasting your time, space and money bringing home outfits the kids are violently opposed to.

• It seems most people have two sets of clothes: the ones they wear now and the ones they wore when they were thinner. If you have such a collection, try once again to recycle the unwearables. (If you're planning a garage sale, price clothes before you store them. When the day for the sale approaches, half your work will already be finished.)

• Be sure seasonal clothes are easy to retrieve. If it's troublesome for you to unearth those stored items, you'll likely put it off and stash things here "for now" until you get the box down. Use under-the-bed boxes, empty suitcases, high closet shelves, large clean garbage cans or hanging garment bags in a seldom-used closet.

When you put things away at the end of the season, make a note on your calendar of sizes and articles of clothing to purchase for next season. This will help you take advantage of end-of-season sales and give you a jump on outfitting the kids for school.

• Put things away only if they're clean and in good repair. Also, if you're undecided as to whether to keep an item, get rid of it. Come next season you'll want it even less than you do now.

• If you have young children who are still growing rapidly, it helps to keep a carton for each child right in their room (if possible). I always kept these boxes on the bedroom closet shelves. Here's how it works. When Jim outgrew something I'd pass it on to Brian. If it didn't fit Brian yet, I'd toss it into his "grow into" box. We'd go through the boxes twice a year (spring and fall) to see if anything for the coming season would fit. Having the boxes close at hand will keep you from piling old clothes all over (until you get around to putting them away) and reduce the likelihood a larger outfit will be forgotten. To avoid the latter, as you rotate seasonal clothes for a small child, hang or store in his drawer all the clothes he'll likely wear before the season is over, even if they're too big at the moment. That way you won't have to constantly check the boxes to see if there's an outfit the child can wear.

• Or, categorize all stored clothing by size, sex and season. Well-labeled containers will further facilitate your storage program.

• Constantly maintain all drawer storage. Keep the contents neatly stacked and separated so clothing is wearable when it's removed. (That's why I straighten drawers whenever I put the laundry away.) Provide drawer dividers to corral socks, underwear, pajamas, slips, hosiery, etc.

• To be sure no one walks out of the house in the morning looking like Bozo the Clown, fold matching outfits together or hang them on the same hanger. (Folding pajama tops and bottoms together is another good idea.) To the clothes hanger attach a small pocketed bag to hold matching socks, belts, hair ribbons or other small accessory items. If you don't have the wherewithal to sew up a few of these organizers, slip one of those sturdy plastic bags with handle holes (used by many stores for carting home your purchases) over the neck of the hanger.

Also, laying clothing out the night before will eliminate much early-morning hysteria.

SUITED FOR SUITABILITY

With the "think before you act" and "discard and sort" processes completed we can move on to grouping and motion-mindedness. Here's where we make the bedroom space convenient and usable.

Start by eyeing things that need to be stored in the bedroom and arrange them into general categories like shoes, ties, purses, jewelry, junk (treasures to the kids), bedding, stuffed animals and so on. Once you're aware of everything that needs to be stored conveniently, you can make the available space work for you.

Let's begin working on the closet.

Did you know you can have a well-organized closet without spending a fortune for costly built-ins? By using inexpensive and versatile organizers that don't require hardware to install (occasionally just a screwdriver), you can get the same degree of efficiency. And store-bought organizers have some other advantages: permanent fixtures, shelves and cubbyholes are OK, but you can't move them into a new house and when new belongings come home, they often don't fit into the "mold" of the former.

As soon as you have a chance, look through a mail-order catalog or browse through a home improvement center. Look at the inexpensive, attractive and adaptable array of portable closet organizers. Plastic "milk crate" boxes can store out-of-season or seldom-used clothing on the top closet shelf. Some of these crates even have removable shelves.

Stacking bins hold, among other things, scores of shoes; rolling three-basket bins hold socks, scarves, shirts, etc.; door- or wall-mounted grid systems with snap-on hooks hold belts and other accessories. Adjustable low-hanging closet rods expand from fifteen to twenty-eight inches wide and move up and down. (Or you can make your own using a dowel, two lengths of chain and two snapping metal shower curtain rings.)

Also, you'll find stackable, sturdy, see-through plastic containers that are individual drawers. (Great for folded sweaters!)

This may seem trivial, but one thing that has helped me more than anything was to get rid of all wire hangers. Those sturdy tubular plastic hangers are more durable than you might suppose, plus they're tangle-free and don't bend, rust or crease pant legs. (They also make your closets look nicer.)

To make your closets even more functional than they'll be once you use more organizers, place several shower curtain hooks over one end of your closet rod. They'll hold robes, purses, umbrellas, tote bags, etc.

Another hint is to have two small wastebaskets in the closet, one to hold empty hangers and one to hold items to be dry-cleaned.

The standard closet rod is roughly 5 feet 9 inches from the floor. If you're at all handy or know someone who is, have the rod and shelf raised up about 7 inches. In your closet (or an older child's) this will increase your hanging space and decrease the wasted overhead space. The extra seven inches of hanging space will allow you to use bi-level hanging storage (suit jackets over shirts, pants, skirts, blouses).

Tension rods (requiring no permanent installation) can also be used for a low-hanging rod. You can divide a closet in half (or whatever suits your needs) by standing a board in the closet vertically. Attach it to the back of the closet and the closet shelf (or ceiling). Tension rods can then be placed at various levels, enabling you to use every square inch of closet space. If the closet is deep enough, a dresser can be placed in the middle and the tension rod can be installed against it. (Unless the dresser is very heavy, secure it to the back wall before mounting the tension rod.)

Scale down a child's closet so it's completely functional for him. Track and bracket adjustable shelving should be installed on one side of the closet to enable the child to reach stored possessions. These shelves can be mounted either on the side wall or the back wall. (Don't install any shelves that aren't adjustable, since children's needs and space requirements constantly change.)

Low closet rods should be supplied, as well, so that even young children can reach and return their clothing. A three-rod swinging kitchen towel holder is a good hanger for small trousers, and they're easy for the kids to manipulate. In an apartment you probably can't

Shower curtain rings placed at the end of the closet rod provide hooks for purses, belts or umbrellas.

deface the wall surface, so use a freestanding shelf of some type. Inexpensive metal shelves aren't very attractive, but they're utilitarian and can be adjusted. (Since hooks are easier for young children to negotiate, look for the type that snaps over the closet rod).

CLOSET CALAMITIES
Spearheading some specific and common problems, let's begin with shoes.

We all know about shoe organizers. There are pocketed shoe bags, freestanding metal racks, tension poles (usually revolving), see-through hanging garment bag types with shelves, open-ended stacking boxes, cardboard shoe files (cardboard units having nine cubbyholes) and a vinyl-coated wire rack that mounts on the back wall of the closet.

Try some of these ideas: Shoes can stand on the existing closet shelf.

(Install a second shelf on top to use the wasted space high up.) Store shoes in their original boxes (be sure to label them).

Stack a bevy of bins from floor to closet shelf and stash away. A simple shoe rack can be made by attaching a curtain rod to a closet wall or on the back of the door: The shoes can then be wedged between the rod and the vertical surface.

Another clever idea is to place a tension rod four inches from the back wall, about six inches from the floor. Place another tension rod seven or eight inches from the back wall and about two inches from the floor (for adult shoes). The shoe heel catches over the back rod and the toe rests down on the front bar. It's fast, easy and cheap!

The best system for kids is to provide each child with a colorful dishpan (or cat litter pan or restaurant dishpan) in which they *toss* their shoes. (Tossing is why the system works.) It takes too much effort to stick each shoe onto a form or into a pocket, but you can throw them into a box with no effort at all. The shoes will at least be penned up, albeit slightly jumbled. As long as the container is fairly shallow, matching shoes will be easy to seize. (It's more effective to make things slightly harder to find than to put away.)

If you don't have enough closet floor space on which to store these shoe containers, stick them on a low shelf, under the bed (not too far

Two tension rods make an inexpensive, yet functional, shoe rack.

under), behind the bedroom door or on the back porch—as a gentle reminder to remove shoes before entering the house.

BEDDING THE BEDDING

Even though the main purpose of a bedroom is to house a bed, that doesn't mean the bed should eat up inordinate amounts of space. Too much or too-large furniture can cause more problems than it alleviates, so when you're purchasing furniture, be sure to consider the size of the room and choose pieces that go up rather than out.

Replace nightstands with headboard storage units; hang a mirror over a desk so it can double as a dressing table. A series of small chests will often use space more effectively than a single bulky dresser.

Bunk beds and trundle beds are tremendous space savers, but they're hard to make up. (Adding casters to bunk beds makes them easier to maneuver.) Beds too close to a wall are also more difficult to make; consider placing the bed on the diagonal—and fit a small storage unit in the open corner.

There are a lot of space-saving beds on the market now. Loft beds can house a dresser, desk, small closet or bookshelf underneath. Murphy beds are still available. (These stand behind a handsome wall unit when not in use and are easily pulled down at night for sleeping.) Sofa beds are another possibility; they give any room in which they're used a dual function. Futons and trundle beds are also good alternatives when space is limited.

Comforters or quilts used for bedspreads and a few throw pillows can make an amateur bedmaker look like an old pro. Fitted bedspreads are also easy for children to handle. I've even seen fitted spreads that cover only three sides of the bed, leaving the open long side to butt up against the wall; this satisfies both the need for saving space and unrestricted bedmaking. Now, here are a few tips for bedding storage:

Store extra bedding in the room where it will be used. Use a different pattern or color for each room to help identify where it belongs. Mark bed linens you already have with an indelible laundry marker or with iron-on mending tape. If you have to store all the extra bedding in the same closet, you can mark the shelf with the corresponding signal.

Fold top and bottom sheets and pillowcases together into one bundle.

If you wash sheets and put them directly back onto the beds, you can get by with a limited supply of extras and you'll spend less time folding and putting sheets away.

If space is a problem, extra blankets can be stashed in between the mattress and box spring or in stored luggage. Colorful afghans, blankets, and throws look pretty stuffed into large open baskets. Under-the-bed boxes keep the bedding clean, yet handy and out of sight, using otherwise wasted space.

Satin comforters (sleeping bags, too) will stay on a shelf if rolled up first and slipped into a king-sized pillowcase. (Put a seldom-used sleeping bag into a plastic bag first and suck out excess air with the hose from the vacuum cleaner. Tie shut. This makes the bundle much smaller.) If you remove your comforter or quilt before bed at night, install a towel bar on the back of your bedroom door and hang it over that. Hanging or freestanding quilt racks display attractive quilts, comforters or blankets.

An old camelback or flat-topped trunk can house extra sheets, towels, blankets and pillows. Because of its decorative quality the trunk can be used anywhere in the house and no one will know it's a linen closet (a wonderful option if you're cramped for space).

Strictly Personal

Personal products like makeup, jewelry and hair-care equipment are often stored in the bedroom. Though makeup and hair products are discussed in the bathroom chapter, I'll give you a few ideas for bedroom storage.

Makeup is best stored in a cosmetic bag if it's going to be toted to the bathroom, to school or to work. Also, in a closed container it's less tempting for little hands that love to smear, paint and squish. If it needn't be portable, makeup can be stored in a basket that sits on a dresser or shelf, or hangs on a wall.

Acrylic makeup trays with built-in compartments and shelves are great for storing tubes, bottles, compacts and pots of makeup. A three-tiered wire basket can hang from the ceiling to accommodate your beauty supplies. A compartmented tray in a shallow drawer gives you the ideal one-motion storage arrangement. A "clean-up caddy" or small tool box also holds makeup and hair equipment.

Hair care products can be stored using some of these same ideas. Curler trays are available with compartments for curlers, clips, hairpins, etc. Use plastic tote caddies (usually used for cleaning supplies) to cart the curling iron, blow dryer, etc.

A shallow box or large dishpan under the bed can slide out for easy access. If electric rollers have to sit out in the open, make an attractive cover for them, or toss a pretty piece of fabric over the appliance.

If these supplies are being used mainly in the bathroom, they really should be stored there. The bathroom chapter discusses how to squeeze out new sources of unused bathroom space.

Jewelry can be handled in a number of ways. Obviously, jewelry boxes are common organizers, though you can also use ice cube bins to separate each piece. Small divided pillboxes (available at any pharmacy) are perfect for tiny pierced earrings. Take a trip through the fishing department of your local discount, hardware or variety store: There are lots of inexpensive divided boxes (made for bait, lures, flies, etc.) that lend themselves to jewelry storage.

You can cover a stand-up picture frame (the entire 8″ × 10″ facing surface) with thick quilted material to match your decor and hang your jewelry on T-pins or drapery hooks (mounted upside down). Cover a piece of cardboard with contact paper and hang jewelry using small self-adhesive hooks. The board can hang on a wall, behind a closet door, in the back of the closet or anyplace that's convenient. A bulletin board for hanging jewelry or memoranda can be made from a foam-backed carpet square or a section of acoustical ceiling tile. (These are also handy for hanging hair ribbons.)

Don't forget about cup hooks, grids or pegboard for hanging storage not only of jewelry, but of any lightweight accessory.

Animal Instincts

Stuffed animals are another cause of lamentation among parents. Piled on a bed, the menagerie has to be removed at bedtime and replaced after the bed is made and frankly, that's a real pain. But if the owner thinks its worth the extra effort, that's fine.

Animals can be nestled in a large wicker basket or an antique cradle. Laundry baskets filled with stuffed animals fit under a daybed and are concealed by a dust ruffle. They can be attached to vertical surfaces with Velcro, or suspended by neck ribbon ties from wall- or pegboard-mounted hooks. A heavy cardboard tube from a roll of carpet can be covered with wallpaper, wedged between floor and ceiling, and used as a surface on which to hang the animals. A hammock made from fishnet or nylon net can be stretched across a bedroom corner to cradle the furry critters. You can always install a high shelf (about two feet from the ceiling) to skirt around the room and hold the display. (This is a good place for trophies, too.)

Dolls can be stored like the stuffed animals. Another way is to sew up a few wall pouches; the fabric and the stored dolls create a decorative effect. (Use a shoe-bag-type organizer for smaller dolls.)

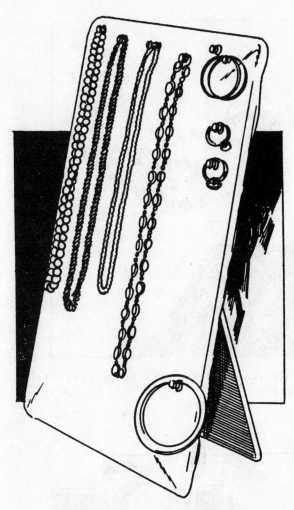

Cover an 8″ × 10″ stand-up frame with thick, quilted material or cork and hang jewelry from it with pushpins.

Posters, Pennants and Pictures

There isn't a kid alive who hasn't begged, cajoled or threatened desertion at one time in his life just to get permission to put something (usually ugly, tawdry or sweaty-looking) on his wall.

If you give your OK (just to keep the family together) but don't want holes pounded into the wall or wallpaper ripped off when the tape is removed, here's a remedy for the situation. Take a large piece of nylon net and tack it up to the wall. (If it matches the wall color, it won't be visible.) Now all the posters, pictures, pennants, and so forth can be fastened to the net with straight pins and changed frequently without damage to the wall. Poster putty is a good product for attaching papers to a wall without damaging the wall or the poster. It also gives the child the option of flexibility when he wants to move (or remove) a poster.

Stretch a piece of mesh, nylon net or pretty fabric across a corner to make a cozy hammock for stuffed toys or dolls.

Put empty wall space to use by hanging wall pouches to hold dolls, toys or storybooks.

Large posters (or "works of art" brought home from school) not displayed can be stored flat in an art portfolio or rolled up and placed inside one of the long cardboard tubes that wrapping paper comes on. The tubes can be labeled and stood in a tall plastic wastebasket.

ROOMMATES

One survey question we asked read, "What bugs you?" A vast majority of the kids named their little brother or sister as the culprit. When kids share a room it's difficult at best; it can create situations that are difficult to solve (one child cleans up his portion, the other child wallows in destruction; one child wants privacy, the other wants attention, and on and on).

What is a parent to do about the roommate trauma? My gut reaction is to say, "I don't have the faintest idea!" I do know, however, that endurance helps a lot.

Review the steps to successful delegation: discussion, eliminating busywork, finding the best person, no dumping, tools, training, consistency, follow-through, avoiding upward delegation, rewards.

Following these steps will help ease any roommate problems you may be having. But if you're still having trouble, reread those particular points about delegation and perhaps you'll discover the weak link in the chain.

Perhaps you and the kids could draw up a constitution or a set of bylaws. Have the kids decide what rules to set (with your input, of course) and what rewards or disciplinary actions will be enforced. When the terms are mutually acceptable, have both the children sign their names. Post the charter where it's easy for the kids to refer to. They should be encouraged to handle the rewards and disciplines themselves, though occasionally you may have to arbitrate.

Moods, however, are another matter. Maybe some flexibility would help. With four boys it's been easy for us to shuffle roommates back and forth: when so-and-so is going through an ornery streak we move him in with the current Mr. Nice Guy. My sister moved one of her six kids into the family room for a temporary stint until the need passed.

Once when I was in Cleveland doing a television appearance, the TV personality who interviewed me showed me around her lakeside apartment. She and her husband had a two-bedroom apartment and two teenaged children (a boy and a girl). In the kids' bedroom she had a wall divider installed right down the middle of the room. It stopped just short of the closet and entry door so both kids could use the closet and enter the bedroom. The effect was both attractive and extremely practical. Room dividers can be made using folding screens, drapes, tall bookcases, modular wall systems, vertical blinds or mini blinds (like

Levolors). While they won't cut out noise or other distractions, they do give the child the feeling of being in control of his own environment.

A general feeling of cooperation will be instilled in the roommates if parental delegation is enforced correctly. And if everyone has a list of jobs, or has to pick up twenty things, or if one child has to pick up everything red and another child picks up everything blue, a sense of fairness and fraternity is bound to emerge. Basically, my plan is to take the good days with the bad and endure my trials as patiently as I can.

One mother I know had a child who was always angry about doing chores she felt were unfair. "*I* didn't make the mess. *I* didn't leave the dishes in the family room. *I* didn't leave the candy wrappers on the end table. . . ."

Talks, explanations and negotiations didn't seem to work. So, Mom took action. Suddenly she started treating her daughter the same way. When Mom set the table, she left an empty place. "I don't use your dishes, so I'm not putting them on the table. I didn't wear your clothes, so I'm not going to wash them. I'm not going to eat your food, so I'm not going to fix it." While this may seem drastic, the daughter got the message quickly. Everyone in a family cooperates and helps each other. Sure, things sometimes seem unfair—but if everyone pitches in, no one person is overburdened. Everyone helps each other.

Two more things will help the children feel like they're being treated fairly. First, be consistent. If you always expect a certain behavior and follow through with that expectation, the children will give up any resistance because they know it won't work.

Second, avoid the tendency to always recruit the most cooperative (or oldest) child. We have one boy who will cheerfully do anything we ask him to do, even if he's doing something else. He's even come and asked us if we want him to do anything. For this reason, I've had to make a conscious effort not to always single him out when I need someone to do something. My natural tendency is to ask Steven because the job will be done with no hassles, no complaints. But, of course, that isn't fair. So, I've had to endure some objecting, some languor and lots of breaks. (One of our children would work at an assigned job for a few minutes, then he'd have to take a break. His "breaks" made any job an all-day affair.)

Now you know how to organize a bedroom without calling in the heavy artillery. Never again will you wonder if there were any survivors as you walk past an open bedroom door. I just bet you can't wait to round up the recruits and get started!

CHAPTER THIRTEEN

Bathroom Blues

H e must have been a brave man to raise six children (five of them girls) with only one bathroom. I'd say my dad qualified for a Purple Heart.

And surely Mother deserves some recognition. As a full-time homemaker, it fell upon her to direct the bathroom traffic—and somehow she managed to do it without using a whistle, firearms or a billy club (though she did keep a switch under the drainboard).

This same bathroom was a small three-fixture job—sink, stool and tub. There was no counter and only a small, shallow medicine chest for storage.

I tell you this sad tale for a good reason. Every day when I step into my bathroom (a step only a trained mountain goat should take) and see the pyramid of towels, clothes, shoes, globs of toothpaste, curlers, blow dryer and wet diapers, I take a deep breath and say to myself, "If my mother could do it, so can I!" And so can you.

There couldn't be a bathroom more inadequate than ours was, but somehow we managed. Mom is a master at using every square inch of useful space and I'll share some of her expertise with you.

First, of course, I'm going to ask you to canvass your bathroom and get rid of everything that isn't being used. No ambivalence here, please, just a lot of cold-blooded pitching into the trash. Toiletries, makeup and medicines, in particular, change chemically over time. Even perfume gets rancid. So if it's not being used, get rid of it!

ADDING STORAGE SPACE

A lack of serviceable storage space is the cardinal sin of most bathrooms, but even that lack can be overcome, and quite inexpensively at that. The bathroom is used more often than any room in the house (with the exception of the kitchen), so we should take great pains to make it as pleasant and commodious (no pun intended) as possible.

First, some general storage ideas.

Start looking for empty places. There are usually generous amounts on the walls (above the toilet or tub, or at the end of a vanity), even in the most Victorian or minuscule bathrooms. Also look under the sink and toilet tank.

The area over the toilet is a universally wasted space, which makes it an ideal site for inexpensive wicker or bamboo shelving units. Or fit the wall with metal standards and insert clear glass shelves on the brackets at varying heights.

If attaching things to the wall is taboo, purchase the shelving installed with floor-to-ceiling tension poles that's especially made for over-the-toilet storage. Freestanding modules sit on top of the toilet tank.

A sturdy, over-the-tank storage unit holds many bathroom storables.

One often overlooked overhead storage location is at the back of the bathtub (one without a shower, of course). Lightweight bookcases, baskets or stock storage cabinets can be used wherever there's room. Open shelving can be made to look more attractive by covering it with louvered doors, swinging latticework doors, bifold doors or curtains.

You can also hang shelves on the back of the bathroom door, or attach a shoe bag or wooden wine rack to an empty vertical space and

A pocketed shoe bag provides one-motion storage for often-used toiletries.

stow bottles, cans and tubes in the pockets or cubbyholes. Look for shower curtains with big storage pockets sewn in. Hang a shower caddy over the shower head. All these organizers hold lots of things that usually take up space in a medicine cabinet.

For more mirror space and wall storage space, replace your old medicine cabinet with a more modern and useful one or get a surface-mounted unit and hang it on a section of empty wall space. (Perhaps two units could flank the mirror that hangs over the sink.) Corner cabinets are effectual for overcrowded bathrooms. If child safety is one of your concerns, buy a locking cabinet or one with a locking compartment inside.

Floor space is apt to be more at a premium than wall space, but check for wasted areas. A bank of bins can stand under a sink (or next to it). One or two bins can be stacked underneath the toilet tank (one or two on each side). Baskets can be stuffed with towels or folded diapers, even dirty clothes.

If you have an old-fashioned sink on legs or wall brackets, attach a gathered fabric skirt around it. (You can fasten Velcro to the bottom edge of the sink with a hot glue gun or use self-adhesive Velcro.) The skirt will conceal bins of supplies, towels, bathroom tissue, a three-bin rolling cart, stacking shelf units, or a container for dirty laundry.

Is there room for an inexpensive chest, bookcases, storage cubicles or a recycled china cabinet? (I know. If you had room for all that stuff you'd have a dressing, sunbathing and exercise area; a sauna; a TV; and an atrium filled with exotic plants, right?)

Counter Space

If counter space is an endangered species in your bathroom, your options are somewhat limited. However, if you're the slightest bit handy, you can at least improve the situation. Counter space can be effectively increased by installing a removable section or one attached with piano hinges over the toilet tank.

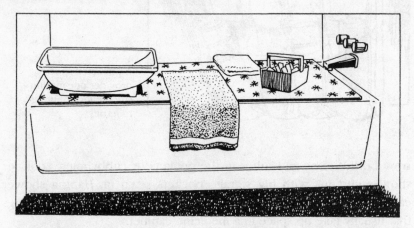

For extra counter space, fit a sturdy board over the bathtub and cover with self-adhesive vinyl.

A cutting board across the top of the sink is a temporary table to use while grooming. A strong board, covered with adhesive-backed paper or wallpaper, can be fitted to span the bathtub. This is perfect for diaper-changing and there's plenty of room for a baby's bathtub (though you'll be doing the job on your knees). Also, it gives you a surface on which to put curlers, makeup, hot rollers or an electric shaver while you're using them. To store the board while bathing, stand it up behind the door, lay it on the floor (it's sturdy enough to stand on), or slide it under a bed. (This idea has some obvious handicaps— but it can be extremely useful to someone with no counter space.)

Portable racks fit over the tub to hold soap, washcloths, magazines or whatever.

Corner a handy person (or roll up your sleeves if you're a do-it-yourselfer) and make an inexpensive storage unit with a drop-down door! Knock out the wall between two studs, build a shallow-framed box to fit, install shelves and the door. (The door is optional, though for safety purposes, a door can be locked.)

Another space-saving method is to hang baskets on the wall—one for each person—in which they keep their bathroom cups, toothbrushes, combs, toothpaste, hand towels and washcloths (hanging over the side edge).

If you use the other three storage alternatives to full capacity (wall, floor, drawer) you won't need as much counter space.

Keeping these general storage concepts in mind, let's consider some specific storage requirements.

Talk of the Towel

Wet or dry, folded or heaped, clean or dirty—in any form, towels are a problem, and the customary one-towel-rod-bathroom just doesn't cut it. For each person using the bathroom two linear feet of towel rod is ideal. Hooks are easiest hanging method for small children. Towel rings, though not as easy to use, are another option.

Cafe curtain or towel rods can be mounted on the back of a door, behind the door or high over the bathtub (be sure the shower spray doesn't hit them). Vinyl-coated steel towel racks hang over the door without making holes in the wood.

Tension poles made especially for towels have outstretched arms at varying heights to hold several towels. Hang some wooden (or plastic) coat hangers over the existing towel bar and hang towels from each of them.

Towel ladders are available that reach from floor to ceiling (or from the vanity to the ceiling). And you can purchase double towel bars (single-mounted).

Standing towel racks or a clothes tree or folding laundry racks can be placed in a corner.

To make the most of your wall space, hang one towel rod above the other. The bottom rod should be in line with the counter or sink and the top rod should be twenty-six inches higher to accommodate hanging bath towels. Towel rods also can be hung on doors, on sides of vanities or be of the type that swing out.

Roll up or fold clean hand towels or washcloths and put them into a pretty wicker basket, stash them in a wine rack or hang them on an expanding hat rack.

Towels are fairly expensive, so when you stock up, get extra hand towels and washcloths. They wear out quicker than bath towels, and matching extras will extend the life of your set.

Remember, towels usually dry off clean people and clean hair. So

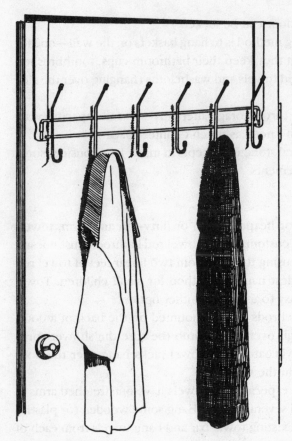

Need extra hooks for towels, robes or clothes? An over-the-door hook gives you plenty (and requires no installation).

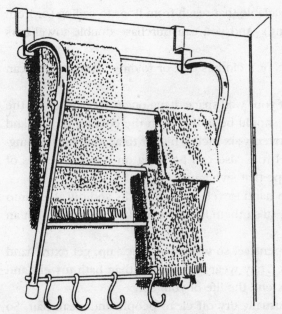

An over-the-door towel rack provides extra towel bars without making holes in walls or doors.

eliminate extra laundering: Hang the damp towels up to dry and reuse them! Common hand towels, however, need more frequent washing.

LASSO THE LAUNDRY

Every bathroom needs a hamper if you can squeeze one in. Aside from the standard ventilated hampers, you can hang a molded plastic tote bag, pillowcase, heavy plastic shopping bag, laundry bag, etc., on a hook behind the door or high over the tub. Or you can purchase a hanging hamper that looks like a giant clothespin bag.

JUST A SPOONFUL OF SUGAR

Since medication is frequently stored in the bathroom, it might be helpful to consider the following pharmaceutical advice while you're working in the bathroom.

• Don't save antibiotics (unless your doctor tells you otherwise). Many of these lose potency or change chemically with age.

• Don't save any drug after you've finished taking it (unless directed otherwise). Sometimes, when symptoms recur, the cause and treatment are different. See your doctor.

• Check to see if the prescription bottle has an expiration date. If not, ask your druggist the shelf life of the product. Note the date somewhere on the bottle.

• The bathroom is not the best place to store drugs. The heat and humidity often speed up drug deterioration.

• In antiseptics containing alcohol, the alcohol evaporates, causing remaining ingredients to be more condensed.

• When buying nonprescription drugs, check the labels for an expiration date. If there isn't one, write the date of purchase on the container. At least once a year, go through your medicine supply and toss out everything that has expired or is over one year old. (If something appears to be perfectly good, check with your druggist.)

• Keep all medicines in their original containers with the labels intact.

• Dispose of medicines by flushing them down the toilet. Never put them in the fireplace.

• Be sure all medications are in childproof containers and placed out of reach of children. Just in case, have the telephone number of the poison control center posted by the phone. (When you're visiting people who don't have small children, take extra precautions; they may be storing medicines carelessly in purses, at bedsides, or on kitchen counters.

Once you've discarded the out-of-date products, it's time to organize. The shallow shelves of a medicine chest are perfect for one-motion storage. However, if there are small children in the house, consider the safety factor.

Another storage method is to place the remedies in a deep container (like a shoe box) and use it as a slide-out tray on a high shelf. (Have one box for internal- and another for external-use products.) You slide out the container, make your selection, slide the tray back. This is even easier if you label the tops of the containers so you can see at a glance what the medications are.

It's sometimes helpful to store disposable cups and spoons with the medicines so everything you need will be in one central location. Also, it's handy to have a marked dosage dropper or test-tube-like measuring container (available at any pharmacy) on hand so you can quickly administer the prescribed dosage.

Save a few old pill bottles. With the lids off and labels removed, they're practical for holding thermometers, dosage droppers and small tubes of ointment. (You can also use these little bottles, with lids on, to hold small tubes of glue; needles; buttons; tacks; ketchup, mustard, salt and pepper for lunch boxes; small nails or screws; fishing hooks, lures and flies; spices; change for parking meters, Laundromats and phone calls; or as stacking blocks for the kids to play with.)

An ideal way to store medicines or small toiletry items is to put them in a recycled spice rack. (Thrift shops are full of previously owned spice racks.) Racks are shallow, ensuring one-motion storage, and can stand on a counter or hang high on a wall, door or inside a cupboard. (Some spice racks even have doors, so the eclectic display is out of sight.)

WATER CLOSET WISDOM

Here, like Heloise of household hint fame, I offer you some random bathroom tips.

• The bathroom is a good place to keep a roll of paper towels. (They can be mounted on a wall hanger or a freestanding dispenser, inside the cupboard door under the sink, or placed in a drawer.) The paper towels are handy for drying wet hands and faces, or wiping up the sink, faucets and mirror. They'll save your towels from wear and tear and extra launderings.

• Other items frequently used first (or needed) in the bathroom are: a clock, underwear, accessory items (ties, jewelry, scarves and other things requiring a mirror to don), a low mirror and sturdy step stool for the kids, and new toothbrushes for forgetful overnight guests.

- Install a shower curtain (using a tension rod) inside a glass shower door. The glass and rubber gasket will always stay clean and spot-free.
- Stick a sponge in every soap dish to absorb water and dissolved soap. (Better yet, use liquid soap in a pump dispenser!)
- Store bathtub toys in a mesh bag and hang it up to dry after the bath is over. If you have no place to hang it, put the toys into a plastic mesh bin or plastic milk crate, drain the bathtub, and leave the toys in the container. When the next person uses the tub, it's easy to remove the carton of toys. Or hang a plastic bicycle basket on the soap dish bar as a toy depository.
- While your child is splashing around in the tub is a good time for you to straighten and polish the bathroom. Or sit on the floor by the tub and use the time to catch up on your reading.
- Use a decorative mug tree to hold individual bathroom mugs. Have the family bring their cups to the kitchen a few times a week for a good washing.
- Display cosmetic brushes like a bouquet in a basket, vase, crock or brandy snifter.
- Use the plastic lids from spray cans to corral tubes of lipstick, mascara, eye shadow, etc.
- Transfer all ingredients from breakable or screw-top bottles into labelled pop-top detergent bottles. This is not only a safety measure, the pop-up lids make liquids easier to dispense. (Ketchup and mustard dispensers can also be used.)
- An extra roll of bathroom tissue can be housed in a bottomless boutique tissue box. (A boutique tissue box is also a handy dispenser for cotton balls.) Two rolls of bathroom tissue will fit nicely in a large oatmeal box. Decorate the container with wallpaper, fabric or adhesive-backed paper.
- Attach an orange juice can to the inside of a cupboard door to hold your curling iron.
- Use an old toothbrush holder to hold your blow dryer. The nozzle fits securely in the space where the cup is supposed to go. The holes for the toothbrushes can hold electric roller clips.
- Remember to look under your vanity; there's a lot of wasted space up there. Pound a few nails and hang pails of reserve supplies out of sight.
- A carpenter's apron can be hung on the wall to hold bathroom provisions, or worn as a hairdo or makeup apron with your needed items secured in the pockets.

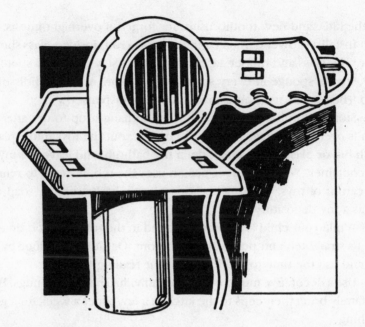

A recycled toothbrush holder makes a convenient dispenser for a blow dryer.

• A compartmented desktop caddy can hold makeup and hair-care equipment on a bathroom shelf or counter.

• Use an appliance timer for hot rollers or coffee makers so they'll be ready to go when you get up in the morning.

• Try some of these ideas for storing hair ribbons, fancy clips, barrettes, coated elastics and combs:

Hang hair ribbons over the pegs on an expanding hat rack, clip them onto café rings, loop and hang them on a clothes hanger or necktie rack, or secure them to a bulletin board with pushpins. Wrap the ribbons around smooth plastic curlers and secure the ends with bobby pins or clips. Keep the curlers in a drawer or in a container on a shelf. The curler "irons" the ribbons while they're being stored. Decorative clips or barrettes can be attached to a wide piece of hanging lace, ribbon or macrame braid. They can be placed in a compartmented box or drawer divider; use them to decorate a stuffed animal or the long braids of a doll. Contain hair combs in a drawer divider, or stick into a hanging length of fake fur.

Coated elastics can be kept handy by storing them around the handle of the hairbrush.

• Place all toiletries and other storables in a container (shoe-box-sized or larger) and use it as a slide-out tray under a sink or on a deep shelf so you can handle several things as one unit.

• If bathroom space is minimal, instead of purchasing giant econ-omy sizes of your favorite products, choose the smaller varieties. It's a little more expensive, but it helps you conserve precious space. If you want to enjoy the cash savings from buying larger quantities and you have serviceable storage areas elsewhere in your house, keep the small containers in the bathroom and refill them from your surplus stock stored elsewhere.

• Clean and sterilize toothbrushes in the dishwasher or soak them in Listerine.

• To organize the space under a bathroom sink, place a plastic crate (or cardboard box) on its side with the front of the container facing forward. Put a dishpan (or another box) into the crate and fill it with any type of supplies. The dishpan slides back and forth just like a drawer. On top of the container you can stack towels, bathroom tissue (or whatever) and make very functional space out of the open hole under a bathroom sink.

• A silverware basket makes a good makeup or hair care caddy.

• Hang a pocketed shoe bag on the outside of the shower curtain with shower curtain hooks. The pockets will provide easy access stor-age for lots of toiletries.

• Wear a wrist sweatband while cleaning the shower stall. It'll keep all the drips from running down your arm.

• Electric roller clips hang over the rim of a mug with no more tangles.

• Attach a magnetic strip to the inside of the medicine chest to hold tweezers, clippers, nail files, pins, etc.

• A recycled pipe rack can become a standing toothbrush holder for a large family. (It should hold six to eight toothbrushes.)

• All bathroom doors should be equipped with locks that can be opened from the outside, in case of an emergency.

• Now that you've thoroughly considered your options and noted your limitations you may need to go shopping. Take a trip through a few bath shops or bath departments in your favorite stores. If you live in a rural area where your selection of products is limited, mail-order companies offer the same choices. Check these resources and see the gamut of products designed to stretch your existing space without snapping your budget.

HOW LONG IS A MINUTE?

How long *is* a minute? As the old story goes, that all depends on which side of the bathroom door you are! While soaking in a hot tub poring over death and intrigue on the high seas, or standing entranced in the shower while steaming jets of pulsing water pound your back, time seems to stand still. But not so for the poor unshaven fellow who's pounding furiously on the door, already five minutes late for work!

Even if your bathroom has enough space for a polo match, without careful scheduling, the orchestration of the family bathroom traffic will look more like a street fight than a ballet.

Common sense demands that we think ahead: the first person out the door in the morning is the first to use the bathroom, and so on. Simple enough. However, be sure everyone knows the scheduled routine and that any prolonged incumbency adversely affects the rest of the family.

To prevent the latter and to avoid frothing at the mouth, put a clock in the bathroom so everyone is aware when his time is up.

To insure privacy, put a shower curtain or opaque glass doors around the tub. That way someone can be bathing while another uses the other facilities.

Perhaps trade-offs will help: someone can shower just before bed, another can shower in the morning. (If "fluffy" hair is a problem in the morning, have that person hurry into the bathroom to wash his hair, then blow-dry it in another room.)

Sometimes, an emergency backup supply (stored outside the bathroom) will alleviate some tension. Maybe extra toothbrushes, toothpaste and disposable cups, bandages, an electric razor, aspirins, hairbrushes and combs and a self-contained potty chair for toddlers would be a few items to start with. In a pinch, the old washbowl and pitcher can double as an extra sink.

If you're one of the fortunate few with more than one bathroom, stock duplicate sets of supplies in each. Marking and color-coding makes the system even more convenient. For example, each child has two toothbrushes. One is in their bathroom downstairs and one is in the upstairs bathroom. They each have a different color of toothbrush and the upstairs brushes are marked with a dot of red nail polish so all ten brushes don't end up downstairs. (Colored plastic tape can also be used to mark.) Keep all the black combs in one bathroom and all the colored ones in the other.

Now, using that as an illustration, expand on the idea. All hairbrushes, shampoo, lotions, etc., marked with a red dot go in the upstairs bathroom. If Mom and Dad use identical disposable razors, always put a signaling dot on one or the other. Even size differences can be used as a labeling code. Long combs upstairs, short combs downstairs; big jugs of shampoo upstairs, small bottles downstairs.

Another idea is to give each child a different colored "clean-up" caddy filled with his supplies. For example, let's say Steven's color is black. He has a black caddy, black comb and brush, black toothbrush, black cup. The caddy also holds any other bathroom items needed by the child: deodorant, toothpaste, lotion, etc. These caddies don't need to be stored in the bathroom. When it's time to get ready, the child grabs his kit and heads to any available bathroom.

Of course, there's no sense getting everything organized if the kids go on a search-and-destroy mission every time they walk through the bathroom door. When you're going through the delegating process, don't overlook an important aspect of training: maintenance. Often we teach the kids how to scrub the tub, sanitize the toilet, hang fresh towels and polish the chrome, but we forget to show them what to do on a daily basis.

Teach them to hang up the towels, put the clothes in the hamper and put away the shampoo, razors and combs. (The ideas you've just read will make it easier for them.)

I have a friend who's trained her kids to polish the faucets every time they turn off the water. Another friend has a sign over her toilet that reads: "I aim to please. You aim, too, please." Another poster hanging on the bathroom door reminds everyone of the general maintenance procedures agreed on in family discussion.

The next time you enter the mass destruction known by childless couples as a bathroom, instead of screaming, put some of these practical helps to use. Defensively armed with this battery of new ideas, you're ready for your attack on bathroom ataxia.

CHAPTER FOURTEEN

Hints for the Harried Home Manager

I get pretty agitated when I read books and articles on getting organized at home. Some experts seem to think we're all wealthy enough to be listed with Dun and Bradstreet or that we have the architectural skills of Frank Lloyd Wright. The purpose of *this* chapter, however, is to show you how you can organize an odd assortment of things without gutting interiors, knocking out walls, going broke or saying words the children shouldn't hear.

Sporting Goods

This covers a wide spectrum of equipment, but let's start with the basics most of us encounter.

One of the best methods I've ever seen for storing balls, mitts, bats, shoulder pads, helmets, etc., is this: Purchase an inexpensive five-shelf metal utility unit and install the shelves upside down. (The installation requires only a screwdriver.) This provides a lip to keep balls, bats, roller skates and skateboards from rolling off. These shelves then become shallow one-motion storage trays. Since you adjust the distance between each shelf, you can modify the unit to house your specific storables. (Heavy things like bowling balls should be placed on the bottom shelf.)

Now, using a few nuts and bolts, attach a length of pegboard to each side of the utility shelf. Here's where you hang odd-sized equipment: skis, poles, fishing rods, racquets, shoulder pads, turf cleats, ice skates, boxing gloves, swim fins, and so on. To make bins for bulky gear, thread heavy twine through holes in the shelf standards. Using this system, all the gear can be stored in a compact area. Anchor the unit to a wall to keep it from tipping over.

For years we used a large industrial bin and all our sports stuff (bats, balls, spikes, mitts, helmets) was tossed inside. It didn't take up much room and kept everything well contained; being an open box, it was

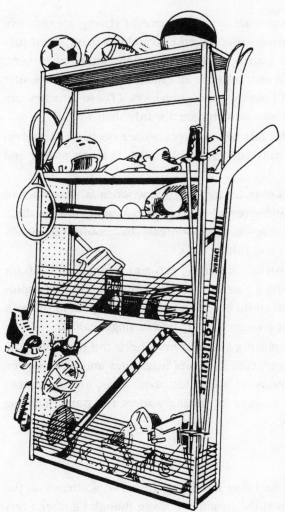

A five-tiered utility shelf is easily adapted for use as a sports storage unit.

extremely easy for the kids to return things. The drawback was that a certain amount of grubbing was required to find something. (But even that was okay, because things can be slightly harder to find than to put away.)

A large toy box is a useful depot for balls and bats. Tote bags, duffle bags and foot lockers can likewise be repositories for athletic equipment. A bar stool turned upside down holds bats, clubs and poles; mitts, helmets and a bucket of balls can hang from the legs. Anchor the bar stool to a wall, if necessary.

The key to maintaining an orderly system is to contain as much of the equipment as possible so several things can be stored as one. Put sleeping bags into "stuff bags;" put tents and cots into duffle bags.

(Army-Navy surplus stores are a good source of strong, inexpensive canvas bags.) Things always used together (catcher's mask, chest protector, shin and knee guards; croquet sets; badminton equipment; horseshoes; or fins and snorkels) are all efficiently stored as one unit in separate equipment bags or other containers. (These pouches can be hung up out of the way or stored on a sturdy shelf.)

Buckets with handles can become receptacles (to hang or shelve) for tennis balls, golf balls and tees, tent spikes, batting gloves and sweatbands.

To hold long sports gear, an inexpensive wooden ladder attached to a ceiling with rope and screw eyes becomes a hanging storage shelf. Since it's see-through, the equipment is easy to choose. (Especially good for skis, ski poles and fishing rods.)

Certain things like backpack frames, skis and fishing poles call for hanging storage. For fishing poles, mount two spring-action clothespins side by side (about sixteen inches apart) and clip the pole in place. A backpack frame is light enough to hang from a single nail.

Browse through a sporting goods store: Check the pages of mail-order catalogs, advertisements in sports magazines and newspapers. There's specialty apparatus for storing just about any sports implement (ski equipment racks, hangers for fishing waders and poles, golf bag caddies, to name a few).

Bicycles

Bikes are notorious for being left in the driveway, scattered on the front lawn or forgotten at the neighbors'. Even though I'll offer a few storage suggestions, a little nagging may still be necessary to see that the system is carried out.

Your first move is to be sure the bicycles have a well-defined place, a specific area well known to each family member.

You can section off parking stalls with paint, or mount the legs of an old headboard (with upright slats) in cement (or on a heavy base of some kind) and use it as a bike rack. Heavy coated hooks can be screwed into wall or ceiling studs for hanging storage during the off-season. Small, lightweight three-wheelers (like Big Wheels) can be hung on a large nail low enough for the children to manage.

Nowadays it seems that bicycle kickstands aren't fashionable, but they sure make it easier to store bikes. Appeal to your children's common sense and install kickstands on all their bikes.

An inexpensive wooden ladder attached to a ceiling with heavy rope provides see-through storage for skis, poles, fishing rods, hockey sticks and water skis.

Coats, Hats, Mittens and Boots

A coat closet is inconvenient. First you have to travel to it, then you have to open the door—too many motions. That's why coats are usually found swinging from the bedpost, thrown over a door, hooked on a doorknob or hung on the back of a chair.

The ideal method for hanging coats, then, is to provide a long row of hooks on a wall just inside the back door (or the door most often used by the family). However, most of us are slightly more concerned with decor, so we tend to make the system a little less convenient. If

Two clothespins serve as a fishing-pole mount.

A wall-mounted bike rack is easily made from 2 × 4s.

this "house beautiful" approach is your idea, then you have to do the harping when the outerwear isn't put back in its proper place.

Whatever your solution, put all the wraps in one central location (space permitting). Hooks will be more readily used than hangers, so use as many as you have room for.

We live in a section of the country where the weather frequently changes. At any given time we need to have heavy coats, jackets and lightweight sweaters handy. If your situation is similar, you'll find that at least three hooks per person works best.

You may even need more hooks if you find there are more than two articles on a hook. You'll notice a greater level of success when only one or two items are hanging from each hook (and then only if the bottom layer is infrequently worn). In other words, the top layer is the one-motion storage area for things worn more often than once a week. For lightweight sweaters or sweatshirts, the hooks can be as close together as four inches; for winter coats and jackets, eight inches.

If space is a problem, another variation is to hook up only those coats and jackets used daily. Use hangers for infrequently worn apparel. Put the hooks up in a convenient spot and little-used articles can be hung in a more remote closet, if necessary. Just have the most commonly used items in the handiest position.

For hats and mittens, you can give each person a small dishpan in which to toss his accessories. Or provide one dishpan for everyone's hats and another for everyone's mittens. It's helpful to store these bins just above the coat hooks, on the floor beneath or nearby. A small chest of drawers tucked into the closet can function the same way.

An expanding wooden hat rack can hold a few jackets and hats. Hats and mittens stored in individual mailboxes or bicycle baskets is another idea. You can also use a hanging purse file or pocketed shoe bag, cardboard shoe file (with nine cubby holes) or stacking plastic drawers.

Hats and mittens stretched over the rungs of a freestanding shoe rack dry in a hurry and are ready for reuse. Or hang an open tote bag or bucket on each coat hook.

Boots can stand in a dishpan or cat litter pan to contain the drips and keep the boots from jumbling into a disorganized heap. These bins should be as close to the door as possible to discourage tracking mud and melted snow through the house.

Although the dishpan method works well, the boots are somewhat slow to dry. To encourage drying as well as order, try this idea. You'll need one brick for each pair of boots (be sure the brick has three holes in the middle), one ¾- to 1-inch-wide dowel for each pair of boots, and plaster of paris.

All you do is cut each dowel in half. Then, with a little water, mix up the plaster. Put one dowel half in each of the end holes and fill the two holes with plaster, making sure the dowels are straight. As soon as the plaster is set, you have a sturdy boot rack. Boots are placed upside down over the dowels; the weight of the brick keeps the unit

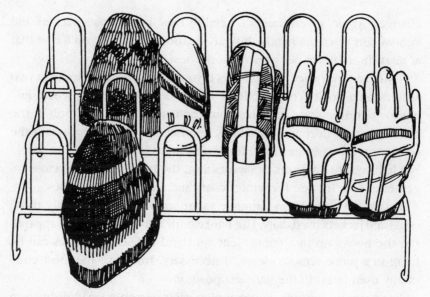

A metal shoe rack aids in drying hats and mittens.

from tipping over. Now, the boots can drain and still be systematically stored while they're drying. (Spray-paint the boot rack and it won't look too bad, either!) Each boot rack can stand inside a dishpan or other waterproof container if you wish, to catch drips.

Another easy storage method for boots is to clip a pair on a skirt hanger and hang them up. Though not great for wet boots, it's a good way to keep dry boots out of the way and orderly. Even wire coat hangers can be bent to hang up a pair of boots.

Miscellaneous Tips and Tricks

Here's a potpourri of miscellaneous storage and general organizational hints.

• If you *must* store magazines (even I have a few too many) try some of these ideas.

Fashion a magazine file out of a heavy detergent box (or buy magazine files) and store the magazines by month—all the January issues together, February together and so on. This is especially effective because all the Valentine's Day ideas will be together in the February issues, spring gardening articles in the March issues, hearty soup recipes in the October issues and so on.

Staple a 3″×5″ card to the front cover noting the page numbers of special articles, directions, recipes or whatever.

Whenever you run across an interesting article or something you

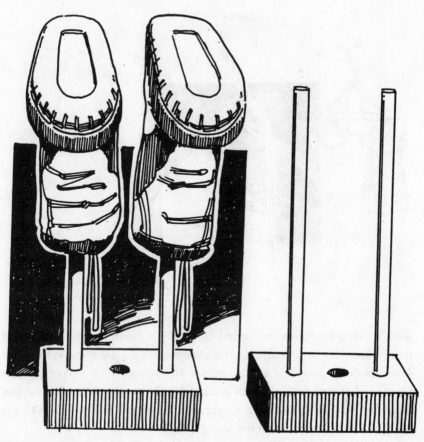

Make a sturdy boot-drying rack from a brick, a dowel and plaster of paris.

Hang up boots on a skirt hanger.

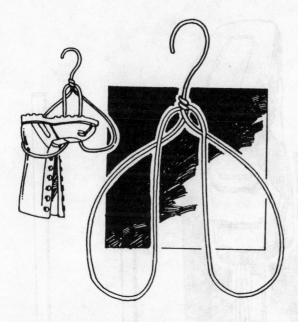

Bend a wire hanger
into a boot hanger.

want to save for future reference, dog-ear the corner of that page. It'll
be much easier to find again. (Details on setting up a filing system are
found in *Confessions of an Organized Homemaker.*) It's okay to keep
magazines if you give yourself a limit. We have a wooden box in the
family room that's filled with magazines. When it's full, we have to get
rid of a few to make room for some new ones.

• If your phone book is receiving a lot of wear and tear, staple a
sheet inside the back cover and jot down frequently called numbers.
Be sure the kids list their friends, too, so you can reach them if necessary. To increase efficient use of the phone book, underline all numbers
as soon as you've looked them up. You'll be able to find them more
easily the next time. Better yet, put the numbers in the family organizer.

Before we started using the family organizer, we had a 5″ × 8″ card by
each phone on which was typed the last names and phone numbers of
about eighty people we called regularly. The front of the card was covered with clear self-adhesive plastic; the back was exposed to note addi-
tions or changes. We made up new cards only once every year or two.

Another clever method is to type or write frequently used names
and numbers on 2½″ × 2½″ cards and slip them into a photo cube.

• Letters can be awkward to store, especially if you like to read
through them now and then. The best method I know of is to keep the
letters in a looseleaf notebook. Using reinforced looseleaf paper, staple
each complete letter to a single sheet. You now have a book that's easy
to store, and each letter can easily be read and referred to.

You can also use file folders or accordion files. Any of these systems sure beat the old shoe-box-tied-with-string method.

- Keep a galvanized garbage can close to your barbecue grill to hold charcoal, lighter fluid and barbecue tools. Include a work glove and scoop for dispensing charcoal without the mess, and a wire brush for quick cleaning of the cooking rack. A stack of bins (covered with a large plastic bag) could also be used for barbecue storables.

- Paperbacks waste a lot of space on the standard twelve-inch-deep bookshelf. Double up and conserve precious space by storing the books two layers deep. In order to see the back row of books, stack two 2 × 4s one on top of the other on the back of the shelf to function like a stair step. This will raise the back row four inches and enable you to see and choose the book you need. If you don't want to use the wood, lay the front row of books down (with spines facing up) and keep the back row standing. You'll still be able to see one behind the other. Video tapes can be stored the same way.

- Store music books in a magazine rack by the piano.

- You can store knitting needles and art paintbrushes by weaving them through the mesh of a loosely woven placemat. Hang up or roll and tie shut. Cut two slits in the front of a ''paint with water'' book and slip the paintbrush through the slits.

- Cassette tapes and CDs (especially the kids') seem to get piled in the most convenient spot, usually on the dresser. Of course you can purchase cassette tape or CD organizers, but I haven't had great success getting the kids to use them; these cases have individual slots into which to slide the tapes or CDs and for kids (ours, anyway) that's just too much work. They always pile up on top of the unit ''for now. . . .'' A four-drawer cardboard chest (one made by Bankers Box is the sturdiest I've found) holds 34 cassette tapes, 58 CDs or 15 video tapes. These are available in the closet department at discount stores. The Bankers Box brand is available at office supply stores.

A rigid briefcase designed for cassette tape storage makes the collection portable. (By the way, any of these ideas are equally effective for baseball or football card collections.)

- We tamed our video games by putting the TV on a sturdy two-drawer nightstand. I drilled a hole through the back of the drawer and then through the back of the nightstand; we put the module into the top drawer, ran the cords through the holes in the back of the nightstand and connected them to the TV. The joysticks and several game cartridges also fit in the top drawer. When the kids are ready to zap something, they open the top drawer, pull out the paddles, insert the

Paperbacks stored two layers deep use space more efficiently, especially when the back row is raised on two 2×4s.

cartridge and they're on their way. When the games aren't in use, all you can see are the TV and the nightstand—as neat as a pin. (I've often wondered just how neat a pin really is.)

• Do you have big or awkward-shaped things? (For example, I have a large crocheted Christmas tree, a stuffed fabric reindeer, antlers, kites, an infant seat, etc.) These things aren't necessarily heavy, but they're awkward to store and retrieve. To solve this storage problem, use a spring-action paper clamp as a hanging device. I place things I want to keep clean in large plastic bags, fold over the top of the bags, clamp them shut and hang them up. Things like kites we just clip and hang as is.

• Super Handyman Al Carrell suggests a couple of ways to store hoses. Nail seven empty coffee cans onto the garage, carport or basement wall. Wrap the hose around the circle of cans and use the open cans as mini storage bins.

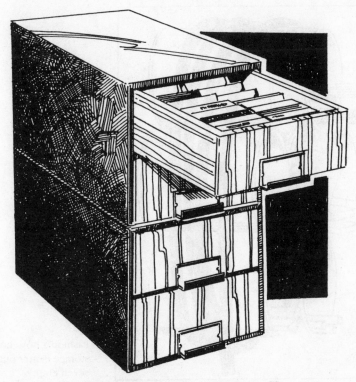

This four-drawer cardboard chest holds many cassettes or CDs.

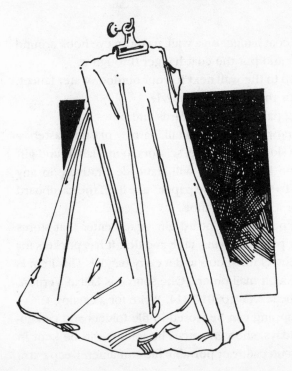

Even awkward items
can be hung up out of
the way with spring-
action paper clamps.

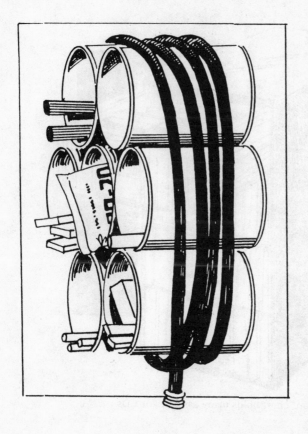

Fashion a hose holder/
storage center out of
seven empty
shortening or coffee
cans.

Or mount a wooden coat hanger on a wall, using an eye hook around the neck. Coil the hose and put the coat hanger through it.

Fasten a broom clamp to the wall next to your outdoor water faucet. This is a perfect spot for the hose spray nozzle.

• Now for wrapping paper, ribbons, cards and bows:

Store long rolls of wrapping paper in a tall, narrow plastic wastebasket. Attach a bag to the side to hold tape, scissors, pens, labels and gift tags. A covered bamboo hamper that will stand decoratively in any room can also be used. To safeguard the paper, take it off the cardboard tube, re-roll it and store it inside the tube.

You can buy an inexpensive cardboard gift wrap center that stores and organizes wrapping paper, ribbons, tape and ties. It has pockets for everything, a wooden dowel for spools and a carry handle. This item is commonly available through mail order. (One source is Lillian Vernon, 534 Main St., New Rochelle, NY 10801-7214. Write for a catalog.)

Folded sheets of wrapping can be stored in file folders and categorized—Christmas, birthdays, showers, etc. The folders can be kept in a file cabinet, box, clean-up caddy or portable file container. Keep extra cards filed with the paper. If you use a box or portable file, you may want to keep scissors, tape, string or other supplies in the container so you can gather everything you need in one motion.

Transfer a roll of wrapping paper into empty aluminum foil boxes. Because wrapping paper rolls are usually thirty inches long, you'll need an eighteen-inch box and a twelve-inch box. Cut through the roll of wrapping paper, forming two rolls—one eighteen-inch roll and one twelve-inch roll. These rolls fit perfectly into the aluminum foil boxes. The wrapping paper is easy to store and especially easy to dispense.

Rubbermaid makes a long, shallow covered container especially designed to hold rolls of wrapping paper, bows and other gift-wrapping supplies. It's only about six-inches deep so it will fit under a bed.

A mounted plastic strawberry box will hold a ball of string or spool of ribbon; the end of the string or ribbon pulls down through one of the holes in the basket, yet the spool is neatly contained.

A plastic strawberry box makes a tangle-free string or ribbon dispenser.

A jumbo foil or plastic wrap box will neatly organize your spools of ribbon. To keep the separate colors tangle-free, stand or lay the spools in the carton side by side. Cut slits in the carton top (one for each spool) and pull the ribbons through—no more ribbon spools rolling off the table.

Store bows in a single layer in crush-resistant, covered boxes. If you have a lot of bows to store, you might consider sorting by color or occasion. Another alternative is to place the bows in a big plastic bag with larger and heavier bows on the bottom. Hang the bag in an out-of-the-way place.

If you have a specific hobby (photography, hunting, woodworking, etc.) that causes some storage and use problems, your best bet is to consult an expert in that field. Talk to people with similar interests and ask them for ideas. Keep your eyes open when you visit specialty shops. How do they store their merchandise? Use the four storage alternative methods to determine the best option for you.

CHAPTER FIFTEEN

Sunrise, Sunset

B e honest. Don't you secretly believe that bedtime should be spelled b-a-d-t-i-m-e and morning spelled m-o-u-r-n-i-n-g?

Every morning is a chance for renewal, a fresh start for the rest of your life. Each new day provides you with a renewed opportunity to scream, "Get out of bed!" fourteen times; to punctuate every sentence with the word "hurry"; to search feverishly for a lost shoe (while you pray the bus waits); to check math problems and unearth an empty oatmeal box for a school art project and help someone construct a model rocket—all the while convincing someone whose hair didn't turn out right that he looks just like Tom Cruise.

My mother-in-law used to say when the kids finally left for school in the morning, it felt like a hurricane had passed. Now I know what she meant, although I realize the peace is only temporary. Though you enjoy the pacific eye of the storm, the fury soon returns—and shortly the quiet repose of bedtime is upon us.

It seems we, as parents, love to grieve about putting the kids to bed, with the distinct purpose of eliciting sympathy: "I have to put Jeff back in his crib twenty-seven times every night!" However, our listeners don't hear this as a plea for compassion but as a challenge to try and top. "I'll see you twenty-seven trips back to bed, and raise you one pillow fight and thirteen stuffed animals covered with diaper rash ointment."

No pity, no empathy, just a lot of "my lot is worse than yours."

No, there's nowhere to turn, no help to be given from the outside world. The problem is yours alone to solve, so let's get busy.

SUNRISE

The success of my day starts the night before. As money is the root of all evil, so is inadequate planning. Start your morning at night by doing the following:

1. *Speak to each family member* alone and ask if anything needs to be done tonight to prepare for tomorrow. (Check homework, find two empty Jell-O boxes for school, sign permission slips, write checks for lunch money or school pictures, make lunches, etc.) Tell the kids to put everything in their in and out baskets or book bags. Before bed ask them if they obeyed your request! Also check tomorrow's schedules so you'll know in advance if Jim needs a ride somewhere, if Brian has to stay after school for a computer class, if Jeff has T-ball practice. Armed with this information, you'll be in better shape to plan and schedule your day.

2. *Anticipate.* Can you foresee any special needs? (Jim has early choir practice; be sure he sets his alarm half an hour early. I have a 10 A.M. lecture; gather instructional materials and have them ready to go. Steven has speech therapy tomorrow; be sure he sets out his manual. Jim is playing racquetball before work; remind him to set out his gym bag, racquet and ball.) Use your calendar to preplan so everyone can work ahead of themselves. A fringe benefit from this practice is a bolster for your patience. It's easier to maintain your composure at the end of a long, trying day when you know the groundwork for a successful morning is already laid.

3. *Lay out clothing.* Get everyone into the habit of putting out the things they're going to wear the next day. Include shoes, socks, accessories, hats, coats, mittens—everything! If someone discovers a missing button or torn seam, he can make the necessary repairs before the morning rush hits.

If this is too much to ask, be sure the laundry is done on a regular basis and that the family knows what the schedule is. Also, see to it that nothing dirty, torn, wrinkled or otherwise in need of attention is put away disheveled.

4. *Pick up the house,* empty the dishwasher and sort the laundry if you're washing sometime tomorrow. Have everyone pick up and put away twenty things, or set the timer for ten minutes and have everyone work at top speed. (You can stand anything for ten minutes, right?) Waking up to a straight house is the nicest gift you can give yourself. Some people carry this a step further by setting the table for breakfast.

5. *Know what you're having for dinner* the next night. If you're going to be away most of the day, post menu instructions so the first one home (or the one assigned) can begin preparations. If you're going to be home, fix what you can for dinner after breakfast.

6. Once again, *check your calendar.* Review your goals, and plan your day. That way you'll have your priorities firmly fixed in your mind.

7. *Provide stimulation* for yourself and discover others' needs so morning will be more enjoyable. (Jim loves a hot shower and the morning newspaper. Jim, Jr. enjoys rock music. I love to exercise. Jeff just wants to be left alone.) Try to meet and understand whatever needs you discover. (Come on. Anyone can put up with a *few* minutes of Van Halen!)

8. Finally, *establish a routine* and a time schedule. Have everyone chart out everything they have to do each morning and assign a time limit to each activity. Here's Jim Jr.'s:

- Up, shower, dress, 20 minutes
- Morning chores, 20 minutes
- Breakfast, 15 minutes
- Brush teeth, gather schoolwork, put on coat, 7 minutes
  (Total 62 minutes)

Now, add a fifteen-minute insurance policy to that total and you get seventy-seven minutes. Jim has to leave for school at 8 A.M.; that requires him to awaken between 6:40 and 6:45 A.M. Oh, sure, Jim's been known to stumble out of bed at 7:30, giving him just enough time to groom, gulp and run, but the whole family pays the price when someone decides to grab a few extra winks.

After determining each individual's schedule, bathroom time limits can be set.

Hints for a No-Mourning Morning

- Give each child his own alarm clock, even if there's more than one child in the room. (With some kids it helps to get the kind of alarm that keeps blaring until he gets up and turns it off.)
- Put on some lively music (John Philip Sousa ought to do it), run the vacuum, sing—just create an enthusiastic "Up and at 'em" atmosphere. (Turning on the TV is dangerous, as it can be too captivating both for you and the kids.)
- Call the child once and tell him breakfast will be ready in fifteen minutes. Behaviorists recommend that you call the child just once and let him suffer (or enjoy) the consequences of his behavior. If he gets up he'll get to eat a good breakfast and be at school on time. If he sleeps, he'll be late for school (he might even have to walk) and may not have time to eat.

Theoretically (if you're consistent with this), the child will choose to get up.

- Have an in and out basket for each child.
- Set a timer for ten minutes before everyone has to leave.
- To motivate a dawdling youngster, read a morning story as soon as he gets himself ready. (You spend five minutes reading a story or fifteen minutes cajoling, nagging and screaming.)

SUNSET

Just as a condemned prisoner sits on death row for years after his conviction, when the kids hear, "Time for bed," they know they can stay up quite a while longer if they put up a good fight. This guerrilla warfare includes ingesting large amounts of water, brushing teeth for five whole minutes; finishing a TV show; remembering big, important assignments; and taking frequent trips to the bathroom (the consequence of tactic number one). This litany of bedtime problems may vary depending on the household, but it's a scenario we all encounter.

My kids have learned from my inconsistencies that my first announcement of bedtime is an empty phrase. They'll wait through each passing announcement and each rise in pitch until the time bomb explodes. Then, when the frenzied, threatening tones rebound off the walls, they decide that perhaps Mother means business (this time).

I've done it the wrong way and I've done it the right way. The right way is faster, but it takes more self-discipline, so I often fall into bad habits and wonder why bedtime is bedlam.

Here's the right way:

1. *Establish a fixed bedtime* for each child (or an "in your room" time for older children) and stick to it. When you've had a great day, you might feel like letting the kids stay up an extra half hour or so. But when you've had an unnerving stint, you strictly impose the bedtime curfew. The message the kids get from your behavior is that bedtime is determined by your moods and is subject at any time to negotiations; thus, the coaxing, arguing and crying.

To further insure a successful morning, schedule bedtimes so the children will get enough rest. When a six-year-old goes to bed at 10 P.M., he makes life miserable for everyone when he gets up.

Set bedtime early enough to give you a little time for yourself. You need to wind down as much as the kids do and some time alone may be just the ticket. (This is especially important for working parents.)

2. *Set the mood for bedtime.* This is a big order, I know, but it helps to have an atmosphere of quiet at day's end, a feeling the day is drawing to a close. Everyone should become increasingly settled down as bed-

time approaches. ("Settle down, you guys," is as frequently heard around here as "Hurry up" is in the mornings.)

Get the kids mentally prepared. Before it's actually time to get ready for bed, warn the children the "bewitching hour" is approaching so they can wrap up whatever they're doing. If bedtime is 8:30, don't let them get involved in an hour-long TV show that begins at 8 P.M. (unless they understand they won't be able to see the program in its entirety).

3. *Encourage cooperation* with an interesting bedtime routine. When all our kids were little we'd play a game as soon as they were ready for bed; then we'd gather together on someone's bed for a story. After prayers, everyone had a loving tuck into bed and a chance to relate the best thing that happened during the day. I used to record everyone's declaration.

One more notable remark was "The best thing that happened to me today was 'Piglet squeezed Pooh's paw.' " At that point I figured I was wasting my time. After all, I was hoping for more profound information—little capsules of their personalities. But as the years have enhanced Brian's words, I'm glad I continued the practice. We've all had many good laughs about that funny quote from Winnie-the-Pooh and now in my middle-aged comfort I realize it's those very things that build and strengthen families.

Bedtime stories are, of course, the age-old tradition, but sometimes you're worn out, too busy or just plain crabby. For those days, purchase or record tapes of your kids' favorite stories or songs. Get some high-intensity lamps that clip right to the bed and let the child look through a group of storybooks, a mail-order catalog or magazines.

Let someone else read to the child, perhaps an older child or a spouse. One evening, ragged and worn, I was sprawled on the couch wallowing in self-pity. With childlike enthusiasm (always more apparent before bed), Steven begged me to read him a story. Sounding afflicted and picked on (and playing the martyr to the hilt), I said, "Why don't you ask your father to read to you?" Somewhat surprised, Steven responded, "I didn't know he could read!" It was then I realized I needed to share bedtime responsibilities with everyone who was warm, breathing and literate.

4. It's easier to put down what you're doing and *take the kids to bed* than it is to sit and shout out repeated directions.

Anticipate all the little tricks and ploys used by the kids to stay up (or to get up). Be sure they brush and floss, go to the bathroom and get a drink. Knowing all their needs have been met, you can confidently stick them back in bed as soon as they climb out.

I've spent many evenings riding shotgun on the bedrooms, ready and waiting for an errant child to sneak out of bed. Armed with a craft project or a good book, I'd sit on the floor in the hallway until the kids were asleep. The more consistent you are at making them stay in bed, the faster they'll learn and cooperate.

Bedtime Tips

- Set a plastic thermos on the nightstand for a child who frequently awakens you during the night for a drink of water.
- Set an alarm clock for the hour your teenager is to be home. Then you can go to sleep and relax. If the alarm goes off, you've got something to worry about, but if the child comes home and turns off the alarm as instructed, you can rest assured of his safety.
- If you've just put a child to bed and he's screaming for attention, stand outside his bedroom door and record his wails. Then give the child an instant replay. He'll be laughing in no time.
- When the bedtime signal is sounded, have the kids play "beat the clock" competing against their own best time.
- Provide frightened children a character night light, or designate a certain can of air freshener or bottle of cologne as "Monster Repellent." The scent will ward off bad guys long enough for the child to fall asleep.
- Let the child listen to soothing music on the radio or stereo. (I have heard from reliable sources that soothing music is still being played on the radio.)
- If bedtime stories are a ritual, occasionally use a map or atlas when telling the story. Indicate where the story took place, where the characters lived, point to the area where you live, and so forth. Other visual aids can add interest, too, such as a toy boat if it's a story about the sea or a toy train, stuffed elephant, etc.

On those inevitable nights when the natives are especially restless and you just want to hide away and hunker down, think of the song "Sunrise, Sunset." Only too soon we'll all be saying with tight throat and a touch of melancholy, "Wasn't it yesterday when they were small?"

A summary of the foregoing would simply amount to one word: plan. Great is the power of a plan. The biggest cause of failure is trading what we want most for what we want at the moment. Plan your mornings and evenings, follow your plans and sit back and enjoy a successful and happy day.

CHAPTER SIXTEEN

B Is for Baby

*"When God wants to have a great work done in the world or a great
wrong righted, he goes about it in a very unusual way. He doesn't
stir up his earthquakes or send forth his thunderbolts. Instead, he
has a helpless baby born perhaps in a simple home out of some ob-
scure mother. And then God puts the idea into the mother's heart,
and she puts it into the baby's mind. And then God waits. The greatest
forces in the world are not the earthquakes and the thunderbolts.
The greatest forces in the world are babies."*

E.T. Sullivan

How can one so tiny change so much? With each new arrival,
lives are refashioned. Schedules are altered to jibe with feeding times, naps, diaper changes and midnight vigils. Physical
surroundings are modified to make room for playpens,
changing tables, cribs, quilts, diapers, outgrown clothes, baby bottles,
small jars of food, lotions, special shampoos, diaper ointment, mobiles,
rattles and educational toys. Yes, one so little changes a *lot*.

Babies not only affect your time and space, they transform *you*. All
of a sudden you find yourself doing things you solemnly vowed you
would *never* do. Your pockets are bulging with color prints of the little
angel. You grab strangers on the bus, corner the parking attendant,
collar a credulous sales clerk (or anyone else whose politeness you
misinterpret as interest). And then you let loose with the exciting details of the first tooth, the first (and *always* precocious) words, the
trauma of labor and delivery and those ubiquitous "kids say the darn-
dest things" anecdotes!

Say! Did I ever tell you about the time Jeff was visiting the dentist
for his kindergarten checkup? Halfway through the ordeal, Jeff stiffened
in the chair and said, "Dr. Orchard, you are despicable!" (I always tell
this story with just enough embarrassment to hide the obvious pride I

take in knowing that my five-year-old could use the word "despicable" in a sentence. Never mind that he learned the word from Daffy Duck.)

Yes, we all delight in our little ones, regardless of the lifestyle changes incurred, and if we organize our time and space right from the start, we'll be able to savor even more of their childhood.

THE TIME OF YOUR LIFE

With infants and young children in the home, you need to relax your standards for the sake of your mental health, especially during the early months of infancy. You're getting used to taking care of another person; your workload is increasing; you're frequently interrupted; and if you are the biological mother of the child, your body is in the process of healing. So relax your standards.

Now is a good time to consider those basic five or six necessary ingredients for a smoothly run home: general pickup, meals, kitchen, bathroom, laundry and entry areas.

Accept any and all help gratefully and without criticism. At this point, something is better than nothing.

Babies take an inordinate amount of time (especially if you're breast-feeding), so don't expect to handle everything with the ease and simplicity of pre-baby days. Right now your energies should be spent maintaining those five or six areas, and delegating as much as possible. A house that's straightened daily can get by for longer periods without a thorough digging-out. Once you get into a routine and form new habits that include this other person, you'll be up to speed in no time.

After our little girl was born (she was number five), I really felt swamped. Here I was this tower of efficiency (on good days, anyway) not knowing if I could keep up the grueling pace. The laundry seemed to double while the size of the house seemed to decrease. I was overwhelmed and frightened. But my experience with four other babies got me through it.

I knew many of these feelings were the same ones we experience during any dramatic change in life. Many of these feelings are also biological in nature and soon pass. New habits are like new shoes: they just don't feel right until they've been well worn and molded. Within a few months I was humming right along, confident in my ability. Rest assured that you, too, will be back to normal in no time.

Before the baby is born, be sure the underlying surface in your home is orderly. Straighten closets, cupboards, drawers and plan menus. This foundation will function as your security blanket during busy days to come. (Of course, if you get a surprise phone call from your adoption agency and learn that you'll be proud parents tomorrow, you'll have to skip this first organizational step.)

Whenever you're in a temporary state of crisis (and having a baby certainly qualifies), jot down the jobs you've had to skip and need to get to when things are back on track. Writing this book has put me in a state of crisis, too, and my "I promise to do" list is beginning to rival Santa's in length, but the list itself has given me great peace of mind. A written list is tangible and manageable. But a head full of nagging mental reminders is fatiguing, unnerving and heralds depression.

TIME FOR TODDLERS

Time management for toddlers takes a different turn. At this stage you have to deal with uprooted plants, the constant dumping of kitchen cupboards, petrified food on the high chair and floor beneath, and rocks, dried beans and small plastic pieces in the mouth, nose, ears or navel. This is when you start to think, "What's the use?"

Because I do a lot of speaking, I'm constantly bombarded with questions. Without fail, parents of small youngsters always ask, "What do *you* do? How do you keep the baby out of everything?" (This type of question is always asked as if life or death hinged on the answer.) I always answer, "I *don't* keep the baby out of everything."

For a few months everything that was low enough for the baby to reach was in a general state of disarray. She'd dump everything out, then when she was otherwise engaged, I'd quickly toss everything back inside the cupboard or drawer. After a while the novelty wore off and the problem solved itself. It's really not a matter of life and death. Relax.

Some of you are probably horrified by this laid-back approach. My mother never allowed us to play in the cupboards and still shudders when she thinks about the prospect. If you take a similar view, the best way to eliminate the hassle is to purchase inside mount latches that prevent the child from opening the drawer or cupboard. Kinder-Gard is a good brand. It's easy to install, inexpensive and widely available in most baby departments. Also, two adjacent cupboard handles can be locked together with a knitting stitch holder or two snapping metal shower curtain rings.

Don't misunderstand; I believe in teaching children to respect their limits and to understand the word "no," but I reserve the word "no" for the sacred and the dangerous (pulling leaves off the plants, smashing the TV with the hammer and playing in the street).

As I followed the trail of blocks, dolls, shoes, clothes and puzzle

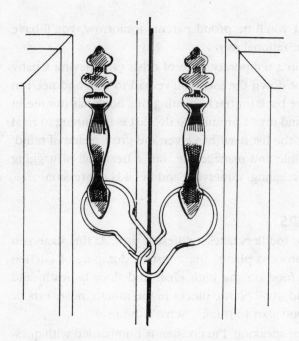

Keep cupboard contents off-limits by fastening door handles together with shower curtain hooks.

pieces left in Schuyler's path, I'd say to myself, "It'll all be over soon," and it was, believe me.

But if you don't want to wait for nature to take its course, begin with a young child and consistently have the tot help you pick up the pieces. Sometimes this dampens the desire to dump.

Learn to work while the child is around. It's tempting to wait until naptime to delve into the chores, but time-wise, this practice can be wasteful. During the baby's nap potentially productive hours pass. Don't waste those moments performing menial, routine tasks. Use that time for projects that require concentration and pay high-yield returns. (Besides, a child is never too young to be influenced by your example. If a youngster is constantly watching your routine, he'll pick up on the system a lot quicker. Imagine—teaching your kids organization while they're still in the cradle!)

Many times when I had a big project going, I'd do the routine, low-productivity jobs while the baby was up. But as soon as she was asleep, I'd stop whatever I was doing and use her naptime to full capacity (working on a book or lecture, reading or studying, sweating through an uninterrupted aerobic workout or putting together a tedious craft project). As soon as her nap was over, I'd get back to any undone essentials.

Never let an imperfect situation be an excuse to do nothing. (Memorize that sentence.)

There are a few jobs, though, I choose to do while the baby is asleep. Dusting knickknacks, or handling anything you don't want the baby to get into, is best left for a time when the child isn't around. For example, we have glass end tables in our living room and if I dust them while Schuy is around, she decides to "help," all the while getting sticky fingerprints on the tables faster than I can wipe them off. So I wait until she's asleep or occupied in another part of the house.

The only other job I try to do without the baby around is to empty or load the dishwasher. We had a neighbor whose child was killed in a dishwasher when he fell into it and his eye was impaled on one of the upright metal prongs. Babies love to climb onto dishwasher doors, but it's dangerous—and impedes your progress besides.

If you want to sew, iron, work on an important report or other project, and need to work freely without constantly stopping to get the baby out of things, put a tension-mounted baby gate across the doorway of the child's room (or other safe location) and make a giant playpen out of the room. Set up your work on the other side of the gate. You can keep your eye on the baby and the baby can see you— but he can't get to what you're doing. He won't be getting burned by the iron or grabbing your supplies off the table.

It's amazing how much you can accomplish when you *have* to. For example, several times I've had early morning TV tapings in my home. With such pressing deadlines I can have the laundry completed and the house in tip-top shape before the camera crew arrives. But without the urgency, you might find me folding clothes at 4:30 in the afternoon. Baby or no baby, we *can* do it if we *have* to.

If you have time demands too pressing to handle, review some of the time management chapters. Often, though, this is a signal that your schedule needs to be modified. Are your standards too high? Can you skip something or maybe improve your methods? Things will run much more smoothly if your space systems are "go." So let's get ready for liftoff.

CLOSE ENCOUNTERS

As I mentioned before, when Baby (and all the baby gear) comes home, you certainly experience close encounters of the crowded kind. Early on I learned to do without in order to conserve space. We've raised five kids without a playpen, a dressing table, walkers, indoor swings, baby bathtubs or bassinettes. Actually, we've managed quite well with a crib, high chair, small chest of drawers and an expanding tension baby gate. So when you're reading through those baby care books and notice the long lists of necessities, be advised—you honestly don't need half that stuff!

If the walls are closing in on you, look around and decide just how much you could live without. Oh sure, those extras (playpens, dressing tables, bassinettes, etc.) are nice to have around, but if lack of space is seriously disrupting the family operation, then these frills are luxuries you cannot afford. Besides, many of these products are only useful for such a short time, you have store them more than you use them.

I enjoy the freedom of wide open uncluttered rooms and unencumbered storage areas. For me, those benefits far outweigh the limited use I receive from the additional equipment.

Here are some baby-care tips that will not only help you make the most of your space, they may even save you some time.

• There are many varieties of infant bathtubs on the market. (One is especially handy-looking and fits right over the kitchen sink.) But here's an idea that will give you double use out of something you probably already have: a dishpan is perfect for a young baby's bathtub. It, too, will fit in the sink and keep you from bending over.

A rectangular laundry basket can be set in a regular bathtub that's filled with about four inches of water. The basket acts as a cage to keep the baby from slipping away.

A shower stall can also function as a shallow bathtub. Cover the drain with a flat circular rubber drain stopper and turn on the shower. (It will hold a few inches of water.) Of course, you'll be on your hands and knees to bathe the baby, but it's good exercise, and think of all the space you'll save by not having a baby tub lying around. (This hint is especially helpful when you're traveling or visiting; just pack a drain stopper with the rest of your supplies.)

• If necessary, you can tote the bathing supplies (soap, lotion, shampoo, towel, brush, diaper pins, etc.) to the bathing area in a cleaning caddy, bucket or the kind of cardboard tote used to hold eight beverage bottles.

• A crib makes a safe dressing table. Whenever the baby needs a change, put a flannelized rubber mat on the crib sheet and lay the baby on top of it. That way the sheet will stay clean and dry. A plastic Frisbee is a good item to keep close by; it's great for holding the wet or soiled diaper while you're changing the baby. The Frisbee is easy to wash and reuse. (Keep one in the diaper bag, too.)

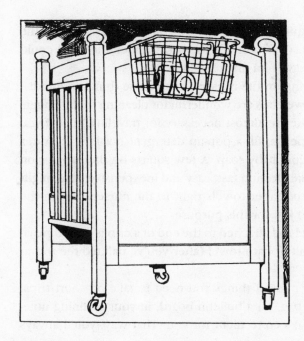

A bike basket fastened to the end of a crib makes a handy storage spot for frequently used baby goods.

Supplies can be close at hand if you attach a bicycle basket to the wall or the crib headboard. (You may have to move this when the child is old enough to reach it.) Supplies could also be kept in a pocketed shoe bag, on top of a dresser, under the crib in a train case, in a diaper bag or wherever it's convenient.

If you live in a house with more than one level, have diaper changing supplies on every floor.

A sturdy card table can also be used as a dressing table. Cover the

A fitted cover turns an ordinary card table into a dressing table for baby.

table with a colorful quilted pad and store your supplies right on the table; there's still plenty of room for the baby. (Since the child could easily roll off, never leave him unattended.)

When you're stocking up the nursery, keep these things in mind:

• Premoistened towelettes are wonderful for cleaning sticky fingers or the diaper area. (They're almost necessary for traveling.) But if you want to avoid the expense, fill a pop-up detergent bottle with water and a few drops of liquid baby soap. A few squirts on the baby or on a paper towel will make cleanup fast, easy and inexpensive. You might want to mount a roll of paper towels right in the nursery (or on the headboard of the crib) just for this purpose.

• A curtain or towel rod attached to the end of a crib is a good place to hang the baby's quilt or bath towel (after you've painted the rod to match, of course).

• Make up a master list of things you need to take on short trips. Keep it in the diaper bag, on a bulletin board, in your planning notebook or anywhere that's convenient for you. That way, you'll always be prepared.

• Are you using a diaper stacker for your cloth diapers? If so, remove all the diapers and lay an ice cube bin on its side right on the bottom of the stacker. Put the diapers back in, piling them on top of the ice cube bin. Next, take all the plastic pants and put them into the ice cube bin. Now you have a divider/dispenser for diapers and plastic pants.

• If some of your liquid baby supplies are in screw-top containers, transfer the contents to ketchup dispensers, liquid soap pump dispens-

A diaper stacker also dispenses plastic pants. Put an ice cube bin lying on its side on the bottom of the diaper stacker and fill it with plastic pants. Stack the cloth diapers on top of the ice cube bin.

ers or pop-top detergent bottles. You can apply the liquid with one hand while the other holds the baby. (Be sure to label the new containers.)

The Lowdown on High Chairs

A high chair can be cleaned easily if you let it sit in a hot shower for a few minutes, or take it outside and hose it down. If you have a wooden high chair, toss a machine-washable nonslip cover over the high chair before the baby sits down to eat. That way, all you'll have to hand wash is the tray. Save a few old newspapers to spread under the high chair when the baby is first beginning to feed himself; baby food (especially cereal) is like cement after it's dry, making cleanup possible only with an air hammer. The newspapers will save you a lot of grief. If the seat of the high chair is slippery, apply some bathtub decals to the seat and the child will sit more securely. Or, use a piece of rubber mesh bar mat on the seat. This shelf liner (sold under brand names of Easy Liner or Firm Liner) is available at discount stores everywhere.

If you need a high chair when visiting, open a low kitchen drawer and put a cookie sheet or bread board across the top. Now you've got a low table for the child to sit right up to. If there's a slide-out bread board in the kitchen, just pull it out and sit the child on a bar stool (one with a back support). For safety's sake strap the child to the stool (using a belt) and do not leave him unattended.

Et cetera

• Rectangular laundry baskets can be used for infant baby beds. Put a slab of soft foam in the bottom and line the basket with pretty fabric. Your newborn can sleep peacefully wherever you go.

• If your grocery store doesn't have shopping carts with child safety belts, take a belt with you when grocery shopping and use that as a seat belt.

• Cut the baby's nails when he's asleep and give him his liquid vitamins when he's in the bathtub.

• If you're tired of folding diapers, after the child weighs twenty pounds or so, just fold each diaper to the desired size and sew. After every wash, they'll be all ready to go. (This idea is only useful, of course, if you don't plan to use the diapers for your next baby.)

• Tie an unused rubber teething ring to the end of the string on a pull toy. It makes the toy easier to pull and the child can't choke on it.

• To avoid changing the crib sheet during the night, make up the bed in layers: mattress, waterproof pad, sheet, waterproof pad, sheet. When the top sheet is wet, just peel it off, remove the pad, and reveal a dry, warm sheet underneath.

• Tube socks or knee socks are long, warm mittens for a young toddler.

• If the baby's bedroom is upstairs and you find yourself running up and down in the middle of the night to warm bottles, try this. Upstairs, keep a few bottles on ice and heat them in an electric bottle warmer when needed. (Or heat up some water in a percolator and warm the bottle in the hot water.)

• After the baby is dressed for an outing, slip some sleepers over his clothing. That way he'll stay clean until it's time to go.

• The tiny hair rollers made for dolls are perfect for short, baby-fine hair. Keep a hair clip in the kitchen to clip up long hair while tying on a bib.

• Tension gates convert entire rooms into playpens or isolate an older child who doesn't want the baby to disturb him. Just stretch the gate across the doorway and the "playpen" is ready. Also, the baby can watch the surrounding activity.

• It wasn't until our fourth child was born that I discovered child-proof doorknob covers and they are the greatest thing since plastic. (As a matter of fact, they *are* plastic.) They slip over your existing doorknob and snap shut. In order to open the door you have to push in while turning. They keep youngsters out of any forbidden room! (These are very inexpensive and usually found in the baby section of most larger stores.)

• An empty Pringles potato chip can holds three jars of baby food. It's a good container for traveling.

• Cut a plastic placemat to fit the high chair tray. It'll make clean-up easier.

• Let your toddler or young child wear an underwater face mask or a pair of goggles while you're shampooing his hair. He'll be more cooperative knowing he won't get soap or water in his eyes.

• If you're taking a toddler or young child to a sit-down event (like the movies or a ball game, etc.) bring a booster chair so the child can see what's going on.

The sum total of my advice is first: Relax. Don't expect so much of yourself and you'll enjoy your baby that much more. Realize that it will take longer to accomplish daily routine tasks and accept it as a matter of course.

Second: Don't overburden your living quarters with too much equipment. Less is better in the long run. You'll save money in the first place simply by not purchasing any unnecessary accoutrements and you'll save again by eliminating repair and replacement costs. And the fewer your possessions, the smaller your space requirements.

Remember, the purpose of homemaking is to provide a warm, comfortable place for the people who live there, so don't be overly concerned with keeping up appearances for the neighbors. Just free up your space and free up your time and you'll be free to relish moments with your baby, the greatest force in the world.

CHAPTER SEVENTEEN

There's Nothing to Do!

The arrival of summer has nothing to do with meteorology. You'll know summer is here when:

1. The morning is only two hours old and already you have refereed five bouts, bandaged three knees, removed six splinters and driven around the block looking for the baby who toddled away.

2. You begin to understand what the world hunger crisis is all about because the first words you hear every morning and every fifteen minutes thereafter are, "I'm starved!"

3. Despite your best efforts, the house always looks messy, the dishes are always piled in the sink and the bikes are always in the driveway (usually right behind the car).

4. The kids never have anything to do, and what is available to do is either too expensive, boring or "gross."

If any of these symptoms persist, read this chapter immediately. While these problems can crop up at any time during the year, they seem to run rampant during the summer, so I'll address them in that context. At first, I'm going to outline the program we used when our five children were young. Because of jobs, day care, year-round schools, etc., you may not be able to incorporate this exact system. However, this chapter has so many ideas, it will be useful for any time the kids are bored or generally unmotivated. The basic system will still work effectively if you modify and mold it to your particular situation.

Identify the Problem

Before you can solve any problem, you have to isolate and define it. When I first set out to do something about our hectic summertimes, here's what I wanted to change:

1. The kids were always in a hurry to get outside to play and they

didn't eat a good breakfast.

2. When lunchtime rolled around, I had to find everyone and drag them (usually kicking and screaming) inside.
3. By early afternoon they were bored which led to quarreling and constant eating.
4. I could never get or keep the house clean with the kids and their friends running in and out all day long.

One afternoon I was complaining to Jim that I was getting nowhere with the housework. He said, "Why don't you just send all the kids outside for awhile?" So I drove everyone out of the house and stood by the door counting heads. Ten little boys walked outside and only three of them were mine! No wonder I wasn't getting anywhere.

With the complaints listed, I began to think of ways to combat and conquer them. What I finally came up with was this main rule: No one was allowed to play outside before 11:30 A.M. That would give us time for housework and a good breakfast and lunch.

When the children were little I hung a bee on the front door. It was made of construction paper and contained the following message: "Sorry, kids, we're busy as bees, come back later if you please."

The children's friends soon learned that as long as the bee was on the door, the kids couldn't play. There were many times I'd see several children just sitting in the front yard, waiting for me to take the bee off the door.

Basically, this one simple rule—no outside play before 11:30— solved every summertime problem I was having. Even boredom was relieved because the kids weren't getting started with their play until after lunch.

For a few years when I was extremely ambitious and home most of the time, I took this rule one step further. I decided to assign each day a special activity. For example, Mondays we'd read a chapter in a book. Tuesday was library day; we'd go to the library, then wade in the stream nearby. Wednesday mornings we went to the park. Thursdays we went to PTA movies and Fridays we went grocery shopping and baked a treat.

Making Changes

The purpose of these activities was to structure the free time before 11:30 and to keep the kids' minds somewhat stimulated. Perhaps you need to modify this arrangement.

One family I heard of sets aside one morning a week for an activity.

Another is *Mom's* activity day; the kids take over and Mom takes off.

One of our friends (a working parent) leaves structured activities (math fact sheets, craft projects, books to read) and a list of household chores for the kids to do in the morning. As motivation for completed assignments, the kids have their afternoons free and a planned family activity on the weekend.

If that sounds too demanding, try a project or activity once a month. Particularly if you're a working and/or single parent, remember when you've done *one* thing, you've done *something*.

IDEAS FOR FAMILY FUN

Here's a list of ideas to galvanize your interest:

- Arts and Crafts. Some of our favorite projects have been working with plaster, making baskets, leather work, models, painting rocks and leaves, and printing with potatoes, rubber bands glued to wooden blocks, Styrofoam meat trays or thumbprints. We've made simple piñatas, jointed puppets from small boxes and string, and toys out of cork and papier maché. We've sculpted things using modeling clay or shredded wheat clay (thin some white glue and pour it over crushed shredded wheat, adding just enough glue to make the mixture manageable).

- *Science and Nature.* Try some simple experiments using common kitchen ingredients. There are a lot of books in the library that tell you how. Scholastic Books *Magic School Bus* series teaches everything from butterfly camouflage to decomposition. Here are two others to check out: Baron's *Science Wizardry for Kids*, and Reader's Digest *How Science Works*.

  Build a solar cooker out of posterboard. Collect insects, identify them and glue them to posterboard. Visit a planetarium, aquarium or zoo. Eat breakfast in a canyon, forest preserve or local park. Look for animal tracks and make plaster casts of them. Stargaze, learn about the environment, develop a recycling hobby or go on a hike.

  Become a bird-watcher. Set up a birdbath: Place a garbage can lid on some rocks and fill it with water. Prepare an after-bath feast of uncooked oatmeal, cracked corn, popped corn, bread and cracker crumbs, or oranges cut in half. Save the fat you trim from meat, hang it from trees in paper cups or mesh bags or pack it in pine cones. Hummingbirds will drink sugar water from a narrow pill bottle tied to a sturdy plant.

- *History*. Study lives and events recorded in history. Visit a pioneer museum and antique shops. Climb a mountain, explore a "new" frontier, pull honey taffy, make slingshots from tree branches and pellets from natural clay. Visit local historical sites, and study the history of your city and state. Visit the state capitol building.

- *Reading*. Go through the classics with your kids—one chapter at a time. Get library cards for everybody and visit the library often. There were times we paid one of our "I hate to read" kids one cent for every page he read. He became a reader, but we kept encouraging him to read by purchasing a new book for him when he finished the one he was reading.

   One family I know makes their children buy their own books; when the books are read, the parents refund the purchase price.

- *Food*. Go through your cookbooks (some cookbooks are written especially for children) and choose some simple recipes to start with. Make letter pretzels, mold a gelatin salad, decorate a cake, cut out rolled cookies, bake a pie, stir up a batch of granola or dry some beef jerky. Not only will the kids be having a good learning experience, you'll be training your employees!

- *Work*. "Work is the greatest wonder drug ever devised by God" (Dr. Orlando Battista). Older children (especially young teenagers) get bored easily. They're too young to drive, and usually too poor to do everything they want to do. To them, the thought of doing a little craft project ranks right up there with sweeping the driveway. Work is one answer to the problem of boredom.

   In their book *Fast Cash for Kids* (Career Press), Bonnie and Noel Drew outline 101 moneymaking ideas complete with business forms and worksheets. Another book with money-making ideas, plus advice on teaching kids about money is *Kids, Money and Values* from Betterway Books.

   Or, try time-tested things like baby-sitting, newspaper routes and door-to-door sales of candy, calendars and cards. If the children act in a professional and responsible manner they can build up their business quickly. There are some excellent books available on baby-sitting that will guarantee your child a corner on the market—if they follow the advice. Try *Kid Sitter Basics* (Westpoint Publishers) by Celeste Stuhring, R.N. She gives information on setting up a baby-sitting business, changing a diaper, getting kids to bed, getting them to cooperate, first aid and just about anything a sitter might encounter.

   The work itself eliminates some of the boredom, and the money the work generates eliminates the rest of it!

There's More

Work on scout requirements (even non-scouts like to be involved). Another organization, 4-H, supplies you with ideas and instruction for just about any subject you can think of. Start an exercise program or work on service projects (visit a convalescent center, invite a lonely child over for a day of play, pick some flowers for the widower down the street). Organize a neighborhood "art" gallery, parade, talent or hobby show.

To this day I remember fondly the neighborhood Fourth of July parades we had when I was a little girl. Every year, our next-door neighbor would round up all the neighborhood kids and we'd march down the street twirling batons, riding decorated bicycles or banging pan lids together.

This is certainly not a do-all, end-all list of ideas, but perhaps you're getting the point. There are thousands of things you can do if you'll just take the time.

Let's face it: We each have to spend a lot of time with our kids. We can spend it arguing, ignoring or disciplining them or we can use a few moments here and there for constructive activities. It takes less time in the long run to be actively engaged with the kids. Leaving children entirely to their own resources can be very time-consuming when you have to deal with the consequences!

But even if you can't be with your kids all day (or don't want to be), you can keep them busy and out of trouble.

Here's how. Consider summer school, basketball (or whatever) camp, YMCA day camp and city recreational centers.

Call your PTA. Sometimes they offer classes, arts and crafts activities and lessons through the local schools.

We had a great summer program when I was in school. One summer I learned to twirl the baton, braid boondoggle, squaredance, do woodburning and play field hockey. Most school districts offer various classes or programs children can participate in.

Every so often have an old-fashioned day at home. On this day no TV or video games are allowed, though radios are OK. Play board games, marbles, jacks or hopscotch. Jump rope, tell stories, bike ride or go on a nature walk. Have a taffy pull. Sit on the porch and sip lemonade or play musical chairs in the backyard. However, instead of using chairs, use dishpans filled with water. When the music stops, the kids have to sit in a dishpan of water.

CHECK YOUR SOURCES

If you're like me, you have the best of intentions, but when the actual "doing" comes, you start with the excuses. "We can't make puppets. I don't have any old socks." "We can't go to the beach. There's no gas in the car." "No, we can't bake anything. I'm out of flour."

The only way to see your good intentions through to fruition is to plan and stock up. This plan needn't be a rigid one—Monday, make rock people; Tuesday, bake bread. Just make a list of various arts, crafts, games and activities everyone would like to do. Then, stock up. Just as in menu planning, have all the ingredients on hand so your excuses will be voided. When you choose an activity from your list, you'll be able to complete it.

Start by gathering ideas. Head to the library. There are hundreds of books containing arts, crafts, simple science projects, hobbies, games— you name it. If you're not close to a library, check with your local school. Often they have many resources most of us never use (or even know about). If your particular school can't get any information for you, perhaps it's available through the school district.

Other sources to check: 4-H, your college extension office, bookstores (books are also available through mail order), magazines, people (talk to your friends, the preschool teacher or someone at the day-care center) and television.

Whenever I run across an idea that looks or sounds interesting, I jot it down, photocopy it or rip it out (of a magazine) and put it in a looseleaf notebook. After years of this practice, we now have an activity book filled with hundreds of pages of ideas—ideas that are especially interesting to our family. It's actually a customized book. What a resource! We use the book for planned and spontaneous activities. When I'm scheduling arts and crafts, for instance, we thumb through the book and choose a few ideas. Then we jot down any materials we need to pick up so everything will be ready when we need it. When the kids are bored, they get the book and choose something they can do independently.

Once you've got a cache of ideas, get a large cardboard box in which to toss cardboard tubes from paper towels and bathroom tissue, pieces of Styrofoam, cork, string, wire, wood scraps, small boxes—anything you can use for a chosen craft or activity.

Of course, you'll also need to keep a running supply of paper, crayons, paint, markers, construction paper, scissors, glue, tape and so on. For my money, these are investments worth making because they keep the kids happy and occupied at *home*.

Following is a list of materials you can get free (or for a nominal cost) and the places to contact. If you need things that aren't on this list, look through the yellow pages. A few phone calls will probably lead you right to the needed source.

Aluminum scraps—window, storm door and siding companies

Appliances (moving parts from)—junkyards, scrap metal companies

Bottle caps—bottling companies

Boxes—restaurants, paper companies, quick copy shops, grocery stores, department stores, packaging companies

Bricks (damaged)—contractors, building supply companies, lumberyards

Buttons—dry cleaners, tailors, garment factories

Cardboard—same sources as boxes; also, bottling companies have large tubes available

Carpet pieces and swatches—carpet companies, department stores (the ones that have custom decorating services)

Circuit boards (printed)—electronics manufacturers

Clothing trim scraps (rickrack, lace, ribbon, braid, etc.)—textile companies, garment factories

Concrete blocks (damaged)—contractors, building supplies, lumberyards

Corks—restaurants

Crates—grocery stores, outdoor markets

Cups—airlines

Doweling—contractors, building supply companies, lumberyards, furniture factories, hardware stores, upholsterers, cabinetmakers

Electronic components (discarded)—electronics manufacturers

Fabric scraps—upholsterers, textile companies, department stores, garment factories

Formica—contractors, building supply companies, lumberyards, hardware stores, cabinet makers, plastic companies

Gears—junkyards, scrap metal companies

Hangers—dry cleaners, tailors

Ice cream containers—restaurants, ice cream stores

Leather scraps and lacings—leather manufacturers

Linoleum—hardware stores, contractors, building supply companies, carpet companies, floor covering companies, department stores

Lumber scraps—contractors, building supply companies,

lumberyards, etc. (see Doweling)

Molding—(see Doweling)

Paint swatch cards—contractors, building supply companies, lumberyards, hardware stores, wallpaper and paint stores

Paper—paper companies, newspaper printing offices, printers

Pipes—contractors, building supply companies, hardware stores

Plastic curlings, scraps, trimmings, tubing—plastic companies

Plexiglas—plastic companies

Sawdust—(see Doweling)

Spools (industrial strength for cable)—telephone company, electric power company

Styrofoam packing—electronics manufacturers, department stores, packaging companies, appliance stores

Tiles—tile companies, floor covering companies, cabinetmakers

Wallpaper—contractors, building supply companies, lumberyards, wallpaper and paint stores

Wheels—junkyards

Wire scraps—contractors, building supply companies, electronics manufacturers, lumberyards, hardware stores, junkyards, scrap metal companies, electric power company

Wood curls and scraps—(see Doweling)

Yarn scraps—garment factories, textile companies

If you've got a lot of empty places to stash this stuff, you can collect and store it to your heart's content. (I don't take great pains here, though. We just toss the stuff in labeled cardboard cartons.)

When space is limited, you'll need to plan your projects in advance and collect the materials as you need them.

Special Activities

Every once in a while I absolutely *have* to have cooperation from the kids (when I'm doing a radio interview by long-distance phone; when I'm getting ready for a party; when I'm putting the finishing touches on a big church assignment). Then I reach into my bag of tricks and let the kids do a special activity. I only have a few of these, but I rely on them so rarely they're always effective and entertaining (and they keep the kids busy, quiet and out of my way).

One such activity is to let the kids play with cracked wheat or corn-meal. I have a large can of each reserved strictly for playing. They dump the grain into a big baking pan and drive their cars through it; they stand up little animals and small dolls in it; they use funnels, sieves, spoons and cups and have a lot of fun. It's clean and easily cleaned up with a broom or vacuum cleaner.

Another favorite is "puff art." (Since using an oven is necessary for this, be sure an older child is supervising, if you're not around.) You make a smooth paste out of 1 cup flour and ¾ to 1 cup water. Then you dip cotton balls into the mixture coating thoroughly (don't wring them out). The kids make letters, animals, snakes, numbers, flowers, or designs by placing the wet cotton balls on a lightly oiled or no-stick cookie sheet. When the design is finished, put the cookie sheet into a 300° oven and bake for one hour. The design (or whatever) comes out hard and dry, all ready for painting.

If I know something important is coming up (like the radio interview), I plan for it and have things ready for the kids to do.

One lifesaver is to go to an appliance store and get some Styrofoam packing forms. (They are molded to the shape of the appliance, which makes them perfect for spaceships, dollhouses, boats, robots, cars, miniature army bases and forts, whatever.) When I bring home a few of these Styrofoam pieces and send the kids down to their room to play, I don't see them for hours!

Anyone can be an impressionist when they do sandpaper art. Using crayons, color a picture on a piece of fine-grained sandpaper. Press hard. When the picture is completed, place it face down on white paper (or light-colored construction paper). Next, apply a warm iron to the back side of the sandpaper for fifteen to twenty seconds. Do not remove the sandpaper for an additional thirty seconds. Then remove the sandpaper and reveal the impressionist drawing. Follow up this activity with a trip to the art museum.

A magazine scavenger hunt is a good activity that will give you some uninterrupted time. Pass out some old magazines to the children and some age-appropriate scissors. Then tell them to cut out everything they find that starts with the letter *D*, for example. Or, you can make up a list of things to look for.

Special activities are effective when they're held in reserve and used only on occasion. If the child is free to do the activity whenever he likes, there's no fascination with the project and it loses its punch.

Try these ideas, and discover others to hold your kids' interest during those moments when quiet cooperation is mandatory!

"I'M STARVED"

Summertime starvation is a common complaint around here, and it's not just the kids who are whining. Often the plants, the pets and the sourdough starter have to beg for food, too.

During the summer of my discontent when I started making changes, I began with our breakfasts. I started fixing good, nourishing breakfasts every morning. (So the kids would still feel in touch with the world, I saved the cold cereals for after-school and bedtime snacks.) With a good breakfast under their belts, the kids easily make it to lunchtime.

Lunches can be made and bagged right after breakfast, so no further preparation or cleanup is necessary. Many times I serve cafeteria-style lunches, too, fixing each child whatever kind of a sandwich he wants. It takes a little extra time to do this, but if the kids eat what they feel like eating, they eat better and afternoon snacking isn't such a problem.

It's a long stretch, though, between lunch and dinner, and I don't expect the kids to make it without something in between. Sometimes, after the kids are in bed, I make up a batch of cookie dough and stick it in the refrigerator overnight. The next day it only takes a few minutes to bake up the dough. Also, rolling and decorating sugar cookies is a good activity for kids with nothing to do.

For more nutritious after-lunch snacks, fill an ice bucket, Styrofoam chest or small camping cooler with ice and favorite snacks. Try carrot and other vegetable sticks, hard-boiled eggs, slices of cheese and chunks of meat wrapped up in plastic or foil, melon or other fruit chunks (in a plastic or glass container) and anything else that comes to mind. Top this off with a basket of rolls or crackers and you have satisfied kids with very little hassle.

Another idea is to give each child a bag or box filled with things you'll let him snack on between lunch and dinner. When his bag is empty, he has to wait until dinner for anything else. If he wants to share his goodies with all the neighborhood kids, that's fine, but when the sack is empty, it's empty.

An insulated jug (preferably one with a spigot) filled with ice water or fruit juice can sit on the counter next to a stack of disposable cups to allow the kids to help themselves. (Keep it on the back porch and you'll eliminate a lot of traffic running in and out.)

My good friend Sherrill went to a bottled water company and purchased a used refrigerated water cooler to keep in her garage. The jug holds five gallons of water (which she fills from her tap), so her children have a constant supply of cold water without running inside, tracking up the floor or interrupting her. (The cooler, jug and cup dispenser cost under $70.)

I hope I haven't painted too rosy a picture in this chapter. No matter what you do, kids will still be hungry, bored and unmotivated at times.

But, with a plan and a stock of supplies and ideas, those times will be fewer.

Occasionally your projects will flop. One such disaster for us was making a device called a "whizzer." We were guaranteed this toy would race across the floor, twisting and turning. Our whizzer, however, went around in circles a few times, hardly what I'd call racing, twisting and turning.

And that's only one example. I could cite many just like it. There have been times, too, when everything seemed to go wrong. One day when an activity was in progress, the baby pulled the paint off the table, Brian slipped off his chair and broke a vase and at that very moment the doorbell rang. The nice man on the other side of the screen apologized for hitting our dog with his motorcycle. While I was straightening up the mess and comforting the frightened dog, I began to wonder if it had all been worth it. But I knew my time had been well spent when Brian said, "Thanks for helping me make my puppet, Mom. You have good ideas."

Yes, I've found many rewards (though they've come in small and simple ways) from spending a little extra time with our children. Actually, kids are like pop bottles: no deposit, no return.

CHAPTER EIGHTEEN

On the Road Again: Family Travel Tips

After traveling (without Dad) in a compact car from Wisconsin to Utah with three kids under six, a dog and four philodendrons, I gave myself an honorary degree in traveling with children. Not only that, I figure I must have fulfilled all the requirements for at least thirteen merit badges (among them Emergency Preparedness, Lifesaving, Bugling and Wildlife Management). With the training and experience I received negotiating dibs for window seats, stalling off full bladders until the next rest stop and shouting threats that would frighten a terrorist, I'm sure I could negotiate peace in any "hot spot" on the planet.

But, after years of healing, I can recall the trials of that trip without pain, realizing that now I know what it takes to make our family trips more enjoyable and relaxing. Let me share a few pointers to guarantee smoother sailing on your next family outing.

As soon as you've decided on a destination, do some homework. Contact a travel agent, your auto club, major oil companies, etc., as sources for literature and maps to help you make the most of your trip. Write to the Chamber of Commerce of cities you're planning to visit to learn about town activities or interesting sights. Write to the state travel bureau (in the capital city) for similar information. Collect brochures and other literature about the areas you'll be traveling through. If you don't, you might miss some of the best sights. (Imagine our disappointment after traveling through Victorville, California, when we discovered we had missed seeing Trigger—Roy Rogers's trusty steed, now stuffed!) Stopping occasionally to visit a museum or other tourist attraction not only relieves boredom, you'll get a little exercise and education as well.

Weeks before your scheduled trip (or as soon as possible if you have short notice), begin making a list of things you want to take. When you think of something, jot it down and you won't forget it. Your list then saves you from repeating the immortal line, "I know I've forgotten something!'' This list also comes in handy when you're returning home, because a quick review lets you know if you're leaving something behind. (Although this will dry up a good source of excitement, because now you won't be receiving packages in the mail containing all your forgotten belongings.)

When you return home, file your list away, and next time a trip comes up you have a tried-and-true list to serve as a starting point. Of course, there might be a few variables, but a master list saves precious hours by giving you a basic foundation. Why waste time making a list for every trip when your file can do it for you?

If you're going camping, a permanently filed list is especially beneficial. There are so many things to take on a camping trip, it makes good sense to have a ready-made chart of necessities.

If you're traveling by car, I've learned the hard way that it's best to pack the car when the children are asleep or otherwise occupied. Excited children and a nervous mom and dad are sure to start any trip on a sour note. You can work faster, more effectively and with less tension when the kids aren't around to share their enthusiasm.

PACK IT IN

When you're ready to pack your suitcases, think small. Most people pack twice as much as they need under the guise of ''better safe than sorry.'' Unencumber your trip from the start by streamlining the number of things you take. In this case, less is more—less congestion and more freedom. You can always rinse things out if need be, or make a few purchases along the way.

Smaller suitcases allow you to locate things quickly, and without the rummaging required by larger pieces of luggage. Also, lightweight luggage is easier to handle and usually less expensive. Whatever type of luggage you use, make sure each suitcase is filled. Half-full bags allow the contents to shuffle, jumble and wrinkle.

When traveling (with children especially), it's a good idea to pack a small cloth folding bag. It won't take any extra room and will provide you with an extra case if you come home with more than you brought— pieces of Indian jewelry from the Southwest, salt and pepper shakers from Niagara Falls, seashells from the Pacific coast and new clothes and toys from Grandma.

As an alternative to luggage, purchase a lightweight (and inexpensive) fiberboard chest of drawers and pack your things in that. Give each person a drawer or two (you may need more than one chest) and store the units in the trunk of the car. Be sure the chests are lying down face up so the drawers won't fall out. If you hate living out of suitcases, this could be a solution.

However, if you opt for using suitcases, have one filled with a change or two of clothes for each person. That way when you stop for the night, you'll only have to bring in one suitcase, rather than the whole load. If you plan to stay in a motel, be sure the swimwear is handy so you won't have to sift through everything looking for swimsuits and robes.

Small pieces of luggage can be placed in the wells between the front and back seats. Place a plywood board (covered with quilt or blanket) over the luggage to make a larger play or sleep area.

If you're traveling with only one child, you might have room for some hanging storage in the backseat. Car closet rods are available commercially, or simply stretch a length of chain from one backseat clothing hook to the other. There you have an inexpensive clothing rod that takes up minimal space when it's not in use, and when hanging in the car it provides tangle-free storage for hangers and easy access to clothes. It also keeps clothes wrinkle-free. A homemade pocket attached to the hanger holds matching belt, jewelry, hair ribbons, socks and any other accessory worn with each outfit.

A tote bag is an absolute necessity for holding shoes, socks, jackets or sweaters, which the kids *always* take off as soon as the wheels begin to roll. Now, when you stop for gas, dinner or a seventh-inning stretch, you won't have to start the mad scramble for the missing shoe and the socks that slipped between the crack in the backseat.

If you stop for short visits with friends or relatives, the tote bag again becomes a central depository that coops up all the clutter you drag in. If the kids are carefully instructed to toss in their shoes, jackets, toys or whatever, departure time will be quicker for you and painless for your host. (Miss Manners frowns upon guests who look under beds, couch cushions and refrigerators to find missing socks, car keys and pacifiers.)

Whenever you receive sample products through the mail, save them for traveling. They're small and usually packaged in unbreakable containers. Travel- or sample-sized products such as toothpaste, mouthwash, shampoo, conditioner, lotion, bandages, cotton swabs and aftershave are plentiful at discount stores or supermarkets. Or, transfer any other needed toiletries into the small plastic containers available at drug, discount and variety stores everywhere.

Dispensing prescription medicines while traveling is simplified by using compartmented pillboxes that have a space for every day of the week. That way you can see at a glance if the daily dosage has been taken. These little containers are inexpensive and easy to find in drug-stores or the pharmaceutical departments of supermarkets and variety stores.

Pack another useful item in your toiletry case—a small night-light. Whether you stay in a motel or with a friend or relative, the surround-ings are unfamiliar to your children. The night-light helps them find the bathroom, their slippers or a favorite teddy bear.

Also, be sure to include a few safety pins and a small thread and needle kit. Frequently the simplest, often overlooked items are the most useful!

ORGANIZED LIVING IN THE CAR

Consider the following when itemizing your list of things to bring along:

Have plenty of extra change for telephones, tolls, pay toilets, tips and vending machines.

Be sure you have current maps of the states you're traveling through. If it's an unfamiliar route, attach the highway directions to your visor with a snap-type clothespin (or use a sticky note).

Washcloths make economical and washable throw pillows for car travel. Hold two washcloths together, stitch around three sides, stuff with polyester fiberfill, stitch up the fourth side, and you have a wash-able pillow for traveling—great for trips to the beach, too.

If you do bring your bed pillows, however, don't forget to pack a few extra pillowcases. Because of sticky fingers, sandy shoes, melted chocolate and french fry sauce, the need for extra pillow slips will soon be apparent.

Speaking of sticky fingers, no trip should begin without a supply of premoistened towelettes, a roll of paper towels or a wet washcloth sealed in a plastic bag. To make paper toweling more convenient, cut the roll in half so it's only half as wide. That way it's easier to keep in the glove compartment, under the front seat or in a remote corner somewhere.

An old metal or plastic lunch pail makes an ideal first aid kit con-tainer. Keep it in your car stocked with essentials.

Take along a few zip-type plastic bags. They keep souvenir rocks, seashells, folded inflatable beach toys and sandals from "sharing" the sand and surf with other packed items. The bags are also useful for carrying wet swimsuits and delicate souvenirs.

Maybe a collection box would cut down on debris. Kids love to save packets of sugar and ketchup, soap and shower caps from motels, postcards, rocks, seashells, empty plastic ice cream dishes, stickers and all types of mementos; a collection box pens up all this stuff.

How about a scrapbook? Pack up an empty scrapbook and every evening paste, tape or otherwise mount the day's collection (photos, postcards, wrappers, drawings, personal notes, etc.).

Have a small diary available for anyone who's willing to make an entry. When your journey is over, you'll have a complete journal of your trip from everyone's point of view. Or, include diary pages in your trip scrapbook.

A laminated card (or other ID) with the following information should be made for each child: the child's name, parents' names, address and phone number, and the address and phone number of the place you're staying. Every morning this identification should be pinned or otherwise secured inside the child's pocket. Should the child become injured or lost, he will be properly identified. (You might want to do this for yourself, too.)

A shoe bag or other pocketed container can hang over the back of the front seat to hold road maps, snacks, entertainment material for the kids, postcards, tourist information, baby bottles, diapers or whatever. It provides easy-access, one-motion storage.

A cake pan with a sliding or snapping metal lid is an extremely functional lap desk and holds coloring books, crayons, dolls and doll clothes, paper dolls, souvenirs, storybooks, etc. It keeps the kids busy and gives them a special place to keep all their belongings in one well-confined area.

Another idea is to hang a clothespin bag on one of the clothing hooks in the back seat. This bag will hold wet wipes, paperbacks, a few snacks, Kleenex, etc., and is especially helpful if you're traveling with a baby. Infants require many extras the clothespin bag keeps up out of the way and within easy reach.

For a disposable bib, make one just like your dentist uses: take a piece of yarn or ribbon (about five inches long for a young child) and tie a small paper clamp to each end. Or, use an alligator clamp. (These clamps are inexpensive and available at hardware stores and home improvement centers.) Clamp a paper towel, napkin or disposable diaper (plastic side next to the child) to one clip, put the ribbon around the back of the child's neck and clamp the other side of the towel. When the bib is dirty, just replace the paper towel. These were so handy when our kids were young I kept one of these bibs in the car.

At the top of your "to bring" list should be some kind of trash

A shoe bag mounted on the back of a car seat becomes a receptacle for often-used travel aids.

receptacle. Have one in front and one in back and empty them every time you stop. That one little act will do more to cut down on car clutter than any other single thing!

Whenever you leave a motel, grab a matchbook or a piece of stationery. That way, should you forget something, you have the address and phone number of the establishment. Usually, lost-and-found items are labeled and stored for ninety days, after which time they're given away or disposed of.

Just for fun, before you leave on your trip, write the addresses of your friends (and your kids' friends) on self-adhesive labels. While you're traveling, just peel off a label and stick it to a postcard. The kids enjoy this activity and friends love to be remembered. (Some folks keep an old phone book in their car to help them find home-town addresses.)

After returning home from your vacation, head to the Laundromat. Mountains of laundry can be finished in an hour and a half—much faster than the load-at-a-time method at home.

FINGER-LICKING GOOD

Eating in the car can wreak havoc with the best-laid organizational plan. Just the sight of greasy french fries under the rubber floor mats, spilled milk shakes dripping down the upholstery, chicken bones carelessly

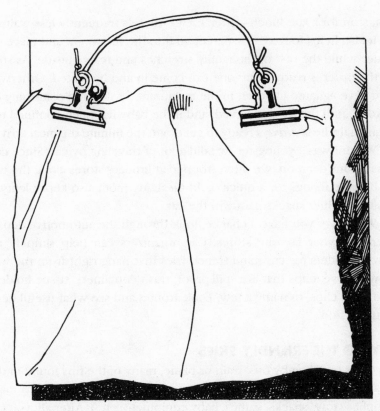

Make a disposable bib from two small paper clamps, a piece of yarn and a paper towel.

dropped in a stray shoe, and the pickles, mustard and lettuce someone scraped off his hamburger would discourage even Horatio Alger. But here are a few ideas for you to try.

The most obvious suggestion is to take your fast-food meal to a park or rest area and keep the mess out of the car. Stretching, exercising, and inhaling fresh air is good for everyone—especially for the driver and active children.

If you don't want to take the time to stop, try giving each child a plastic shoe box. These help the children hold and balance their entire meal without continually asking for help. The high sides of the container eliminate spilling, but should something overturn, the mess will be contained in the shoe box. After eating, wipe out the containers, stack them and slide them under the front seat.

If you eat in restaurants, you might want to have your big meal at lunchtime. Luncheon menus are generally less expensive than dinner menus, and cost is usually a factor when you travel with children. If you stop for a late lunch—after 1 P.M.—there's frequently less waiting.

It also helps to have one parent go into the restaurant and place the order while the rest of the family stretches and rests outside. As soon as the order is ready, everyone can come in and be seated. Otherwise you have agitated children in the restaurant fussing and disturbing everyone until the food is served, and if the baby has been confined to a high chair, he is *always* ready to get down the minute the meal arrives.

When I was a youngster, we did a lot of traveling by car. Since cost was a consideration, we often stopped at grocery stores along the way to buy the fixings for a quick, cold meal. My mom also kept plenty of fruit and other snacks handy in the car.

Whenever you have a chance, look through the automotive departments in your favorite stores. Car organizers can help simplify car travel: holders for cups and french fries that hang right from the window groove; cups that are spill-proof; trash containers; tissue holders; and visor clips, to name a few. Look around and see what useful items you can find.

FLYING THE FRIENDLY SKIES

If you're traveling by bus, train or plane, many of the tips found in this chapter are still valid. However, you won't have easy access to many supplies (toys, snacks, games, baby equipment, etc.). After all, you can only carry on so much, right?

Pack a small carry-on bag with the bare necessities and be sure to include something to entertain the kids. (Some specific suggestions are coming up and many of them require little or no room.)

Be sure the children have their ID cards. This is especially important for bus travel, because the children are getting on and off the bus every so often. Air travel, too, has a few special peculiarities you should consider before you leave. First and foremost, use a travel agent. Agents have the knowledge and skills necessary to get you where you want to go, when you want to get there and at the cheapest rate! Many people mistakenly believe travel agencies are expensive. Not so! Rates are the same whether you use a travel agent or not.

Let your travel agent know what you want. Tell them you're traveling with children—there may be special discounts and/or services. Children's meals can be requested, usually at least six hours before departure. Specify direct flights or connecting flights with minimum delay. In larger cities there's usually more than one airport; tell your agent you prefer to land at the least busy airport in the city of final destination. (The last time I flew to Los Angeles everyone laughed or groaned when

I said I had flown into L.A. International. Yes, the Orange County airport is about an hour away—but at LAX it took us two hours to get back to the car!) On business trips, of course, this advice might not be practical, but when you're dragging your family along, it could be a lifesaver!

Keep in mind, also, the hour of your arrival or departure. Will there be rush-hour slow-ups or delays? If you can't avoid them, at least allow yourself extra time.

Flying first class with children would be delightful (I can only imagine), but if that's out of the question, there's extra leg room in bulkhead seats, on the aisles, and by the emergency exits. Ask your travel agent to preassign those seats to you, if possible. Children under the age of fifteen are not allowed to sit in a row with an emergency exit, though.

Also, be sure everyone uses the rest room before boarding the plane. On an airplane you can't pound your fist on the bathroom door, screaming at the occupant to hurry up (because "*this* is an emergency") like you do at home.

When checking your luggage, avoid checking it at the curb. While this is extremely tempting and seems convenient, your chances of losing your bags are far greater. When the ground attendant tags your baggage, be sure he puts the correct destination on it. If you see a big black ORD (Chicago's O'Hare Field) and you're going to Portland, you may be without clothes for a few days.

If you're traveling alone, carry-on luggage is great, but with the kids you might want to take on as little as possible, particularly if the children are small and need to be carried or held onto.

No matter what your mode of travel, a little forethought and careful planning make the experience so pleasant you'll be glad to do it again some day!

MANAGING TRAVEL TIME

"If you guys don't stop fighting, we're not going to Disneyland. How many times do I have to tell you?"

"Mom, Jimmy's touching me."

"Brian, if you don't let Steven sit by the window for a little while, I'm going to turn the car around and we're *all* going home."

"Jeff, please leave the baby alone. She does *not* like that stocking cap pulled over her face."

The foregoing is part of a script from many of our family vacations. But I just said that planning and forethought would make traveling with kids a pleasant experience. . . . It will. Trust me. Now that our surroundings are organized, we need a game plan.

Keep in mind nothing short of phenobarbital will turn red-blooded kids into sweet, calm, considerate angels, with their arms folded and heads bowed. Excitement and anticipation are half the fun on a trip— so let the kids expend their energies. Your job is to channel that energy. Here's how. Check through the following list of activities to see how many of them provoke your interest.

Weeks before your departure date, start to gather coloring books, crayons, arithmetic fact sheets, writing tablets, crayons, paper dolls, comic books, card games and anything else compact to occupy the kids' time. Check local bookstores, school supply stores, toy departments and office supply stores. You'll find all sorts of workbooks (math, science and reading, at least), word puzzle books, travel games and trivia books. If you're bringing video games, it's much less annoying if the sound can be turned down (or they're equipped with headphones). This is especially important if the children are using public transportation. Also, electronic games must be completely turned off during plane take-off and landing.

Don't forget the possibility of using children's magazines (*Highlights for Children, Sesame Street Magazine, Nickelodeon Magazine, Disney Adventures* to name a few). They have interesting stories and articles for the kids to read, quiet activities, riddles, hidden pictures, poems and other things that lend themselves nicely to travel. One magazine I highly recommend is *The Friend* (a Christian children's publication), 50 E. North Temple St., Salt Lake City, UT 84150.

When we travel with the kids I keep all these materials inside their cake pans. The surprise contents are waiting when we start. (I've always wondered which the kids enjoy more—opening their cake pans or going on the trip!)

The cake pans keep things running smoothly for a while. But when the novelty wears off, it's time for your backup plan. Have a box or tote bag filled with things to pull out when the need arises. Keep in mind that this is for your use only, to distribute at just the right moment. If the kids are allowed to rummage through your backup box, it will lose its effectiveness. Here are some ideas for your backup plan:

Separate little bags filled with dried fruit, marshmallows (large and small), raisins, O-shaped cereal, gumdrops and round toothpicks provide materials for edible creations. Let the kids build a monster, robot, space ship, building or solar system; then they can eat their grand designs. Edible jewelry can be made from string licorice and O-shaped cereal.

Small, inexpensive wrapped gifts can be distributed every two or three hours. New things seem to hold the kids' attention longer than old ones. If your budget won't permit the buying of a few new things, weeks before your trip, pull a few of the kids' toys out of circulation. When they reappear on the trip, they'll be like new. (Don't forget secondhand shops, cereal trinkets, free refund or send-in offers and garage sales as sources for inexpensive novelties.)

Or have these items wrapped and use them as grab-bag gifts. Have the kids pull out one a day, or one at breakfast and one after lunch.

Sewing cards take little space and promote quiet activity perfect for traveling. To make the cards yourself, simply mount coloring book pictures on heavy posterboard and punch holes around the picture. The picture can be "sewn" with a shoelace or piece of colorful yarn.

A small blackboard and dustless chalk are good for drawing pictures, playing hangman, tic-tac-toe, or for keeping track of letters and numbers in alphabet and counting games.

A ball (for use during rest stops) is great for helping the kids work off voltage.

A tape recorder provides hours of fun. Before our trips I purchase new storybooks, or dig out some old ones we haven't read for a while. Then, disguised as Ding Dong Mama, I record them on a cassette tape, ringing a bell when it's time to turn the page. Also, be sure to bring along a blank tape so children can record their own voices. (That alone will entertain the kids for a long time.)

Check with your local library to see if they have tapes of old radio shows like "The Shadow" or "Ellery Queen." Bring them on your trip for added entertainment. Books are available on tape: check the library or order your own.

The Guinness Book of World Records is an interesting and entertaining book to bring along. Have everyone guess the length of the world's longest fingernail, the record time for lying on a bed of nails, the duration record for continuous clapping or the greatest distance achieved by the national spitting champion.

A small, paperback dictionary is another possibility for fun. Whoever is "it" picks out a word and gives a definition for it. (The definition can be real or imaginary.) Everyone tries to guess if the definition is true or false.

Tie a blindfold around someone's eyes and put an object in his hands. The child guesses what the item is, just by its feel.

Photocopy maps of the United States (one for each person) and have everyone begin a license plate hunt. When you see a particular state license, cross out that state on the map. The first person (or team) to have the whole map filled in is the winner. This is not only fun, but a good geography lesson.

Games on the Go

Here are a few suggestions for traveling games that need no advance preparation or extra equipment. These games are just as good for trips across town as they are for jaunts around the country.

When I was a girl, my sisters and I spent hours playing the alphabet game. We'd look at road signs along the way, searching first for a word that started with *A*, then *B* and so on. *Q*, *X* and *Z* were the real killers; sometimes we'd allow each other to find those letters in the middle of a word rather than at the beginning. The first one to find all twenty-six letters of the alphabet was the winner.

Another version of the alphabet game is to locate an object that begins with each letter. (If you want to eliminate the competition, each person can take a turn locating something.)

Roadside cribbage is a dandy. (Before interstate travel became the norm, this game was less challenging than it is today.) Each person (or team) chooses a side of the road to watch. The object of the game is to score one hundred points, which are accumulated as follows: A herd (any number over ten) of animals counts ten points. (When fewer than ten animals are seen, score one point for each.) A school or a church counts ten points. If you see a white horse, you double your score. A graveyard wipes you out and you have to start over from zero.

Mileage games are fun, too. Have someone choose an object in the distance (a farmhouse, viaduct, flashing light). Then that person closes his eyes and says "now" when he thinks the car is passing the object. Or have everyone guess how far it is to the object, then watch the odometer for the exact answer.

A scavenger hunt is also fun. Before the trip, make up a bunch of lists with things like: horse trailer, train with forty-two cars, mobile home, green-and-white car, a man riding a horse and so on. (Everyone can have the same list, or make them all different.) The first person to spot everything on his list wins the scavenger hunt.

Print a long word (or city and state of your destination) on a piece of paper. See what words you can form with the letters.

Go through a storybook and cross out some nouns, adverbs and adjectives with a pencil. Then ask the family to supply you with different nouns, adverbs and adjectives. Lightly print all the new words in the storybook and read the "new" story out loud to the family. This is always good for a few laughs (and it's educational).

Squiggle pictures are so much fun and will be used so often it's smart to "invest" in a good set of them. Draw squiggles in various shapes on individual sheets of paper (one squiggle per sheet). Have them laminated. Give one of the sheets to a child with a dry erase marker and have him make something out of the shape: a fish, a monster, a dinosaur, a flower, an ocean liner—anything that pops into his imagination. Wipe off the picture and it's ready to be used again. It's also fun to give the kids a pad of paper so they can make their own squiggles and challenge each other.

Travel bingo is another inexpensive activity that will keep everyone occupied for a while. You'll need some slide pages. These are clear plastic sheets with thirty-six pockets in them to hold slides. They're available at photo shops. Or, for a less challenging bingo game, you can use pages with nine pockets for sports cards.

Cut pictures from magazines (or draw them) and slip them into the pockets. (Be sure the pictures are things that they'll likely see on the trip: school, flag, white horse, army truck, detour sign, etc.) Give each player (or team) a bingo card and dry erase marker. When they see one of the items depicted, they cross it off. Then, the first person or team to cross off all the items in a row is the winner. (Or make the game harder by asking that all boxes be crossed off.)

There you have it—a plan for organizing your space and time. Keep in mind what your objectives are. Usually you're striving for family fun and togetherness and a chance to get away from it all. So when the kids get rowdy (and they will), relax and keep your cool. As long as things aren't too far out of control, you're probably meeting your objective for an enjoyable family time together.

HOW TO TAKE YOUR DAY OFF OFF

A year is a long time between chances to "get away from it all," and I for one (and you, too, probably) need to escape more frequently.

"I can't wait until I get back to work so I can rest up from my day off! Every weekend I get two days off and how do I spend them? Cleaning the yard, washing the car, picking up the cleaning, grocery shopping, washing windows, cooking and doing the laundry. Is *that* my reward for a hard week at the office? What can I do?" the wearied woman complained to me.

I think we've all felt like that at one time or another.

While there *is* no permanent escape from the rigors of family life, you can still spend an occasional day off enjoying rest and relaxation. And you can do it without going into debt or depression or having to call in the heavy machinery to dig out the house when your day off is over! Here are three basic ways to help you take your day off off: just do it, plan for it or pay for it.

Just Do It

Remember the time management principle we talked about—the Pareto Principle? Pareto stated that 80 percent of our time is spent doing things that aren't vital. So what would happen if you didn't mow your lawn Saturday afternoon? Would the neighbors circulate a petition to drum you out of the neighborhood? Probably not. What would happen if the windows weren't washed, the garage not swept, the cleaning not picked up? Would you be investigated by the Board of Health? No. Absolutely nothing would happen.

Most of our trivial pursuits could easily be delayed for a day or two (at least) with no severe consequences, so why not just do it—take a day off and let things go.

Suppose you, your spouse or one of the kids were involved in an accident and laid up in the hospital for a spell. You'd be forced to put all but the most consequential tasks on the back shelf for a while and you'd do it without hesitation, wouldn't you? I'm suggesting you do the very same thing—only for a better reason! Do only those things that absolutely cannot be postponed and neglect the rest until your day off is over.

Imagine your family's response to the declaration that "Saturday we're taking the day off. No cooking, no cleaning, no yardwork, no bedmaking. We're all just going to relax and have a leisurely day, doing whatever we want to do!"

(Be sure to tell the kids that this rest and relaxation is for *your* benefit, too. If they suppose you'll taxi them and a carload of their friends back and forth to the water slide and make pizzas for everybody afterward, they've got the wrong idea—so set them straight from the start.)

Just do it. Go ahead and take a day off. What needs to be done can wait until your day off is over.

Plan for It

Maybe you're not quite so impulsive and prefer a more premeditated approach to your day off. Here's what you do. Together with the rest of the family, set aside a day or two in the near future when everyone will enjoy the day off.

First decide what you're going to do with your free time. Let's say Mom wants to read all day, Dad wants to spend the day golfing and the kids want to go to the mall. When everyone has expressed their desires, it may be necessary to work out some compromises. (Dad will drop the kids off at the mall on his way to the course. Mom will pick them up at 2:30. Then you'll all go out for a late lunch.) Or choose a family activity everyone can be involved in.

In any case, it's important to plan what you're going to do so you won't spend the entire day off negotiating who's going where and when, entertaining (or refereeing) bored kids and wishing your day off was over!

Next, establish the rules and guidelines: we'll all make our beds, we'll eat all our meals at restaurants, snacks at home will be eaten on paper plates, the house will be cleaned the day before and so on.

Then, brainstorm and make a list of all the things that need to be done a day or two before the day off (e.g., laundry, housecleaning, yardwork, car washed, stock up on fruit and other snacks). Assign jobs or have everyone sign up for a few. It helps to point to a few jobs on the list and say, "I'll do this and this. Which will you do?"

As soon as the chores are divvied up, note the assignments in your planning notebook and on the kids' weekly planning sheets. This breeds a spirit of family unity and togetherness because everyone is working for a common goal. The thought of having a bona fide day off is usually all the motivation the kids need to carry through with their responsibilities.

Getting these chores out of the way will make the day off much more relaxing by eliminating those nagging reminders we give ourselves: "I just can't sit here, the house is a mess." "Look at all those weeds in the strawberries." "This car is so dirty, I'm embarrassed to park it in front of the house." And, when your day off is over, you won't have all those bothersome jobs waiting for you.

So try a plan. Plan when your day off will be, plan what you're going to do and what you're not going to do, and plan the chores so they can be completed before the big day comes. Then, plan to have fun— because you will!

Pay for It

With a little extra cash you can indulge in a more lavish day off. Though this is a pay-as-you-go approach, you still need to do some planning.

Decide when the day off will be and what chores need to be completed in advance. If you're feeling especially extravagant, hire out as many of the chores as you can: Have the groceries delivered, call a cleaning service to wash the windows, hire a neighborhood college student to run those last-minute errands.

Then, decide what you're going to do. Here are a few ideas:

One summer we checked into a local motel for a few days. Though we were close to home we were away from the phone, the mail, the housework, and the kids were away from their friends. We spent the days swimming, we ate at restaurants, we went to a movie. In short, we had a great time together as a family. By removing ourselves from our home and work environments, we eliminated any temptation to let other things claim our attention, and everyone had a chance to unwind.

Another idea is to turn your house into a hotel. Dress up the place just a little with scented guest soaps, chocolates on paper doilies by each bedside and fresh-cut flowers. Get out the guest towels and the good silver. Eat at restaurants (try out some new ones), shop for souvenirs, hit all the local tourist traps the "natives" seldom frequent. Get some picture postcards and send them to your friends. If your town has historical sites or guided tours, pretend you're tourists and rediscover the place where you live. Go to the zoo, the beach, hike through the forest preserves, browse through that antique shop you've always wanted to see. With this sense of adventure, your in-town day off will leave you with the strong determination to do it again.

Take an occasional day off, and during those times when there's just too much to do and time off seems impossible, take it easy, at least. Simplify meals by relying on soup, sandwiches, salads, leftovers and freezer meals. Hire a baby-sitter and (if nothing else) lock yourself in your room for a few hours. Can you take a half-day or a few hours off? Time off now and then is invigorating and renews your resolve to keep plugging away.

What about those times when you're locked into a big, high-priority project and stopping midstream is out of the question? When I can't change my circumstances, I just change my attitude.

Stop and remember the value of good hard work. A wise man once said, "Work is the tonic that tones the systems for play. Work is not merely a means to an end, it is an end in itself. Blessed is he who loves his work, for he shall know great joy from day to day."

Many times I've longed to be free from the insidious interruptions that plague my days. After *Confessions of an Organized Homemaker* was published, I got my wish: I was sent across the country on a book-promotion tour and spent many hours alone in hotel rooms. And do you know what I discovered? It wasn't as great as I thought it would be. How I longed for even one small interruption!

Here's a favorite anecdote. After an especially long stint at work, Thomas Edison returned home, where his wife begged him to take some time off. She told him to think of the place he would most like to be—and go there. Next morning, Thomas Edison took his wife's advice and returned to the laboratory.

So you see, "work" is a state of mind. If you can't change your circumstances, try changing your attitude (at least until your circumstances change).

Every once in a while take a day off. Make the most of it and get as much rest and relaxation as you can. But when a day off seems like "Mission: Impossible," be grateful that you're able to work and that you've got something to work for. And while you're feeling grateful, sit down and schedule a time when you'll take your day off off!

CHAPTER NINETEEN

Move It!

Name an event that turns women into unyielding shrews, makes men weep and gnash their teeth, and fills the hearts of children with anguish, fear and lament. During this event muscles are reduced to jelly, dishes broken and thirteen years of *National Geographics* discarded (maybe). The answer is: a) World War III; b) the NFL draft; c) moving.

While a) and b) might be considered correct, if you answered c) moving, you're right on! Moving an entire family seems to bring out the beast in people. The mere mention of the word "move" and well-meaning friends respond with, "I'm glad it's *you* and not me!"

Why is that? I suppose it's because when you decide to move, your life suddenly becomes one giant "to do" list. At this point it pays to remember anything that seems unconquerable is just a series of small, manageable steps. Swimming the English Channel starts by finding out about swimming lessons. Getting into medical school starts by getting into college. Writing a book begins with an idea. And moving begins with writing down that "to do" list.

Most people let the pressure build, reminding themselves over and over what must be done. They lie awake at night stewing and fretting while they suffer from cold sweats or hot flashes. The task then seems overwhelming. So let's begin by seeing exactly what needs to be done.

Moving can be broken down into three basic categories:

Stage 1: Getting the house ready to sell, selling the house (or terminating your lease), house hunting and packing.
Stage 2: The trip.
Stage 3: Settling into your new surroundings.

Due to space and intelligence limitations (mine) I won't discuss the specifics of buying/selling a house; leave that to a qualified professional.

However, let's investigate each stage involved in a family move.

STAGE 1: GETTING READY

As soon as the decision to move hits, wait until the dust settles. (Any hyperventilating can be relieved by breathing into a paper sack.) Then gather your wits, roll up your sleeves and start planning.

Get a brightly colored folder with pockets to use as a central moving file. (Depending on the amount of things you'll collect, you might want to use an expanding file with several pockets.)

Use this file to house the following:

- All receipts you collect for moving-related expenses. (You may be entitled to a tax deduction.)
- Estimates from moving companies or truck rental rates and information.
- Floor plan of your new home. (You'll want to decide in advance the final resting place for your belongings.)
- Information on schools, parks, recreation, community calendars and maps for your new area. (Contact the Chamber of Commerce or Visitor's Bureau.)
- Copies of medical and dental records you'll need to take with you.

Next, create a "moving" section in your planning notebook, or set up a separate diary just for that purpose. This is where you'll keep that massive "to do" list I mentioned earlier. The heading for your first list is: Getting the House Ready to Sell. (If you're renting, check the terms of your lease. You, too, may be required to repair damages.) Go through every room in your house or apartment and jot down everything that needs attention before you vacate the premises: repair torn wallpaper in bathroom; have living room carpet seams resealed; paint the hallway; call a repair company to fix drain in laundry room; replace cracked garage window; caulk shower and tub. Be sure to include a thorough housecleaning on your list. And, yes, call a pest removal company, if need be.

Your real estate agent can advise you as to what repairs and improvements will help you get top dollar for your home. (A renter hoping to have his security deposit returned in full should check with the landlord to find out exactly what's expected.)

Now, begin a second list entitled Wrap-Up. What loose ends need to be taken care of before you move away? To stimulate your thinking, consider the following suggestions:

Contact your doctors, dentist, lawyers, insurance agents, bankers, real estate agent, brokers, etc. Ask if they can refer you to similarly qualified professionals in your new area. Also, find out how to get your records transferred.

Notify your children's schools. If possible, give them the addresses of the new schools so they can send transcripts. Speak to guidance counselors, speech therapists, special education teachers, etc., about any recommendations they have for your child.

You might want to call your priest, pastor, rabbi or minister. Ask for a letter of transfer.

Don't forget to notify the draft board or Social Security Administration (if you fall under their jurisdiction). Also, the Division of Motor Vehicles needs to be informed if you're moving within the state.

Change of address notices need to be sent to all correspondents: friends, relatives, magazines and other publications, newspaper agencies and national credit card companies. (Local companies can be notified when you pay your final statement. Then destroy your card.) Notify your postmaster.

What services will have to be terminated? Call or write each company, indicating your moving day. Here are a few memory joggers to help you begin: telephone, gas (or fuel), electricity, water and sewer, private garbage service, milkman, bakery delivery, in-home shopping services, newspaper, diaper service, lawn and garden service.

Do you have any pending business to wrap up or turn over to a co-worker? Do you have to train a new employee, update a training manual or familiarize a subordinate with a client's account? (This can lead to a whole new "to do" list when you get back to the office.)

Do you belong to organizations or clubs you'll need to resign from? (Hospital volunteers, Girl/Boy Scouts, car pools, committees, Sunday School staff.)

Are there any special needs to consider? Will you need to hire someone to mow the lawn after you move (until the new owners arrive)? If you're moving out of or into an apartment, inquire about the availability of the service elevator. Will you have to make special arrangements for the dog, the canary or the goldfish?

If you're moving a pet out of state you must consider Interstate Commerce Commission (ICC) regulations, and possibly state and local laws that apply to pets. Check with your veterinarian before you move. If your pet is going to be transported by air, make the reservation well in advance.

Speaking of the ICC, they also have regulations affecting perishable plants. (Yes, plants have rights, too.) While it's OK to take your Boston fern across town, you may need a state of origin certificate (by state or federal pest control officials) to get it across the state line.

To find out exactly how much the ICC is involved in your move you can write to the ICC, Consumer Information, Washington, DC 20423 (or contact a nearby ICC field office). Ask for their current public advisories regarding for-hire carriers. Another helpful booklet is "Summary of Information for Shippers of Household Goods." (Moving companies should also have copies of this publication.)

Some more reminders:

Refill any prescription drugs so you'll have a supply until your medical records are transferred.

Your appliances (washer, dryer, air conditioner, stereo, satellite dish, etc.) may require special preparations for transporting. Will you make arrangements to do this, or will the mover handle it?

Do you have family members with special needs, physical handicaps or learning disabilities? Are there organizations in your new area that can help or continue with ongoing therapy?

Lest we forget Uncle Sam, check with the IRS. They have regulations and forms concerning tax-deductible moving expenses.

Now that you have something to chew on, we're finished making out lists for stage one. Maybe you feel a little green around the gills, but cheer up, it looks worse than it really is. I know what you're thinking: "Where do I start? There's so much to do, and I can't do it all. I can't even start." Sure you can!

Getting Started

Start first thing tomorrow by streamlining your life. Your number one job right now is getting your family through the next few months without pills, alcohol or suicide. Tomorrow morning start making phone calls. Resign from the PTA, the Rotary Club and the League of Writers. Call your neighbor and ask if he'll canvass the neighborhood for the Heart Fund this year. Call Roto-Rooter, the carpet layer and the paperhanger to schedule those needed repairs.

Now, get out your pocket calendar or complete planning notebook and start scheduling. As with any major project, you begin by scheduling backwards. That's right: backwards. First, schedule your target— the moving date. Now, count back at least thirty days and schedule the following:

- A thorough housecleaning. (If you're going to show your house, this job may have to be done sooner.)
- Investigate and choose a moving company. Or check out truck

rental rates and information if you're making the move yourself. If you're moving across town, call Uncle Joe and make arrangements to borrow his pickup truck.

- Notify the post office. Send out change of address cards to everyone on your list. Notify online services of your change of address. Also, get a local dial-up number for your new location before you leave.
- Gather your records or make arrangements for their transfer (medical, dental, school, financial, pet immunizations, etc.).
- Clear all tax assessments.
- Make your travel plans. (See chapter 18, "On the Road Again: Family Travel Tips.") Make hotel or motel reservations (if needed) to confirm later. Or call Grandma and tell her you'll be converging when you come through town.
- Start using up your frozen food.
- Return borrowed items discovered during your thorough cleanup (library books, Jack's garden hoe, Susan's eight-piece snack set, Ed's gourmet cookbook, Marilyn's motivational tapes).

Now, count two weeks backwards from your target date and schedule the following:

- Subscribe to newspaper in your new area. Secure a copy of your new white and yellow pages.
- Photograph wall groupings to duplicate the arrangement in your new house. Use masking tape to secure screws and hardware to the backs of pictures, etc., when you remove them.
- Begin gradual packing.
- Collect things you've loaned to other people.
- Transfer bank accounts and release safe deposit boxes.
- Make arrangements with local utility companies to disconnect services to your home.
- Make arrangements in your new area to connect utilities.
- Call an appliance service representative and make an appointment to have your appliances prepared for transport (unless the movers are going to handle it).
- Get your car into shape for the trip. Give it a good inside cleanup. Schedule a regular maintenance checkup and tune-up.
- Donate all castoffs to charity or have a garage sale.

One week before you move, schedule these final arrangements:

- Set aside a box of things you'll need for the last few hours in your old home and for the trip to your new home. Some suggestions:

- Tools (hammer, screwdriver, pliers, wrench, flashlight—check batteries)
- Paper plates, cups, plastic flatware
- Snacks, canned food, can opener, cooking utensils
- Towels, washcloths, soap, bathroom tissue, aspirin
- Lightbulbs, fuses
- Travel alarm
- First-aid kit
- Cash, credit cards, checkbook, ID cards
- Keys to both houses (old and new)
- Things to occupy the children. See "On the Road Again: Family Travel Tips" for a more complete list of ideas.

- Set aside things to put on the van last (so they're the first things unloaded), like the vacuum, bedding, essential kitchen items, TV, baby furniture and a bucket of cleaning supplies.
- Defrost deep freezer.
- Dispose of flammables.
- Seal opened packages of food.
- Empty gasoline from lawn mower and other power tools.
- Take down curtains, rods, drapes, shelves, TV antenna.
- Schedule a baby-sitter for moving day.

The day before the move, clean and defrost the refrigerator and clean the stove. Throughly clean the bathrooms. On moving day all they'll need is a quick wipeup. Wipe out closet shelves, kitchen cupboards and drawers.

On moving day you should be available to answer questions if you're dealing with a professional mover. Take the children to the sitter's. Vacuum bed rails, piano back and under large appliances or other hard-to-move furniture. Pack the car. Before leaving the house, check each room to make sure windows are closed and locked, lights are out and nothing is left behind.

Now you have everything carefully scheduled. Relax. Most of the assignments can be handled over the phone or through the mail. Those jobs take only a matter of minutes. OK. All the physical plans are made, but before the actual labor begins you need to prepare the rest of the family for the rigors that lie ahead.

Preparing the Family

Just by reading this book, you've proved that *you* are the home manager in your family. With that job goes an important responsibility: your attitude.

When you discuss the move with your family, present a cheerful, positive attitude. Stress the benefits: new experiences, sights and friends. Make it sound like an exciting adventure. Maybe you're going for a better job and a bigger house. Now *that's* exciting!

Remind your family of the problems you're leaving behind: no more crabgrass, no more car pools and no more cranky Mr. Evans (the neighbor who keeps all the balls that bounce into his backyard).

This experience can give everyone a sense of unity and a renewed sense of family spirit. Your feelings are contagious, so make the most of your new adventure and others will, too.

Moving is especially hard on children. Glance through the following list of ideas and choose a few to make the adjustment easier.

Tell your children before you tell anyone else. You don't want them to get the news secondhand.

Let the kids help with the plans. They can suggest features they'd like in their new house. Have them write to the recreational department in the new area for information about swimming facilities, golf courses, racquetball courts and recreational programs.

Perhaps you could arrange for pen pals through the new school. Weeks before the move, subscribe to your new town's newspaper. That way everyone becomes familiar with the new store names, town activities, school functions, auxiliaries, etc., ahead of time.

Find out about the local radio stations. What's the format? What type of music do they play? This is especially helpful if you're moving with teenagers.

Plan a special family purchase after you're settled into your new surroundings (a basketball standard, video recorder or season tickets to the ballet). That way the kids will have something to look forward to.

Before pulling away from the old homestead, take pictures of your house, the kids' schools, friends and other favorite sights. Also, plan a time when your children can come back for a visit.

Moving With Small Children

Younger children have special fears about moving, so be careful to explain every detail to them. They need to be told that every*one* and every*thing* goes.

Check with your local librarian to see if there's a storybook available about the experience of moving. Go to a professional moving company and look at the big trucks. Maybe they'll even give you a tour. When driving around town, stop and watch a move in progress if you happen to stumble across one.

If possible, show the children pictures of their new house, their room and their green backyard (or better yet, the dirt—if there *is* no backyard). Get out a map and show them where you live now and where your new house is. Teach them to say their new address and phone number as soon as you can.

To add some excitement to the whole affair, have a "countdown to moving day." This can be done very simply: A month before the move, put thirty raisins in a dish and have the child eat one a day. When the raisins are gone, it's time to go. Or make an Advent-type calendar or a paper chain and tear off one link per day. The whole idea is to eliminate fear and dread.

When the time comes, let the children pack some of their own toys. Colorful comics can be used for wrapping their "treasures."

Moving With Older Kids

Logically discuss the circumstances causing the move—a better job, a chance for advancement, moving into an area you can better afford— whatever the reason, explain it to your child.

You may encounter some self-pity, particularly if Sarah was just elected president of the junior class or Steve was about to letter in football. Don't encourage the self-pity, but be patient. Children are pretty resilient if you roll with the punches for awhile. Some families have an older child finish out the school year with a close friend or relative. Perhaps that's a possibility.

An older child might enjoy helping you hunt for the new house— especially if it requires missing a few days of school.

Maybe you can tempt the older child with YM/YWCA summer camps, classes or sports that are available in your new town. Scouting; church activities; music, dance, art or gymnastics lessons; sports associations; choral or community-theater groups; bands or symphonies; drill teams—to name a few—are activity ideas that will encourage the kids' interest and get them instantly involved with new friends.

Getting the House Ready

Let's see. So far you've made a list and scheduled your activities, and you've taken care of the emotional requirements involved in moving your family. Now what? Up until now, nothing has been too taxing, has it? Good, because now you need all your strength for the housework.

No matter the season, now is the time to do your spring cleaning with a vengeance.

Ruthlessly go through closets, drawers, cupboards and shelves throwing out, donating or selling unused articles.

Do not move torn or broken articles. Mend clothing and repair broken toys, tools, and equipment. If you don't want to fix it, get rid of it.

Organize and group things into logical categories (put the books together, put extension cords by the power tools, put all the action figures in the same toy bin). When it comes time to pack, this underlying organization greatly simplifies things. You'll be able to find things when you need them, and when you unpack, everything will already be organized and ready to put away.

Scrub cupboards, shelves and drawers. Wash off sticky cans, ketchup bottles and bottles of syrup. Thoroughly clean the refrigerator, range and oven. The day before the move, only a once-over will be needed.

Go through your collection of stored prescription and over-the-counter drugs. Unless otherwise directed by your physician, throw away anything over a year old.

Air draperies, bedding, bedspreads. (Send drapes and curtains to the cleaners *after* you move into your new house.)

Keep the ironing, mending and washing current. Make those necessary repairs (the leaky faucet, the loose linoleum seam, the cracked plaster).

Now, when "Pack" comes up on your calendar, you're all ready!

Packing

You should be aware at the outset that hiring professional movers to handle the packing will add another five years to the life of your marriage. However, if your last move already destroyed your marriage, professional moving services will add at least five years to your *life*! The stress of packing all your belongings is, at best, life-threatening. Let's face it. Professional movers know what they're doing. They have equipment to do the job right and insurance if they do the job wrong.

Moving companies usually charge by the hour for short moves. Long-distance moves are based on weight and distance. They offer many additional services that add to the total cost, e.g., packing, unpacking, servicing appliances, housecleaning, special shipping and storage services. You can receive a binding or a nonbinding estimate from the moving company before you make your final decision.

If at all possible, avoid peak periods when you move. The busiest times are from June 15 to September 15 and the first and last days of every month.

Mayflower publishes a marvelous moving kit that's free for the asking. It comes with a set of brightly colored carton labels, a household inventory, a ready-made "to do" list and information about their moving services. To receive a copy send your name and address to Aero Mayflower Transit Co., Inc., P.O. Box 107, Indianapolis, IN 46206.

Now, if you're doing your own packing, start rummaging for boxes early on. Call a few local grocery stores and ask them to save some cartons for you. Often photocopy stores will sell the boxes reams of paper come in; they're nice-sized boxes and have removable lids. Your local van lines also sell packing cartons. They have one for every need: books, dish packs (with sturdy cardboard dividers), wardrobe cartons with a hanging bar, mattress boxes, large telescoping boxes to hold various-sized frames and pictures, etc. Moving companies can also make customized packing crates for such odd-sized valuables as chandeliers, grandfather clocks, antiques and heavy tabletops.

With their heavy cardboard dividers, liquor cartons make excellent packing boxes. Also, round oatmeal or cornmeal boxes can be put to use. Different-sized wax milk cartons can hold stemware, figurines, vases, candlesticks or small plants.

Have a good supply of newspaper, unprinted newsprint (roll ends are available at your local newspaper office) or tissue to wrap and protect breakables.

Begin by packing daily the things you're not using. (If you've got time to spare, just pack a few boxes every day.) Things used every day will have to be packed at the last minute. Keep each box light enough to be handled by everybody—not just the strongest person. Heavier items go in smaller boxes, lighter items in larger ones. Close up the boxes so they can be stacked. Clearly mark all cartons, noting especially those boxes that contain fragile items, things to load last and boxes that are not to be loaded.

If you're moving a long distance, take pains to ensure your belongings' safe arrival. Breakables should be carefully and individually wrapped and placed in divided cartons or on top of unbreakable items. (Fragile pieces may be placed loosely in undivided boxes provided each piece is wrapped and empty spaces are filled with crumpled paper to prevent shifting. Be sure the box doesn't get too heavy.)

Popped popcorn and Styrofoam pieces provide excellent padding for delicate pieces. Do not stuff drawers with breakables.

Pack brooms and garden tools by tying them together in bundles.

Before you take down your pleated drapes, open them up so all the pleats are close together. Then, starting at the top, tie them together (or use masking tape) right under the pleats. Then tie them together again about two feet below that point. Continue tying about every two feet. Fold lengthwise and pack; this will keep your drapes wrinkle-free and ready to hang in your new home.

When packing a computer, store backup copy in a safe place. You might want to take the backup and other diskettes in the car with you. Contact your dealer and find out how to "park the heads." This prevents damage to the computer's moving components.

After you turn off the computer and all attachments, unplug the power cords and label all cables before you disconnect them.

If possible, pack the computer in its original box along with the packing materials. Mark the box boldly: *computer, fragile*.

Extreme temperatures are not good for a computer. For every hour the computer is subjected to extreme conditions (below -50° and above 125°F.) it should have a corresponding number of hours (up to 8) at room temperature before using.

Check your manual. The manufacturer may have specific recommendations for packing your particular model.

Don't leave spillable bottles of perfume, lotion or boxes of powder in your drawers. Remove the containers, tape them shut and pack separately. If extra precautions need to be taken (medicine bottles or other bottles you fear will spill), seal the tops by dipping them in melted paraffin, or seal with adhesive tape.

Don't forget to pack an old phone directory. Should you need an address or phone number (doctor, bank, schools, friends and such) you'll have a ready reference.

Packing containers can be labeled in any number of ways. The contents of each box should be clearly printed on the side of each carton. Also, if you're moving into a large home, the destined room should be indicated (kitchen, family room, John's bedroom, etc.).

Or you can number the cartons—K-1, K-2, K-3 (K is for kitchen). List all the items packed in each box on a separate list. For example, if you wanted to find the electric blanket you'd check your B list (B is for bedroom). A quick scan down the list would tell you the electric blanket is in box B-4. It's helpful to put the marking (B-4, for example) on each side of the box.

We use the Smooth Mover when we move. It is similar to the idea above, but it's color coded by category. It comes with color-coded labels and indexes for each grouping—kitchen, bedroom, toys, household (cleaning products, garden equipment, tools, etc.) furnishings and decor, crafts and hobbies, holiday decorations, office supplies, bathroom, books. (For ordering information, write to Home Management,

P.O. Box 214, Cedar Rapids, IA 52406.)

Sometimes (particularly if movers are involved) the person unloading the truck won't know which room is Susie's room and which is your office. For that reason, some folks assign each room a number and post it on the doorway. All boxes and furniture marked #1 go in the room marked #1, and so on.

If you can't be there during the unloading, provide your help with a diagram of the house. Tag furniture and boxes and key it to the diagram. Another variation on this theme is to color-code boxes and rooms.

The main point to remember is that boxes need to be clearly identified so you can find what you need when you need it.

STAGE 2: THE TRIP

This subject is nicely handled (if I do say so myself) in chapter 18, "On the Road Again: Family Travel Tips." The only added precaution is that you'll have a double dose of nervous energy and the kids will have a triple dose (at least). So plan carefully to ensure a pleasant family trip.

Since, because of the move, you'll have extra cargo, pick and choose those traveling ideas that don't require much space.

STAGE 3: SETTLING IN

Now is the time to reach for your copy of *Confessions of an Organized Homemaker*. If you don't have one, now is the time to get one! Therein you will find a complete guide to organizing everything in your home so you can find it in less than a minute! Remarkable claim? Try it and see.

Next, you may find it desirable to get a baby-sitter the day you move in. He can keep the small children occupied in the backyard or out of the way while you and the older kids unpack and direct the furniture placement.

Since it's a new environment for the kids it's better to have the baby-sitter and the children there with you rather than sending the kids off somewhere. I'm sure the new neighbors, the newspaper or a temporary employment agency can refer you to someone. Or call the local senior citizens' center. Somehow, a person who seems like Grandma or Grandpa is more comforting to a small child in a new environment.

If possible, do any last-minute cleaning (of cupboards, shelves and bathrooms) before the truck is unpacked. Here's a list of things that need to be done the first day:

- Connect appliances.
- Assemble and make up beds.

- Unpack kitchen and bath necessities.
- Unpack suitcases.
- Put major pieces of furniture in place.

With these jobs completed and out of the way, you'll be able to get along nicely while the rest of the unpacking is underway.

Here's a terrific settling-in system. A friend of ours worked for a national retail chain as a manager; he and his family were transferred often. But they had it down to a science. Whenever they moved, they immediately had the furniture put in place. Two or three boxes containing only necessities were brought in and unpacked. All remaining boxes were left in one area (the garage, basement, closet or separate room, depending upon the particular house). Whenever time allowed, they'd bring one box in and put it away. When neighbors dropped in to welcome them, they were amazed at the instant order—no crates to step over, no wadded hunks of newspaper, no piles of garbage towering in the corner. Nothing! What a great system—especially if you've got kids, careers and limited time.

Here are a few more tips for settling in:

- Get a map of your new city.
- In your planning notebook or pocket notebook, jot down notes to help you remember certain things (the day garbage is picked up, your new office phone number, bus and train schedules) and directions to various places.
- Get a library card.
- Call the Chamber of Commerce and find out what's going on.
- Call Welcome Wagon or other such organization.
- Call the Avon lady or other in-home shopping services.
- Call the PTA president to volunteer or to find out what activities are upcoming.
- Get in touch with your minister so your family can quickly become involved with your new congregation.
- Measure and record room sizes, window sizes, wall and floor space (for paint, wall and floor coverings). Make a list of needed goods and pick up things as your budget allows.

Now that your move has been a total success, relax and enjoy your new surroundings. Remember that the whole process is much like surgery. You forget the pain after a while!

INDEX